Harvesting Silence

A journey from being 'hushed' to being heard

Sarah Cook

Ark House Press
arkhousepress.com

© 2025 Sarah Cook

All rights reserved. Apart from any fair dealing for the purpose of study, research, criticism, or review, as permitted under the Copyright Act, no part may be reproduced by any process without written permission.

Unless otherwise stated, all Scriptures are taken from the New International Translation (Holy Bible. Copyright© 1996, 2004, 2007, 2013 by Tyndale House Foundation. Used by permission of Tyndale House Publishers Inc., Carol Stream, Illinois 60188. All rights reserved.)

Some names and identifying details have been changed to protect the privacy of individuals.

Cataloguing in Publication Data:
Title: Harvesting Silence
ISBN: 978-1-7640542-5-6 (pbk)
Subjects: BIO026000   BIOGRAPHY & AUTOBIOGRAPHY / Memoirs; FAM001010   FAMILY & RELATIONSHIPS / Abuse / Child Abuse; REL012040   RELIGION / Christian Living / Inspirational.

Design by initiateagency.com

Endorsements

'I've known Sarah for nearly twenty years, and *Harvesting Silence* is a powerful testament to her journey. With raw honesty, she shares how she overcame a silenced and painful childhood to become a professional speaker with a passionate voice for healing. This memoir is both shocking and inspiring—a beacon of hope for anyone seeking freedom from their past. I highly recommend it.'

Sam Cawthorn - Founder of Speakers Institute Group and Speakers Tribe

'Wow.... this book is absolutely amazing. It made me laugh and it made me cry, it also made me angry at what Sarah had to endure. I felt genuinely privileged to be involved as a proofreader for such a powerful and moving memoir.'

Nerida Wynne-Primus – Editor

'I've had the privilege of knowing Sarah for over 30 years, and I am deeply moved by the courage it took for her to share her full story. Harvesting Silence is a powerful, unflinching account of the abuse she endured and the lasting effects of shame, grief, and inner turmoil that followed. Her honesty will resonate with many who carry the hidden wounds of childhood trauma. This book is not only raw and real—it's a beacon of hope and healing, offering comfort and strength to those who need it most.'

Sheralyn Bucknell - Senior Minister, The Avalon Church

'Sarah has the gift of storytelling. This book is a courageous and deeply moving testament to the human spirit. With grace and honesty, grit and humour, Sarah shares her journey through unimaginable trauma and what it takes to find justice over 50 long years. Hiding behind the wood pile, the uncomfortable story of Bobby Dazzler, stowing away to Cape York, being silenced by the Nuns, her arrested development and mental health journey, breaking her silence to the Royal Commission, the bravery required to endure the medico-legal and mediation processes, and her courage to never give up despite her distress and exhaustion. This story shines a light on Sarah's quiet resilience and unwavering faith, it is not only a powerful witness to survival, but also to the redemptive power of Christ's love. A must-read for anyone seeking hope in the darkest of places.'

Amanda Allen - Triple Crossfit World Champion, Champion for Health, Founder of Amanda Allen Nutrition

'Sarah Cook has written a brave and compelling account of her own life that I could not put down until I reached the end of the book! Somehow Sarah has managed to write of the crimes and injustices she experienced from childhood with clear objective perspective, yet at the same time succinctly capturing the raw fresh perspective of the one who experienced such things. Hers is a big story of a lifelong journey to discover healing and freedom to be the girl she was created to be. Her story takes on larger dimensions because of her underlying heartbeat to see others also set free from sad, silent prison walls of shame.

There is so much for us all to learn from Sarah's story both as individuals and as a society. Shining through her story, it becomes clear what really counts in life and where peace and restoration can be found.

Thank you, Sarah Cook for courageously sharing your story and for becoming the strong, confident, caring woman you are today with passionate commitment to serve and see others discover their voice of freedom.

Bev Spence -Pastor, Australian Christian Churches

Table of Contents

Endorsements... iii
Acknowledgements.. ix
Dedication xi
Author's Note xiii
Preface: Silenced.. xv
Prologue: The Wood Pile.. xvii
Chapter 1:   First Day of School... 1
Chapter 2:   Family.. 4
Chapter 3:   Doctor's Daughter.. 17
Chapter 4:   The Red Dress... 21
Chapter 5:   Secret Adventures... 28
Chapter 6:   Sunday Church 36
Chapter 7:   The Cane 40
Chapter 8:   The Gate.. 43
Chapter 9:   The Pool 47
Chapter 10: The TV Room... 52
Chapter 11: The Royal Princess 55
Chapter 12: Friends 60
Chapter 13: The Lie 64
Chapter 14: The Numbing.. 68

Chapter 15: The Reporting ... 70
Chapter 16: The Wooden Bench ... 75
Chapter 17: Under the Bridge ... 80
Chapter 18: The Tutor ... 86
Chapter 19: The Interrogation ... 90
Chapter 20: The Holiday ... 96
Chapter 21: The Nurse ... 102
Chapter 22: Around the World ... 111
Chapter 23: Bobby Dazzler ... 120
Chapter 24: Speed ... 127
Chapter 25: Island Life ... 134
Chapter 26: The Top End ... 146
Chapter 27: Three men and a baby ... 165
Chapter 28: Salvation ... 180
Chapter 29: New Beginning ... 194
Chapter 30: A Single Mum ... 207
Chapter 31: The Royal Commission ... 212
Chapter 32: Seek and you shall find ... 230
Chapter 33: The Reunion ... 243
Chapter 34: The Arrest Warrant ... 246
Chapter 35: Revisiting the Wooden Bench ... 252
Chapter 36: The Assessment ... 255
Chapter 37: The Results ... 266
Chapter 38: Mediation ... 272
Chapter 39: The Harvest ... 289
Epilogue: Sarah Cook's Impact Statement ... 295
Supports ... 305
Footnotes ... 307
Appendix ... 309

Acknowledgements

I would like to acknowledge the Nash family, along with all the families who have lost loved ones due to the devastating trauma of child sexual abuse. The Nash family's story deeply moved me when I first encountered it in the award-winning documentary series *Revelation*, an investigation into Catholic paedophile priests, presented by Sarah Ferguson. Andrew was just 13 years old when he tragically took his own life, unable to express the unbearable pain caused by his abuse.

May God bless all those who have suffered because of this evil. Your pain is not forgotten, and your stories matter.

Dedication

I dedicate this book to my parents Peter and Wilhelmina Cook. I want to honour them for being my God chosen parents and for parenting me the best way they knew how. I also dedicate this book to my two daughters whom I love with all my heart.

Author's Note

Most names in this book have been changed. My deceased parents and grandparents carry their real names to honour them and so do a few other significant people.

This book is a work of non-fiction based on the experiences and recollections of the author. In some cases, the names of people and other identifying details have been changed to protect the privacy of others and for legal reasons. Brother David 'Dave' Davenport is a fictious name as this person in my story has a current criminal charge in the Australian legal system.

Except in such minor respects, not affecting the substantial accuracy of the work, the contents of this book are true. As a warning, a few of the stories in this book portray details of abuse which may trigger some readers.

Preface
Silenced

'Children should be seen and not heard' is an adage drawn from the Victorian era which was common practice in the 1960's and 1970's. This means that, 'Children can be present in a conversation but should not speak, particularly when they are around adults.'

The accepted belief of this era sadly gave power to some adults to abuse children and keep them silent.

I was silenced.

Countless silenced children carry pain, trauma, and secrecy into adulthood and sadly to the grave. The burden of their 'buttoned lips' twisted inside causing knots of addiction, both physical and mental sickness, strained relationships, homelessness, and suicide. Some make it through life, some do not but none are left unscathed.

I have two adult daughters navigating the 21st century - a generation continuing to fight for the rights of women, standing for equal opportunity, having a voice that is valued. The "Me Too" movement started as a movement for women to be heard #MeToo. Yet I am horrified to hear stories of women continuing to be abused and silenced today. They are afraid of not being believed. There is a fear of a tainted reputation, intimidation by pornography and media fueled false body expectations, and a lack of trust in the law and the justice system along with AI images to compete with. This can be a road to despair and self-destruction. There is an absence of knowledge on how to stand up and speak your truth. I hear stories of date rape, spiked drinks, inappropriate sexual touching, sexist remarks, and sexual expectations through social media. The horrific case of Gisele Pelicot, in France in 2024 screams for women to be heard and believed for "shame to change sides" (1). I write this book for the shamed and the silenced—for the survivors of abuse, and for those who know someone still too afraid to speak. The statistics tell us: we all know someone.

Children should be seen and *HEARD*. Survivors—men and women of all ages—should be seen and *HEARD*.

It is time for the **New Voiced**.

A movement of truth-tellers, screaming light into the darkness.

Your story matters.

Your opinion matters.

Your pain matters.

You MATTER.

Those who have been wronged deserve justice.

The historical failings of institutions that were meant to protect children—and the present-day practices of the Australian legal system—are laid bare in this book to raise awareness for generations to come.

This is the journey of a life that was once harvesting silence…

Now, it harvests a **victorious voice.**

Prologue
The Wood Pile

The bitter wind whips around the woodpile sending violent chills over my exposed skin. My light cotton school uniform offers inadequate protection against its unrelenting blows. Cold with aching numbness, I shiver uncontrollably with terror. This overwhelming sensation begins to engulf my body, transporting me from the conscious to the semi-conscious. I am now in a realm I have never experienced before. I am out of my body in a black void, a blackness blacker than black.

Time has vanished.

A new dimension, a place of haunting quietness. What is this place? What is happening to me? My eight-year-old mind is lost trying to make sense in a senseless space.

I tell myself, "I know where I am" - but I am not there. The spider webs brushing against my face are not seen, the sticky mass is only felt. The bitter cold bites again like a stinging nettle, yet this is not my main distress.

My thoughts begin to race beyond any physical reality.

I picture my mother's face twisted in anger,

"Where have you been?" she growls.

What will I tell her? Why am I late home from school? What is my excuse?

The wood pile seems like a safe place to hide – a strange choice of escape drawing me into the darkness. This is the only option. Go into my home and face him or hide by the woodpile.

My father loved to light a fire in our fireplace in winter. It was the centrepiece of the living room, the heartbeat of the family home. The glowing embers would heat up my small, reddening face causing me to retreat inch by inch — wanting to be close but not to burn. I was taught to be careful of fires, they could be dangerous. The wood was carefully stored in a neat pile against the side of our family home. Where this wood came from, I never knew, but as a child the knowledge of its source was not important. All that mattered was that this wood was the making of our warmth.

But tonight, I am hiding. Huddled behind the chopped pile, with splinters catching on the threads of my school uniform. There is no warmth in this outside darkness. No spark to ignite a flame.

The terror beyond my mother's questioning awaits. His car is in our driveway, and I know if I go inside, I will have to face HIM.

Fear shifting in the shadows has a power so strong I can no longer hide from it. The fight against it is lost. I don't know if I am more terrified of 'him' or of my mother's wrath.

I stand, dust the spider webs off and walk towards the house — towards him, the enemy, my abuser.

"Hello Brother Dave," I tentatively greet him, my eyes down cast to the floor, with shivers sending electric shocks through my veins.

"Hello Sarah."

Chapter 1
First Day of School

"Sarah, time to get up. It's your first day of school," my mother called. Her voice was gentle yet firm at my bedroom door. The warm January sun peaked through my pink and cream curtains, slowly ushering me out of a deep sleep.

I snapped to attention remembering the conversation with my mother the night before.

"Now Sarah, you need to wake early tomorrow as it is your first day of school. You must get up, put on your school uniform, have your breakfast, clean your teeth and then I will do your hair." The list of orders seemed militant, an essential check list that I was to learn to follow five days a week for the next 13 years.

Villa Maria Primary School was a lovely local Catholic school situated in the affluent enclave of Hunters Hill – a suburb whose streets were lined with brush box trees, creating a canopy of bright green shade. Grand historic cottages of the 1800's featured white wrought iron verandas circling the inhabitants safely inside. Magnificent sandstone mansions, having been in families for generations, dominated the foreshores of the Lane Cove and Parramatta Rivers. Their perfectly manicured hedges towering twelve feet high, strategically planted to mark out the boundaries. Many boasted extensive driveways leading along smooth river stones which would crunch and crackle under the tyres of the Rolls Royce cars alerting the owners of a guest's arrival. A double tennis court and inground pool were standard along with the commanding Alsatian or Doberman Pincer dogs, to either greet or warn.

My family home was within walking distance of the school, yet my mother chose to drive my brother Matthew and me up the steep hill to the school. The incline was a little bit too steep for my small kindergarten legs. The excitement I felt was mixed with concern, an uncertainty of what lay ahead. My mother ordered us to sit on the garden bench to pose for the first day at school photo. I forced an expected smile.

"Say cheese," mum said.

"Cheese."

Matthew was 11 months and 26 days older than me, so for five days every year we were the same age. I took delight in reminding him of this fact every year.

"Ha, ha I'm the same age as you," I would chant.

My five days of teasing made him very annoyed, but then he seemed annoyed with me most other days of the year too. I was the much wanted daughter who had inconveniently interrupted his only child status.

Mum had decided, in her great wisdom, to send Matthew and me to school in the same year. This made me only four years old when I commenced school, which in 1969 was considered too young, but the nuns made an exception.

Matthew had a speech impediment that made him quite hard to understand. I had no problems with his strange mutterings; I understood him perfectly. I was allocated the role of Matthew's primary school interpreter.

FIRST DAY OF SCHOOL

This was a tough job for a younger sister, a position I had not put my hand up for. I often wished I was still at home playing with my dolls.

The family Chrysler Valiant Station Wagon pulled up out the front of 'Villa', the affectionate name given to our new primary school. Our little school stood directly opposite the large conspicuous St Joseph's College known as 'Joeys'. I looked up at its huge ornate iron gates that seemed to reach up to the heavens. The thick sandstone walls were equally as high, keeping intruders out and the elite Catholic boys locked in.

I clutched onto Mum's hand so tightly that her wedding ring sank into my flesh leaving a reddened dent, a separation scar that I carried into the classroom. The indentation gradually faded as the roll call was taken and I was shown to my spot on the floor to sit quietly cross legged.

"What is your name?" a nun in a long grey tunic asked, her face struggling to look kind.

"Maaa-tt-eew," my brother stammered.

"I beg your pardon," the nun enquired.

Oh no, it had begun.

"His name is Matthew Cook," I interrupted at the risk of speaking out of turn.

The nun wheeled around and glared at me. Another woman in the classroom quickly moved towards the nun and whispered something in her ear. A knowing sigh rang out as if to acknowledge that this was the 'brother and sister act'.

It was to be a long first day at school.

Chapter 2

Family

My father, Peter Cook, was an identical twin, both brothers serving in the RAF during the Second World War. He and his brother John loved the trickery of their likeness and would often fool the teachers at school with identity confusion. A mirror image of the other, they were both very bright boys with cheeky dispositions. Boasting blonde locks with cool blue eyes, their boyish faces would wink and grin at each other before the impending identity switch.

"Peter, stand up and recite a Shakespeare verse," the teacher would command.

John would leap to his feet and in a loud voice bellow out,

"To be or not to be that is the question."

Children's giggles would echo through the vast wooded classroom with an expectation of the constant swapping game the boys seemed to never grow tired of.

When World War II commenced, the two boys were eager to represent their country and escape the drudgery of Shrewsbury, a small country town in northwest England. They lied about their age, falsified documents, and went off to war. They were seventeen.

FAMILY

Peter headed to Canada to train in the bomber command, returning to the UK to perform many operations as an air bomber in the RAF commencing on 17th June 1943. He had always wanted to be a fighter pilot, so a co-pilot in Bomber Command was good enough. The operations were numerous times a week, including both daytime and night flights. He flew various crafts including Tiger Moths, Halifax, Wellingtons and Lancaster planes.

On 2nd February 1945, Peter's plane was hit by enemy fire. The smell of burning metal filled the fuselage, a thickening smoke screened all vision. The plane began a rapid descent. The seven men on board rapidly executed the procedures that they had been trained to do in an emergency. These men had flown many operations together over the past two years, their connection can only be described as brotherly. When men face dangers daily, a bond of trust is formed. Peter felt a violent shove on his back as one of the crew pushed him out of the aircraft. His world went black.

The remote field in The Hague was soft and green. Peter's parachute had miraculously opened moments before he impacted with the ground. He suffered concussion along with numerous broken bones, including fractures in his shoulder and neck. He laid still, fading in and out of consciousness. His plane had crashed, killing the remaining six crew onboard.

The crash was reported to the UK, informing all the families of their loved ones' deaths, including Peter's. His parents, Ernest and Sally, received a letter from King George the sixth, it read:

"The Queen and I offer you our heartfelt sympathy in your great sorrow. We pray that your country's gratitude for a life so nobly given in its service may bring you some measure of consolation, signed George R.I."

A grave site was established in Holland, burying the bodies of the crew. Peter's name was engraved into a tomb stone next to the other six. It was believed there were no survivors.

Muffled sounds surrounded him, and he later found out that he had been discovered by a farmer who had carefully moved him to a nearby barn. There he was hidden from the German soldiers. Two days later, a collaborator in the village heard of the English airman hiding in the barn and reported him. He was rewarded with a 60-gilder ransom. Peter was taken on a motorbike to Essen, a large city in Germany. Here he was admitted into a hospital for treatment of his injuries from the crash. Slipping between consciousness and unconsciousness, drowning in waves of pain, Peter was disorientated. As soon as he was able to be moved, Peter was transported on a train to the German city of Frankfurt under German guard.

Frankfurt had been badly bombed by the British. Peter was escorted through the city streets in his RAF uniform for everyone to witness. Mobs of people surrounded him, jostling and screaming accusations while spitting in his face. With his hands tied tight behind his back he was unable to wipe the warm liquid away leaving it to run into the corners of his mouth. The taste of hatred was sour to swallow.

"Murderer," they yelled in unison.

"You killed my wife and two children," one man cried in grief holding a family photograph. His uncontrollable shaking was on the verge of convulsions, the agony of loss becoming a physical manifestation.

Peter was fully awakened to the devastation of war. The innocent deaths that nobody wanted. As the bomber, he felt responsible and full of sorrow. Buildings crumpled around him as he fell to his knees, weeping in the dust. The crowd began to punch and kick him trying to take his life.

"Swinehund," they yelled.

"He's only a child, leave him," a woman cried in German.

The German guard led Peter away from the angry crowd, a decision that spared his life.

FAMILY

Peter was taken to the infamous POW Camp, Dulag Luft, for interrogation. One of his military assigned boots had a cover on the toe concealing a knife. Peter discreetly removed the cover, with the intention of unpicking the lock to his cell. He was seen by a nearby guard who swiftly removed the knife, slapping Peter's face with a harsh backhander. The force left a sting that would linger for hours.

'The Sweat Box' was a small interrogation room used to gain information through various methods of torture. Denial of food, along with hot and cold torture would torment the captured air crew. Blood curdling screams from adjacent cells would resonate in the pitch darkness.

"Hey Limy, give them the information," a man with a Yorkshire accent called out.

This man had been planted by the Germans to assist in gaining intelligence. Screams of Americans continued from the cells around him, gun shots fired, a constant mental torture to break them.

But Peter would only give his name, rank, and serial number even when he was offered cigarettes and chocolates as bribes.

When the weeklong interrogations were over, Peter was commended by the German guard for remaining strong.

"Well done," the guard said as he kicked Peter's leg hard with his steal capped boot.

It was early April when Peter moved to the main POW camp, Stalag Luft, a more permanent site. The conditions were horrific with overcrowding, hunger, and brutal treatment. The stale stench of death was ever present in the oppressive thick air. As a prisoner of war, you were rationed one meal a day of German sausage, black bread, and soup. There was no hygiene, no access to any kind of washing. Red Cross parcels would arrive once a month to the delight of the prisoners. Jam, biscuits, cigarettes and condensed milk would be evenly distributed. Peter didn't smoke so he would use his cigarettes to trade for other items he enjoyed. He would keep fit by walking up and down the campgrounds, plans of escape were always in the cell's whispers. Concealed microphones had been hidden by the Germans in the hope of catching them out.

"The American troops are getting closer. The war is nearly over," the guard said.

The bitter cold forced the prisoners to burn their beds for firewood, desperate for warmth. This left them sleeping on the floor snuggling into each other for body heat. Peter buddied up with an injured French soldier for his survival. They would share stories of their families back home in the few common words they shared.

A decision was made to march the prisoners to a neighboring camp. Rumor spread that the Germans were going to use 100 prisoners as hostages on Hitler's life. The men were gathered to parade through the snow in the bitter cold. The holes in their boots invited a damp numbness leaving their toes white and bloodless. They were given no food for the 300-mile journey, having to pick up food along the way. Turnips were growing freely so the starving men began to eat them raw. This resulted in violent diarrhea which they aptly named 'squitters'. A German guard with an Alsatian dog, allowed the prisoners to go into the ditch at the side of the road to relieve themselves. Peter and a few others decided to use this opportunity to attempt an escape. Jumping down into the ditch, they remained there hiding for the entire night. The freezing mud oozed around them, as they dared not move or make a sound. On the break of day, the escapees ran as fast as they could away from the gunfire to the west. Peter kept his head low as his legs carried him in an adrenaline rush. It was 5th April, Peter's 20th birthday. He had escaped, no longer a 'POW', Prisoner of War. A taste of freedom sweetened his lips as he smiled in victory.

FAMILY

Drunken Americans on tanks were a welcome site. Already celebrating the impending victory, they took Peter onboard over the Rhine River to Brussels. A short flight on a familiar Lancaster and Peter was home on 1st May 1945.

With no communication during wartime, Peter was eager to get back to his hometown of Shrewsbury to inform his parents that he was safe. He knocked on the front door.

"John," his mother cried.

"No, it's Peter," he corrected.

"I know. It's terrible. Peter's plane was shot down. He's dead."

His mother was choked with emotion as she stared at Peter. The bagged redness of her eyes indicated many hours of despairing tears.

"It's me. I'm Peter," Peter said.

The son standing before her was her identical twin, not John but Peter. Elation bounded out of her as she wrapped her arms around a ghost. Her son had returned - alive.

On 8th May 1945, the Germans unconditionally surrendered, ending the war in Europe. The returned soldiers received a wonderful reception with shouts of victory. Flags were flying from every house, as the people rejoiced and danced in the streets.

These early life experiences moulded my father into a man of great courage and purpose. He was a war hero. I later found a tiny Bible that he had been allocated in Starlog Luft. It was a copy of the New Testament from the American Bible Society. Inside the front cover written in pencil was:

F/O Peter Cook, Hut 69, Block 4, Stalag Luft 3, Germany.

Peter had highlighted one scripture, Acts 24:15:

> "And have hope toward God, which they themselves always allow, and there shall be a resurrection of the dead, both of the just and unjust."

I wondered if my father had reflected on the bombs he had dropped on Germany. The innocent lives killed, the man with the photograph screaming "murderer" in his face. Only a few years earlier he was a young boy holding falsified documents, excited and proud to be fighting for his country. While locked away as a POW, he was pondering this scripture about the God of the Bible, a God of justice.

Many years later, a photograph of the wreckage of Peter's plane, displaying the deceased bodies of his comrades, was obtained from a museum in Duxford, UK. On a return visit to Holland, Peter visited his grave site where 'Peter Cook' was chiselled into the head stone. He took a photo to mount on the wall alongside the framed letter from King George VI. He was assumed dead, yet defeated all odds to become a survivor, a war hero.

After the war ended, Peter pursued a career as a doctor at Guy's Hospital in London, a reputable teaching hospital producing dedicated doctors. Still with adventure in his spirit, Peter sailed the seas as a ship's doctor to Australia. He had a season as a Flying Doctor, visiting many outback towns until he finally settled in Sydney as a GP in Top Ryde.

My mother, Wilhelmina, was born into a life of privilege and stardom. As the daughter of an amateur opera singer, William Bermingham, she was taught the skills required to launch her into fame. Her angelic soprano voice was seen as a gift from God. Her singing career began on 2GB radio station as an 8-year-old child. She was known as a child prodigy. The range of notes she could effortlessly reach left people mesmerised leaving no question of her destined future. Winning a scholarship at the age of sixteen, she travelled to Rome to study Italian Opera. This is where her adventures truly began.

In Italy she discovered the delights of fine foods, wine, and men. Stunningly beautiful she had many suitors chasing her. But Wilhelmina had no interest in settling down, the enjoyment of stardom, keeping her single through her twenties and into her early thirties.

Until Hector, an Italian Doctor from New York appeared, sweeping Wilhelmina off her feet. They were to marry and return to New York as soon as possible. The telegram arrived unexpectantly. William, her much adored father only in his late fifties was at the hospital in a terminal condition, the emphysema from years as a smoker increasing its death grip. Wilhelmina rushed home to Australia to be at the bedside of her beloved coach and father.

One fateful day, the resident doctor was unable to attend to William, so an intern Dr Peter Cook, was sent in his place. Now well settled in Sydney, Peter had just celebrated his 40th birthday. His time at war had delayed the commencement of his career. Studying to become a doctor did not allow much spare time for courting a wife. He was a handsome man with a boyish face. His English complexion contributing to his lingering youthfulness. The skin on his arms was absent of hair, it was pale and smooth. He had entertained many casual lady friends back in the UK but had left them all behind at the dock.

Peter entered the small hospital room, a vision of beauty appeared before his eyes. Wilhelmina's golden hair was carefully backcombed into a style of height and elegance, her skin radiating a flawless translucence. The fluorescent lights shone bright, illuminating her high cheek bones and the softness of her eyes. Even though they were wide with sadness, she was perfection in Peter's eyes. He had to know this woman.

"Hello, I'm Dr Cook, you can call me Peter," he said, his eyes transfixed on hers.

Over the following days, Peter and Wilhelmina engaged in pleasant conversation, a welcome distraction for Wilhelmina from her father's impending fate. Peter soon discovered Wilhelmina's love of opera, a passion they both shared.

"Would you like to come to Madame Butterfly this evening at the State Theatre?" Peter asked.

"Yes, thank you," Wilhelmina accepted.

The evening was electric, with elaborate costumes dancing their magic while voices cascaded delightful sounds to the ear. Wilhelmina was swept away into a world she knew and loved.

William's final hour came suddenly, stealing his last laboured breath. His wife and daughter by his side, Dr Peter Cook searching for a pulse that was no longer there.

The formalities were concluded over the following week. A death certificate was officially signed, a cremation was decided upon, to be held at the nearby crematorium at North Ryde. Wilhelmina remained somber yet also relieved that the long suffering was over.

Peter loved anything foreign and exotic, the more spice the better. Wilhelmina accepted tentatively his invitation to an Indian restaurant, a first-time experience for her. Raised on a staple diet of meat and three veg, she was hoping the Asian menu wasn't going to be too hot and spicy. The waitress, dressed in a shimmering sari of golden threads, reds and aquas of sheer satins, caught Wilhemina's attention. Her bare belly displayed a gold ring, pieced into her skin just above the belly button. A welcoming gesture broke Wilhelmina's stare directing them both to a table for two by the window.

Peter looked deeply into Wilhelmina's hazel eyes and drew breath.

FAMILY

"You need to write to your fiancée in New York and tell him you are not going to marry him," he said.

"Why on earth would I do that?" she replied, startled at his statement.

"Because you are going to marry me," he proposed.

Hector's ring was returned, and the two were married on 20th July 1962. Wilhelmina's decision to marry Peter also included a decision to stay in Sydney to comfort her newly widowed mother.

She was to marry a doctor, one way or another.

The winter wedding was a small affair with a hand full of relatives on my mother's side of the family and no relatives on my father's side. Dad's family all resided in the UK, the distance and cost of travelling well out of their reach.

Arch Campbell was the best man. 'Archie' had been one of Dad's patients and they hit it off while Dad was examining him for skin cancer. Archie's pale Scottish skin had seen too much of the Australian sun as he enjoyed numerous hours on his 80-foot yacht sailing on Sydney Harbour. His wife Mary was a sweet lady always elegantly dressed, frequently joining the other Hunters Hill ladies for a game of bridge. She was an excellent golfer, and her body was trim. She always chose carefully from the menu at social luncheons. Archie convinced Dad that Hunters Hill was the only suburb to reside in.

Hunters Hill was considered one of the best suburbs in Sydney at the time. A leafy peninsula of land, surrounded by calm royal blue waters where most homes enjoyed a view along either the Lane Cove or Parramatta Rivers. You would be the envy of all if you could afford to get a plot of land in this neighbourhood.

The wedding ceremony was held in a local school classroom with Wilhelmina walking past the school desks, which stood in a perfect line forming a makeshift aisle. She wore a pale blue chiffon dress, her hair in its usual back-combed style, a pearl necklace and white leather shoes with a modest heel. Her makeup was impeccable, as she spent a full hour carefully applying each stroke of powder and blush to highlight her prominent cheek bones. She held a small bouquet of white carnations wrapped with a blue satin ribbon tied into a large bow. There was no veil, no flowers decorating the school room, no bridesmaids, no flower girls, no photographer, no fuss. I later wondered why my mother, a life of performing on the stage, chose to have such an understated wedding. I could only guess it was because they had very little money and my mother was embarrassed about some secret relatives who came from the wrong side of town. But doctors had the potential to make good money, which Peter looked forward to once he had completed his Australian internship.

Not long after the wedding, my grandmother mortgaged her modest home in West Ryde to give the newlyweds the deposit needed for their Hunters Hill home. A property came on the market not far from Archie and Mary's place and Archie was quick to let Peter know.

"This is a gem, Peter," Archie cried down the phone in a bellowing voice that matched the bagpipes be played.

"If you don't jump on it, you will miss out," he added.

The waterfront dream home was purchased. Wilhelmina and Peter could not have been happier. Beaming with pride; Wilhelmina was now a doctor's wife from Hunters Hill.

Matthew was born the following July in 1963, followed closely by me in July 1964. Mum had gone to hospital early with Matthew thinking she was in labour. She did not enjoy waiting around a full week, then having a difficult breech birth. Her first few weeks of motherhood were spent sitting on a round blow-up cushion that resembled a large donut. She was grateful to have a husband as a doctor who made sure she had access to plenty of strong pain relief.

Wilhelmina wasn't going to make this mistake again, so with me she waited until she was sure she was in labour. Heavily pregnant she had hosted a dinner party for three of the doctors and their wives from Dad's surgery where he worked in private practice. The evening was uneventful, the usual talk boasting about what their children were achieving.

"Douglas has been accepted into Sydney university to study law next year. He was awarded dux at Scotts College," one of the wives gloated.

The last of the farewells were made in the driveway, BMWs and Mercedes reversing carefully up the stamped concrete. A sudden gush of warm fluid spilled down Wilhelmina's favourite blue velvet slacks.

"Peter, I think I need to go to the hospital!" she cried with an urgency.

Peter quickly realised that my arrival was imminent. Grabbing some twine and his medical bag, he assisted Wilhelmina into his Mini Minor, taking off at full speed to Hornsby Hospital. He was ready and expecting to deliver me on the way.

'Buzz buzz'. Peter's pager went off. The expected confinement of Mrs. Jones' third baby was also imminent. Pushing harder on the accelerator, Peter exceeded the speed limit. Wilhemina's eyes were shut tight, consumed by violent contractions. The 'Minnie' car flew into the Emergency entrance as if it had wings, Peter leaping out of the driver's door frantically waving his arms above his head.

"This way. I have a woman giving birth!" he shouted.

A young man pushing a wheelchair at high speed swept Wilhelmina onto the seat. Peter leant forward to kiss her on the forehead.

"I love you," he gently spoke panting, then jumped back into the Minnie to rush off to deliver Mrs. Jones' baby.

My near birth in a Mini Minor had been avoided, my entrance into the world delighting my mother minutes after arriving at the hospital. The delivery was so quick that my head was pointed like an elongated mango, and I was bright yellow with jaundice to match. I was Wilhelmina's much wanted daughter and the apple of my father's eye. Bubbling with personality and a free spirit, my mother found me challenging. Babies were foreign to her, and I was a strange creature for her to try and tame. And tame me she could not.

Full of life I had no time to waste. Sleeping in a cot was certainly not on my to-do list. My mother would shut the door to my room and let me cry - battle cries I was determined to win. My father would sneak in, going under my mother's radar, pick me up, place me gently in his bed and begin to sing sweet songs. My favourite song was the one he wrote himself, the limited sounds would wash over me, 'By by buba, bubity boo ba ba, bubity boo ba boo ba ba, bubity boo ba ba'. If mother caught us, she would be very cross. That cross face with a deep furrow between the eyes, a look of disapproval, would follow me throughout my life.

Chapter 3
Doctor's Daughter

Renovations and decorating occupied all my mother's time. Floral wallpaper, dark wood panelling and golden carpets completed her signature style. My father on the other hand was not a decorator, he was a collector, later developing into hoarding. He collected all kinds of things from ornaments, war relics, books, records, buttons, stamps, antiques, you name it. His favorite past time was visiting secondhand stores. 'Tempe Tip' was a huge store of unwanted bits and pieces in Tempe, Sydney.

Most of these wares came from deceased estates, piling up the items that the families no longer wanted. Dad would take Matthew and me, allowing us to fossick through the piles of discarded stuff in the hope of finding a valuable gem. Dad had an eye for that special find. He would spot first edition books and other sought out collectables of the time. He would pride himself on the large box full of treasures he would lug to the counter.

"Five dollars," a woman would say, Dad's chest puffing up, as he smiled at the bargains before him.

Mum would roll her eyes when his catch arrived home whilst mumbling under her breath, "Where on earth do you expect me to put all this junk?"

As a full-time mother of two, Dad did not expect his wife to get a job. It was common at the time for women to be stay-at-home mums, especially in Hunters Hill. Mum therefore had time to decorate and meticulously clean the house from top to bottom. Every surface gleamed. The chandeliers were dusted on a regular basis and the carpeted floors vacuumed almost daily. Housework was her pride and joy. Cooking was not her strength. As a young woman travelling the world, the opportunity to learn to cook eluded her. In our house, all food was to be fried. A large metal pot sat permanently on the stovetop – three-quarters full of some kind of lard. The metal was dark and burnt at the edges, the heating and cooling turning the contents from liquid into a solid mass. Fried potato chips were a staple. Mum meticulously washed, chopped, and peeled potatoes every night. They would sizzle violently when dropped into the bubbling pot, spitting hot fat at anyone daring to come near. Then the chicken would be added. Crumbed chicken legs that had been coated in flour, egg, and breadcrumbs. The token green vegetable would be frozen peas which were boiled to a soggy death.

Deep in the bowels of my family home was Dad's home-based surgery. It was a place of intrigue — a small dark room with one window where my father would occasionally see patients like the kids in our street who fell off their bikes needing to be bandaged. I recall one kid who had been using a slug gun when the bullet ricocheted off a wall and embedded in his forehead, only slightly missing his eye. I was shocked by the amount of blood pouring from this boy's head. I was Daddy's little nurse called to assist in these bloody emergencies.

On display in Dad's surgery was a small baby in a jar. This baby was curled in a fetal position, the umbilical cord still attached. A perfectly formed little boy, his genitals visibly on display. As a young girl I would visit the surgery and stare in wonder at every detail of his fully formed body, the fine fingers so tiny and yet so exquisite, the nails formed at each tip of the ten fingers, his tiny penis resting on his scrotum sack.

This was someone's child, a precious baby, but it sat on a shelf as an ornament or science experiment in my family home. As a young child myself, I never thought of this baby as a human being. It was an exhibit to stare at in awe. I was so mesmerised by the 'Baby in the Bottle', as I referred to it, that one day I decided to take it to school for show and tell.

Looking back, I am amazed that my parents and my teacher allowed this exhibition. There was no emotional connection with a human life that had been denied a proper burial. I surmised later in life that this was a still birth or perhaps from an abortion, an unwanted pregnancy from a teenager. This child was discarded, losing all rights and respect. He was placed in a jar to be pickled and preserved as a specimen to be viewed in fascination, all dignity lost.

I'm not sure what eventually happened to the little boy tucked up in the bottle, but I think the liquid methylated spirits may have dried out and he was discarded.

I think of all the discarded babies in the world. The baby girls in China, born then left on the side of the road, in the gutters, not valued not heard. Left to die. With a broken heart I wrote a poem for them:

LAST CRY

Light so bright all around
Engulfing ears with enormous sound
Take a breath, expand the lungs
Rejoice a birth, a life begun

Cast aside, warmth denied
Suckling lips, no breast beside
Searching eyes, gazing space
Discarded life, female race

Fear inside, hunger pain
Crying out, but in vain
Blackened world, passing by
Hardened hearts, blinded eye
Screaming pain, freezing wind
Precious life, never sinned
Weakening heart, not a say
Life, now death, in just one day

Chapter 4

The Red Dress

"I'm here to pick up Sarah," my mother's voice broke the silence of the classroom.

You were deemed lucky if you got to leave before the end of school bell. An early mark was a reward.

I had been told I was leaving school early to have my photograph taken.

Once in the car, my mother glanced sideways at me with a look of concern as the vegemite smears were still lingering on the corners of my mouth from my lunchtime sandwiches. When we arrived home, the instructions followed:

"Hurry up, Sarah. You need to get ready. Go and wash your face and put on your dress. It's on your bed."

A red dress with white polka dots and a large white collar was laid out neatly on my bed. It was made of a cotton rayon blend that was soft to the skin. The fabric would swirl from side to side in an elegant dance when I swayed my hips. Sitting slightly above my knees it oozed of sweetness. A matching belt was tied into a large bow at the back. Mum had to help me with the zipper to make the outfit complete. It was a special dress for special occasions. Other than my school uniform on school days, mum liked to dress me in pants and a shirt. She seemed to like brown tones while my brother was often dressed in the exact same matching outfit. I think mum liked the attention she received from people asking if we were twins. Having us dressed in the same clothes brought this question to her regularly. I hated being thought of in this untruth and Matthew hated it more. The red dress, waiting patiently on my bed had only been worn on one other occasion. A friend of the family was christening her new baby daughter, and this special dress was purchased for the occasion.

Mum began brushing my long blonde hair frantically into a high ponytail pulling firmly securing each hair into a tight elastic. This was my mother's selected hairstyle for me, giving me headaches by the end of the day from the excruciating tightness. I don't ever remember getting my hair cut as a child as Mum wanted my hair as long as possible. It was a golden mane of glory for her to admire.

Every night before I got into bed, my mother would put a small plastic roller in the end of my hair to create a defined curl for the next day. This practice was insisted on, even when I had sleepovers with friends, which became increasingly embarrassing as I got older.

Mum seemed flustered, fussing in her dressing table draw, eventually pulling out a red ribbon, which she tied neatly in my ponytail.

"Hurry! Let's go," she ordered.

I climbed back into the car, and we raced to the church. Villa Maria Church was a five-minute drive, then if you got the red light at the top of Mary Street. Arriving at the large historic sandstone building, I scurried along beside Mum, trying to keep up with her quickening pace. Following her lead, she took me down a pathway into a side entrance leading to a room next to the main church altar. This room was used for confession, a familiar space I had only previously entered from the main body of the church.

THE RED DRESS

The sacrament of Penance, 'confession' as it is known, is where a parishioner would confess their sins to a priest. This sacrament was a requirement for the Catholic Church from the age of approximately seven years. The commencement date was usually just before the partaking in the first holy communion and confirmation ceremonies. If you had unconfessed sin, you were not permitted to take holy communion at Mass on Sundays. I sometimes disobeyed this requirement, taking holy communion anyway so that everyone in the church would think I was a good girl.

At the confessional booths you would await your turn to confess. You would enter through a door into a very small dark room. A small window inside was covered with a sliding screen. Behind the screen was an equally dark adjacent room. A musty odour was always present as the ancient wood was deprived of light or fresh air. Waiting quietly behind a sliding window, was a silhouette of a man. A stranger not to be identified. The only option was to kneel on the hard wooden step close to the window that would creak under your body weight. The window would slide open revealing the silhouette behind the darkness.

"Tell me your sins, my child," the strange voice would command.

This command would send me into a panic. My heart pounded in terror while my mind raced with plans of how to get out. To run. The hidden figure held an authority I knew I had no choice but to obey. What were my sins? I couldn't think.

"Um, I was.... mean.... to my brother," I stammered. But he was always mean to me, so that was not really a sin I concluded.

"I have been naughty," I added after a lengthy silence. This overarching confession I thought could cover any other sins against God I had committed since my last confession. I paused, waiting for my judgement and consequential punishment.

"You are to say one Our Father and three Hail Marys," the dark voice instructed.

I would quickly jump to my feet reaching to open the door, hungry for air. The penance prayers were to be carried out in the pews beside the confessional booths on your knees, head bowed. The strange darkened anonymous man had the power to forgive my sins. He scared me and I dreaded confession times.

Mum tapped her fingernails looking back and forwards across the room then to her wristwatch.

A man swiftly entered the room, my mother immediately switching from an impatient glare to a beaming smile. His eyes widened as he looked directly at me.

"This must be Sarah. Isn't she pretty," he said.

My mother beamed back at him; always soaking in any compliments about me as if they belonged to her. He was not dressed in priestly robes but was wearing casual beige loose pants and a black untucked shirt. He looked professional with all the photographic equipment he was carrying in a black duffle bag. A large umbrella was placed to the side of a camera he began to mount on a stand. A small table covered in a red cloth with three ceramic statues was positioned in front of the camera. He instructed me to approach.

"Now look up at the baby Jesus, Sarah," he said.

I moved gingerly towards the table noting that Joseph, Mary, and the baby Jesus were waiting for me.

"Move closer," he urged.

"Closer. That's it! Closer. Now look up."

I was so close now the statues were a blur. I felt very uncomfortable in this position and my eyes watered from trying to focus on something so close. My body felt so unnatural conforming to this strange positioning. "I want to go home," I thought to myself.

Click, click click. The light flashed over and over. The man allowed a short rest before it began again. I was repositioned, *click, click, flash, flash.* After what seemed like a ridiculous amount of time to take a photo, I was finally released.

Gratefully back at home, I took off the red dress and placed it carefully on a hanger in my antique wardrobe. As a reward, I got to devour hot buttery toast with vegemite. I could never get enough vegemite toast. Mum explained I was to be on the cover of the Marist Father's 1972 Christmas edition of HARVEST Magazine.

"You are to be the cover girl!" she announced with pride.

I was glad the photo shoot was over. I never wanted to pursue a career in modelling, and this day cemented my belief.

* * * * *

Villa Maria primary school held a strong connection to the local parish Villa Maria Church, both being overseen by the Marist Fathers. The Marist Fathers was a religious order of Roman Catholic priests dating back to the 19th century. One of the more regular visitors to our school was Brother Dave, a handsome clean-shaven man in his late twenties. He was in training to become a priest. All the young girls seemed to flock around him when he visited, enjoying his warm charismatic charm.

We never questioned why he was visiting our school as it was commonplace for the Marist Priests to come and speak with the nuns. The teaching positions at my school were dominated by nuns. Brother Dave seemed to take a special liking to me. I was so delighted when he caught my attention and said hello to me ahead of the other students.

Other girls would flounce around, swinging their regulation knee length skirts, skipping back and forth, trying to catch his attention. But he only had eyes for me. With flushed cheeks and chin tucked, I'd look up at him returning his sweet smile. I was shy around this man, yet I felt strangely safe. He was studying to become a priest, the highest calling for a man in the Catholic church, a position to be admired. He was holy, special to God, and because of that, I believed he could be trusted.

Not long after my eighth birthday, I noticed an unfamiliar car in our driveway and was pleasantly surprised to learn that Brother Dave had come to visit. He was in the music room with my mother. The room was aptly named as it was the hub for gathering to enjoy music. A large pianola was the centrepiece standing boldly next to an antique wooded chest filled with various musical instruments for visitors to choose from. There were tambourines, triangles, castanets, recorders and bells, and a delightful array of percussion pieces. Many nights were enjoyed pumping the two peddles, billowing out sounds from the hundreds of pianola rolls in Dad's collection. I attended piano lessons but found practicing scales tedious and quite boring. I would much rather be outside playing and making cubby houses. Later, I was placed into flute lessons because Mum loved the sound of the flute. Again, I struggled with the necessary practice.

This afternoon, Brother Dave was sitting at the piano while mum was standing close behind him.

"Hello, Sarah," they both echoed in unison.

"Hello, Brother Dave," I replied quietly.

I discovered that Brother Dave played the piano beautifully. He was accompanying Mum as she sang her favourite tunes from the musical South Pacific. Mum had starred in this musical touring New Zealand and sang like an angel. I never tired of listening to her voice. She sang like the sounds of beautiful birds reaching each high note with perfection, bringing delight to my soul. I would sit captivated by her.

Mum had met Brother Dave at church, and they soon shared their love of music. Mum would gather on the grounds outside the front of the church at the end of mass and mingle with the other parishioners. Brother Dave would come and say hello soon chatting to Mum about the musical pieces he enjoyed. I was already familiar with Brother Dave from his many visits at the school gate. A friendship developed between them, and the duo soon became a weekly performance in our music room. Brother Dave playing the piano seemed to bring my mother so much joy as she would bat her eyelids towards his handsome face. His visits were on Wednesdays, when Dad was working late, and Mum was always delighted when the doorbell rang.

I would tell the girls at school of these 'special' visits, and they would glare with envy. I had won the attention of the handsome man of God and now he was coming to my home. I felt special. I had worn my special red dress because I was chosen to be the cover girl. Maybe Brother Dave had seen the Harvest magazine and noticed how special I was?

Chapter 5
Secret Adventures

Growing up on the Lane Cove River was always an adventure. My father bought my nine-year-old brother a small dinghy with an outboard engine. Not wanting to miss out or be treated as unequal, I pestered Dad endlessly until I convinced him to get me one too. I was the apple of Dad's eye, so my sweet charm got its way.

As an eight-year-old girl, I was now the proud owner of a 10-foot Savage dinghy with a six horsepower Evinrude engine that came with a big responsibility. This gateway to freedom suited my adventurous spirit perfectly as I found being at home drudgery. Going out on my boat was an escape and I would venture out every moment I could.

The purr of the engine was music to my ears and its speed was an adrenaline rush. I would fly up and down the estuaries with not a care in the world. My friend Jean often joined me on weekends for some crazy adventures. Jean Thompson arrived from Tamworth in grade 3, at Villa Maria. She had red hair and freckles and seemed to gravitate towards me. She was very clever and yet had a sense of mischief that intrigued me. Her parents were recently divorced, and we became thick as thieves as we schemed our naughty antics. Under strict instruction from my mother, we were told not to leave the Lane Cove River. The river terminated at Lane Cove National Park, a popular picnic spot just past the weir.

From our family home it was a nine-kilometre trip down the river, winding and turning as it narrowed. At low tide the water became very shallow with the propeller often banging against submersed rocks as we hit the bottom. By watching my brother get out of tricky situations I soon learned some boating skills. I would pull my engine up to the first click on the leg, allowing the dinghy to go further into the shallows and mangroves.

The entrance through the mangroves was only as wide as the boat so we believed if we breathed in deeply this would help us fit through the tight passage. The narrow creek was fringed by massive roots, a maze of twisted limbs distorted out of shape, with no end in sight. Deep into the mangroves, an eerie stillness was in the air as we travelled into the belly. The pungent smell of filthy mud made us pinch our noses tight with our fingers for as long as we could. Eventually, a desperate deep breath was needed which engulfed our senses again with the putrid stench.

Despite the smells, we would continue to venture deeper, using the oars to push against the foliage, the branches smacking our faces. The aim was to see how far we could get up into the dense green jungle. Tiny crabs would scurry along the banks over the stinky mud. The excitement of pretending to be lost captivated us as we toyed with fear.

One day, Matthew and his friend Edward, his school 'bestie', confided in Jean and me telling us that they were going on a secret adventure. Edward was a follower and was always happy to tag along with Matthew's adventures. He had a mischievous laugh that would boom out from under his jet-black hair, cut into a bowl cut. I think his mother exercised hairdressing on her two sons over the kitchen sink.

"Please, please, please let us come too," we pleaded.

"Ok, but you can't tell Mum. Go and get some pocket money, we are leaving in five minutes," he instructed.

I was a good saver, having a suitable stash of coins under my bed in an olive green, round metal tin. I checked the petrol supply for my dinghy in the red plastic tank to make sure it was full. We were off. At top speed we headed upriver in the opposite direction to the weir. I followed closely in Matthew's wake enjoying crisscrossing, jumping over the waves. The Sydney sun was beaming down on my freckled face.

The end of the Lane Cove River finished with Woolwich to our right and Greenwich to our left, opening to the vast expanse of the Parramatta River. I had never ventured beyond this point before. To my concerned surprise, I could see Matthew and Edward still at full speed ahead bouncing over the increasing wakes of the large boats busily heading out to Sydney Harbour. I quickly turned the handle on my engine to reduce the speed. What was Matthew doing? The longer I hesitated the further he disappeared, and I feared I would lose sight of him. I squeezed my fist on the throttle to increase speed again, looked at Jean for reassurance and stepped into disobedience.

Carefully, I navigated the huge waves coming at me from all directions, the product of the numerous pleasure crafts. Suddenly at high speed, the Sydney Harbour Ferry was approaching. Instinctively, I knew it was my job to keep out of its way. My level of concentration was at its peak for my eight-year-old brain, as I desperately tried to catch up to Matthew's dinghy in the distance. His dinghy was 12 feet long, only two more feet than mine and I now desperately wished I was in a bigger boat.

Matthew hadn't even turned to look back to see if his little sister was following. I was scared but there was no turning back. The huge grey arch of the Sydney Harbour Bridge was ahead in the distance. I could vaguely see Matthew now, way ahead of me, heading straight for it. "Oh no, where are we going?" I quietly thought to myself so as not to alarm Jean.

The pleasure craft waves became more frequent and bigger, forcing me to slow my boat to a near stop so as not to be swamped by their whitewash. I knew I was committed to keep going, too terrified to turn around and head home without Matthew with me. What seemed like an eternity, I finally saw Matthew turn towards the shore. He was heading into Watson's Bay to the famous Doyle's fish and chips waterfront restaurant. We were now 20kms away from Mum's fury. She would have a heart attack if she knew where we went, and I could never tell her. We tied up the dinghies to the long wharf jutting out from the white sandy beach lined with multimillion dollar homes. I was hungry by now so rushed to join the queue of Sydney siders waiting for takeaway food. My box of fish bites and hot chips coated in fresh lemon with white tartare sauce to dip in was heaven for a hungry kid. The treacherous journey was now worth it. I ate ravenously and at the same time scolded my brother for not waiting for us.

As soon as we had finished, we knew it was time to head back as Mum would be questioning our long absence. As my dinghy bounced back across the busy harbour, I saw a large blue and white vessel heading towards my boat. A beefy uniformed man on the bow was waving at me. Matthew and I both slowed down only to discover it was a police boat commanding us to stop.

The vessel came close as the officer called out,

"Show me your life jackets please."

In the rush to get on our adventure and checking I had fuel I had totally forgotten to put the two life jackets into the bow of my boat. We were in trouble. The officer asked lots of questions, "Where do you live, where have you been?" and "How old are you?"

It shocked him when I told him I was eight years old.

"Do your parents know you are out here with no life jackets? It's against the law not to carry life jackets," the officer informed us of this fact I was already fully aware of.

Both Matthew and I said very little, trying not to incriminate ourselves further.

I wanted to cry but somehow kept a brave face pretending I was mature. After a brief telling off, the police officer let us go. I was so relieved that our secret trip out of the Lane Cove River would go undetected.

Back at home, I hooked up the large metal winch and with my skinny arms manually turned the handle to pull my boat on its trailer out of the water. It was exhausting. I used all the strength in my tiny-framed body, frequently stopping to catch my breath. I disconnected the fuel tank, then lifted the heavy engine off the boat onto a trolley to be flushed out with fresh water from the hose. My arms trembled under the weight. It was then wheeled up the side of the house to be locked into the shed. Matthew never offered to help me and seemed to be amused at my struggle. Jean would assist but I enjoyed the independence, proving I was strong and capable. Mum watched from the upstairs, always detached from any strenuous activity. It was no surprise when I required a double inguinal hernia operation later that year.

The day after our secret adventure, Dad arrived home from the surgery, had a quick talk with Mum, then called me and Matthew into the kitchen. He was frowning.

"Did you both go to Watson's Bay yesterday?" Dad asked in an unusual firm tone.

I looked at him blankly, quickly thinking I would blame Matthew for making me go with him. Dad continued,

"Jeff Peters, one of my patients, called me today to say he saw you near the Harbour Bridge."

SECRET ADVENTURES

It turns out that Jeff Peters was the police officer who had pulled over Dr Cook's children who he quickly identified when he asked for our names and address.

We were busted. Our mission was detected. We were both promptly sent to our rooms with no TV for a week. The worst punishment possible in our minds.

"Noooooo!" I screamed inside.

I was born with an adventurous spirit and my life was to be filled with many more adventures.

One other adventure stands out not so favorably.

Now 10 years old, my school friend Emily had come over to my house for the day. Emily also loved the water and adventures. We had planned a day out in my dinghy, but my engine had broken down. My boat was out of action. Matthew was getting his dinghy ready, the fuel tank full and life jackets stuffed in the bow.

"Would you girls like to come for a ride?" Matthew asked.

"Sure," I replied.

The summer sun already had a bite turning my fair skin a shade of pink. I quickly raced upstairs for some sun cream. Emily stood on the shore untying the rope while Matthew pulled hard on the starting cord. The engine hummed as he adjusted the throttle to idle at a smooth pace.

"Hurry up Sarah, we're leaving," he shouted.

Emily was well versed at playing the deck hand role, releasing the rope, and launching herself into the boat effortlessly. I followed with a leap as the boat pulled away from the waterfront of our family home. Matthew putted slowly to the other side of the river, opposite our house. The houses on this side made up our view from the bay window in the TV room. I would get Dad's binoculars and peer into the windows hoping to be entertained by spotting people unawares in their homes. A mother in the kitchen preparing a meal, a man watching TV, kids playing games, any action was a delight.

As we approached the shore opposite my home, Matthew stopped the engine and reached for one of the wooden oars. He held it high above his head, his eyes becoming fierce red.

"Get out," he said threatening me and Emily with the wooden weapon.

Wide-eyed in shock and terror, we obeyed, scrambling out of his boat into the stinky mud. I instantly sank deep up to my knees, the gooey mass all consuming. The squelching goo sliding between my toes sent shivers up my spine. Unknown sharp objects hidden below the mud touched against the soles of my feet, sending me into a panic. My heart pounded with a deafening beat.

"No, Matthew, please," Emily desperately pleaded in vain.

The smirk on his face said it all. We were doomed to be left in the mud.

The only hope we had of getting back home was to wade through the putrid mud along the shoreline, then to climb over treacherous rocks to get to the bridge. We could then walk across the Figtree Bridge and get back to my place. The rocks were covered in oysters, their shells sharp as razor blades. Fighting back tears, we began to navigate the 100 metres ahead of us. One foot in front of the other, we slowly moved forward, each step sinking deeper into the quagmire.

"Why is Matthew so mean?" Emily questioned, her tears blending with snot, resulting from her gut-wrenching sobs.

"I don't know," I replied.

Over an hour had passed but we were pleased to be making ground. Our feet were bloodied from oyster cuts, which I feared would become infected from the festering mud. Suddenly Matthew returned, offering an olive branch.

"Sorry girls, get in. I'll take you home," he said.

Exhausted from our efforts yet relieved, we climbed into the boat. Matthew guided his dinghy back to the original place where he had forced us out. Again, he reached for the oar.

"Get out," he said with a shout.

"No," I screamed in horror.

The large wooden oar was swinging just missing my skull.

"Ok," I whimpered climbing back into the putrid mud. Emily fearfully followed.

Taking the same treacherous route, we finally made it home hours later. The blood seeping from our sores blending into a muddy soup.

"Where have you girls been?" Mum exclaimed.

She won't believe me, I thought as Matthew was her golden boy. I felt defeated and remained silent.

Chapter 6

Sunday Church

My mother was a devout Catholic, therefore a Catholic School education was a nonnegotiable in our home. Dad, being brought up in the Church of England, was given no choice but to accept her decision. He was non practising in his faith, so Mum won the decision, and we were sent to Catholic schools.

Wilhelmina was brought up in a Catholic home by William and Eileen Bermingham. William owned a small block of flats in Randwick containing eight units where his wife and daughter resided. Eileen worked at the Greyhound Control Board where she was much loved and respected. Young Wilhelmina attended Brigidine College, Randwick a prestigious Catholic girl's school.

As a child prodigy, Wilhelmina was known at her school to be a gifted child. Whenever any dignitaries came to the school, Wilhelmina was quickly removed from the classroom and asked to perform. Her voice would stun all as she sang complicated arias in her flawless soprano voice. Already singing on radio, her future as an opera singer was destined from an early age. Wilhelmina also had a flare for English. She wrote beautiful poems that

SUNDAY CHURCH

won prizes in competitions. Songwriting was also a passion with her songs so simple and pure that she continued to write into adulthood.

Dad liked to keep the peace and had the wisdom not to take Mum on with this difference of opinion, especially involving 'religion'. He preferred to let her make the decisions regarding the care of the children. He was a compassionate doctor dedicated to his patients, with deep concern for their wellbeing. He trusted Wilhelmina to take care of their children.

My brother and I had to attend Mass every Sunday, no questions asked. Our morning would begin at 9am with a compulsory fasting before we received the sacrament of holy communion. I never understood why the church and my mother enforced this cruelty. The hunger pains combined with light headedness were unbearable.

At 10am, Mass was about to start, and Mum would bustle us into the old sandstone church. Its huge stained-glass windows stood luminating the story of Christ's journey until his gruesome death on the cross. I used to look up at the shining glass story in horror. The hour-long service seemed to go for a lifetime. My groaning stomach and my complete boredom made church a dreaded experience. The solid wood church pews were rock hard on my small bony bottom with no cushions in sight.

Inadvertently, I was being taught that suffering and discomfort was pleasing to God as His son Jesus also suffered. To complain would only undermine the great sacrifice that Jesus endured for my salvation. One of my strongest memories is of my brother poking me over and over and pushing his pointer finger deep into my side. He would conduct his annoying attack discreetly not to be noticed by Mum. I would eventually crack and slap him.

"Stop it!" I would shout.

My foolish outburst would now have to reap the punishment. With her long brightly painted nails Mum would dig them into the flesh on my thigh, bringing me to tears. I knew that another sound made in church would be punishable by death, or so I thought. My mother would not even cast her eyes sideways as she continued to sing ancient hymns and recite repetitive chants.

Coming home from church was the best part. My Dad would be waiting preparing food for the starving children with a warm smile. He delighted in telling us that he was once a choir boy, making us laugh with his stories. Mum would get annoyed as his stories had a tone of mockery.

Every night Matthew and I were called by Mum to the parental bedroom for the Rosary. Dad knew to stay well away. The beads were carefully removed from a hook on her dark wooden antique dressing table and dished out to each of us. I always wanted the pair with clear crystal beads, Matthew grabbing for the green ones and Mum was left with the mission brown pair. The prayers would begin after the making of the sign of the cross, a ritualistic movement of a hand moving from forehead to chest then crossing the chest from left to right.

"Our Father who art in heaven hallowed be thy name," Mum would recite. Matthew and I were quick to join in the prayer, which was easily parroted as it rolled off our tongues. Another ritual learning that had been indoctrinated into us as children. Next mum would begin:

"Hail Mary full of grace, the Lord is with thee……" Then the next prayer would commence.

One 'Our Father', followed by ten 'Hail Marys' and concluded with a 'Glory be to the Father.'

After the first round the cycle of prayers would start again. Our fingers would move around the beads until all the beads had been visited. We would finish with another sign of the cross. This seemed very tedious and meaningless to me as a child, and my mind would wander off thinking about all kinds of interesting things I would rather be doing. This evening

SUNDAY CHURCH

ritual eventually ceased when the teenage years arrived, and both Matthew and I would rather pick a family fight than say the Rosary. Mum gave up inviting us kids and went into her bedroom alone to continue the ritual each evening by herself.

Chapter 7
The Cane

During my school years, in the 1960's and 1970's corporate punishment was the norm. The cane, also known as the 'sixes' was a dreaded punishment. Six hits 1,2,3,4,5,6 were inflicted either across the back of the hands or the backside.

The nuns dished out these punishments mainly to boys for behaviours such as chewing gum or snickering when being spoken to. These poor boys would skulk out of the principal's office red-faced, blotchy, and completely humiliated whilst bravely holding back the tears from their peers. The girls would heave a sigh of relief as they rarely fell victim to this assault. That's not to say we escaped the wrath of the nun's discipline, because we didn't. Psychological and emotional taunts would leave deeper scars on our impressionable young souls. It was also common for the girls to get a hard whack from a ruler across the knuckles, a surprise swipe while chatting to the child sitting next to you.

Nuns were a big part of my young life. As teachers at my school, I was fascinated by the habits they had to wear. Some of them wore full habits where only the face was exposed, while some wore a veil over the head showing the face, hair, and neck. Made from a thick fabric in navy blue,

THE CANE

the garments were fitted tightly around the neck with long sleeves and floor length tunics. These heavy garbs were designed to hide the body's form. In the summer I would feel sorry for them under this mound of material, faces puffed and red as they wiped the sweat from their brows. Yet my pity would soon be dispersed when their judgement fell upon us.

One day a group of us seven-year-old girls were playing in the back field in the school yard. This was a dusty large paddock of mainly dirt where the boys had dominion. It was known to be out of bounds for the girls, which made it even more enticing. We were having so much fun chasing the boys that we didn't hear the end of recess bell. Sister Theresa, my third-grade teacher, was not impressed by our tardiness. The look of disgust on her face as we rushed through the door was concerning.

I knew we were in trouble and my whole body trembled. Her lips were pursed into a snarl, saliva visibly dripping from the corner of her mouth. With a long stick in her hand, she was ready to perform her disturbed method of punishment. Humiliation was a common method to teach disobedient children a lesson.

Lining up in front of the classroom, we were ready to have our wrong doings broadcast to the entire class. This was to be a public hearing, a community flogging so that all the children would know that naughty children would always receive their due punishment.

The hearing began while Sister Theresa paced back and forth tapping her long stick on her hand. I was hypnotised by its swinging movement and didn't hear a word she was saying.

"Put your hands out," was the command that I knew would eventually come.

Warm pee dripped down my leg in an uncontrollable response. Oh no, I wanted to disappear or self-combust. Shaking all over, I looked to my right and left to see all the other guilty children. They were also responding with trembling hands outstretched in front of them, tears welling up in girls' and boys' eyes alike. In that moment, I remembered a story from a brave previously spanked boy who told us if you wet your hands the stick would not hurt.

Sister Theresa turned her back momentarily giving me a rare opportunity to act. I quickly put my hands to my mouth and spat into them, but my mouth was so dry from fear that it took a deep nose and throat inhale to conjure up spittle from deep within.

My hands, now dripping in saliva, I was ready to face my fate. But Sister Theresa decided to give leniency this day and called off the caning. I walked back to my seat carefully wiping my soggy hands on my tunic, feeling foolish, yet relieved to have been shown mercy.

Brother Dave was waiting at the school gate that day.

Chapter 8
The Gate

Inside the gate of Villa Maria Primary School, sat a large tin box with a thick black rubber flap. The box housed small individual milk bottles that were delivered daily to the school. Each bottle was tightly sealed with a silver foil cap to keep the liquid from curdling.

The old truck rattled up the road, bottles clanging together to announce its arrival. The middle-aged driver looked old and tired with his white unkept beard and hair that had not seen a comb. His forearms were hairy and solid from carting the crates of milk to all the schools.

Once the milk had been placed in the box, the flap would be pulled into place and his job was done. The milk would often sit in the extreme heat inside the tin box for hours. By the time the milk was delivered to the children, it was warm and curdled making me gag with each sip. The disgusting smell and mucus forming in my mouth was a daily ritual I dread. This was a nationally ordered milk scheme established by the Australian Government and no child was exempt. I later discovered I had a milk allergy, and this health directive was making me, and I am sure other children, sick.

When the final bell rang, the rush to leave the school would begin. I would be jostled along by the boys who would push past never considering anyone. The only thing on their minds was to escape as fast as possible. It was every man or child for themselves. I preferred to say my farewells to my friends and wait for the rush to be over before slowly making my way to the gate.

The children seemed to know that my special 'uncle', Brother Dave, would be at the gate waiting for me. His growing familiarity toward me gave him the nickname 'uncle' from my school friends. They would enjoy teasing me.

"Oooh Sarah, your Uncle Dave is here," they would gleefully chant.

Mum worked as a volunteer at the Marist Father's Missions Center, a Catholic charity that supported poor children in Japan and other nations in need at the time. This organisation was affiliated with Villa Maria Church, located in the same street. Mum would dutifully turn up every Thursday to assist with office duties.

This required a full make up application and setting her hair in rollers, followed by a back combing ritual. Mum would never leave the house without her presentation being immaculate. As she had never had a job in her past, other than being a professional singer, she would use her limited office skills doing filing and putting newsletters into envelopes. Mum seemed to find satisfaction doing 'God's work' for a few hours a week.

The parish priests often frequented the offices to give instructions while having cups of tea with the ladies. This wasn't the only commitment my mother made to the church. Our home was often used for fund raising events. The generosity of this offer was received with gratitude as our home's waterfront location was perfect for events. I remember one event called, 'Night of Nights'. We had a large chocolate wheel with many donated prizes including a chook raffle. The crowd shrieked with excitement when

THE GATE

a number was read out and a lucky person got to take home a wrinkly raw frozen chicken in a plastic bag. I watched in wonder from the upstairs verandah, at a distance so as not to be seen, as this was an adult only event. Other priests from the Marist Father's presbytery would frequent our home leading up to events and after. I never questioned why these men were in my family home.

I grew up in a generation where children were to be seen and not heard. I remember many times my brother and I being shuffled to our rooms just before the visitors arrived for dinner, with a stern warning from Mum not to be seen or else. Children were not a part of nighttime adult activities. My mother would sternly say,

"Nobody wants to see children."

One night, I needed to use the bathroom. The glass doors to our lounge room were in the path of my destination and there was certainly a high risk that a quick dash past the doors would have me spotted by an adult guest. This created a dilemma as I processed my plan to use the toilet.

Once the guests had been moved from the lounge to the dining table my risk of being sighted would diminish. Matthew came out of his room to find me standing, back firmly against the wall peering anxiously through the glass doors into the lounge room.

I was agonising over my decision to make the dash or not. After quiet whispers, Matthew promised to act as my watchman and give the command to run when the coast seemed the clearest.

Mr. and Mrs. Wilson, the Smith family and Dr Ainsworth and his wife, were all enjoying their pre-dinner drinks. Progressive dinners in the street were a popular undertaking. This was where the neighbourly group would start at the first home for an entrée, then move to the second home for the main course then finish up for dessert and liqueurs at the final home before staggering back to their own homes.

Finally, in a lull of silence, I inched forward. A sudden roar of laughter sent me fleeing back to my starting position.

Then, the command from my brother came,

"Go!!"

Matthew had given me the go ahead for safe passage. As fast as I could, I launched myself across the gap between the two glass doors. I had made it, my mission accomplished. No one saw me, thankfully.

My childhood upbringing, characterised by a generation of silencing children and hiding them away, only embedded a deep belief that I was not to be seen or heard.

I don't remember ever being cuddled or hugged by my mother. She was physically distant, showing no affection. I never saw her showing affection towards my father or brother either. The words, "I love you" were never uttered. As a child I felt like a trophy. In my mother's generation, it was a woman's duty to marry and to have children; my mother had achieved both. She had married a doctor, had two children, a boy and a girl which ticked her boxes. She lived the dream of a successful career in music and now she had her husband and children. But the children had to look good, achieve and make sure she would be seen in a glorious light. She would beam when speaking highly of her family life, even if what she was saying wasn't quite true. Exaggerating the truth or embellishing a story with a few white lies was her style. I would cringe inside in silence as I listened to her embellished praises while her audience gasped in awe adding congratulations.

Brother Dave noticed me. I didn't feel hidden or silenced around him. His beaming smile, waiting with questions about my day, was at the gate. I was a child, and he was an adult who saw me. I knew he liked me, and I felt special. I returned his smile as I approached him.

"Hello Sarah."

"Hello, Brother Dave."

Chapter 9

The Pool

The stifling heat, a heavy blanket of thick moist air, weighed upon me drawing me closer to the oiled black butt floorboards. Each breath was shallow and labored, I was gasping for life.

'*Click Click Click*'.

The seemingly amplified sound of the classroom ceiling fan as it rotated off center, pounded in my head. A muffled distant voice of my teacher told us the temperature had reached 37 degrees Celsius and at 38 degrees Celsius we would all be sent home. The room was spinning, smothering me. I desperately attempted to fill my lungs.

"Are you alright Sarah?" my teacher enquired.

"Quick get her asthma inhaler, she can't seem to breathe," the teacher exclaimed with urgency.

I developed asthma at the age of eight years old, the same year I met Brother Dave. My mother was also an asthmatic, which she developed as an adult not long before my first attack. This affliction can come on suddenly, with no warning, as the airways constrict, limiting access to oxygen, which can lead to death. I always carried an asthma inhaler to rescue me from the grim reaper and from the embarrassment of gasping and splattering on the floor in front of my classmates.

February in Sydney can be very hot, and this particular year, was an extraordinarily humid hot summer. The walk home from school was mostly downhill, so my brother and I often took the journey on foot. Mum would pick us up on occasion, but on this day I was disappointed not to see our car parked in the school street. The heat had nearly killed me. I slowly began my trek home, one foot in front of the other.

The air was thick with heat and the deafening sounds of cicadas, their vibration pulsating into an overpowering hum. I cupped my hands over my ears to reduce the loud impact on my eardrums. The male cicada spends up to seven years underground before surfacing, breaking out of his exoskeleton to scream for a mate at over 120 decibels. Then after six weeks of this ceaseless noise, he is dead.

Matthew ran ahead of me, not wanting to be seen walking with his little sister. He had not taken any interest in my near-death experience earlier in the classroom. Joubert Street, named after Didier Joubert a French photographer, and Hunters Hill's first Mayor, was a treacherous part of the walk home. A park lining the street, dotted with tall gum trees, was home to nasty magpies. These birds would swoop down on me from great heights, pecking my head and drawing blood. There was no way to avoid them, only waving a stick over my head as I ran down the hill seemed to keep them at bay. Today, they were extra mean, perhaps stimulated by the cicadas' mating cries. Puffing and panting, I began jogging; my school backpack bouncing hard on my back – the pointy edges of my books piecing into my flesh with each bound. But there was no way I was going to stop and let these evil creatures get my blood. Safe under the Fig Tree Bridge, I could slow my pace, catch my breath, have another puff on my asthma inhaler and walk 20 metres home to safety.

THE POOL

When I got home from school, I made a beeline for the pool to cool down from the internal booming heat that had been with me all day.

Brother Dave was visiting again! Dressed in small tight swim trunks he walked to the edge of the pool, eagerly jumping in with a splash. His face lit up with delight as he plunged into the cool clear water. Already in the pool myself, I was surprised to see him in a swimsuit, assuming Mum had suggested he cool off after such a stifling hot day.

He seemed relaxed and calm as he glided towards the shallow end where I was standing. Putting his hands around my tiny waist, he guided me toward the side of the pool so I could not swim away. Pushing his body against mine from behind, with both arms wrapping around me, he slipped his hands down the front of my pale-yellow floral bikini pants. I froze as his fingers fondled my genitals. Pinned against the side of the pool, I was breathless with shock, terrified, unable to scream.

"Where was my mother?" my thoughts raced.

Even if I did scream, the chance of her hearing me from inside our large family home was slim.

His unspoken power was enough to silence me. My body stiffened hoping he would stop. When he'd had enough, he released me, backed away and swam to the other side of the pool. Pulling himself out of the water, he briefly sat on the side of the pool before leisurely walking to a towel hanging on the back of a chair. He dried himself off and left.

No words were spoken.

My body numb, I stood in vacant time. Lifeless, motionless, my mind spinning in uncontrollable confusion. There was no way for my childish mind to comprehend what had just happened to me. A deep wave of nausea swelled up from my belly catching in my throat. I felt the blood rush from my face as a chill came over my body. I was shaking in shock. The heat of the day was now dark coldness. I gently pulled myself from the pool pausing momentarily before standing to my feet on the side of the pool. I was unstable launching sideways having to catch myself to stabilise. My Snoopy towel seemed so far away on the blue sunlounge.

Snoopy was my favourite cartoon character. A fun beagle from Charles Schulz comic strip Peanuts. I acquired many comic books which sat in piles on the bookshelf in my bedroom. There were no speaking adults in the series as Schulz believed adults would ruin the magic and were simply not needed. I agreed. Snoopy would go on missions by slipping into daydreams where he would fight the Red Barron, his arch-nemesis. His doghouse would transform into a Sopwith Camel airplane as he headed into battle against the ruthless Red Barron. Snoopy was sometimes the clear victor, but other times, the Red Barron triumphed. Snoopy would call out,

"Curse you Red Barron."

"Curse you Brother Dave," I silently cried.

I managed to slowly move my body to reach the towel, the warm terry towelling comforting me as I wrapped it around my trembling small frame.

Brother Dave had left. I didn't want any dinner that night. Mum put my strange behaviour down to the incident earlier at school with the asthma attack and suggested an early night. When would he come over for another swim I questioned? It was to be a long, scorching summer. Flooded with fear, I waited in anticipation for his next visit.

"Children are not to be heard," echoed in my head as I stared out of my bedroom window.

As evening came, the darkness engulfed the light as the predictable cycle of night approached. A black winged creature in a majestic form began its flight across the sky. One lonely bat was followed by another, then another and another as the black mass increased in number. The Grey-headed Flying Foxes were awakening to begin their nightshift.

THE POOL

I lay still on my bed and watched them. An eerie sense came over me as they extended their rubbery wings in that distinguishing shape. My friends and I used to love to watch Dracula horror movies with blood sucking vampires who would drain all the life source from the human body. A sudden attack from the darkness, as their long sharp fangs pierced the carotid vein in the neck, while the victim became limp and powerless.

I lay limp and powerless. Life sucked out of me. In silence, I eventually drifted off to sleep.

Chapter 10
The TV Room

The family TV room was my favorite room in the house. With its enormous bay window showcasing a view that stretched all the way up the Lane Cove River, it was the perfect location for watching the ever-changing scenery. Boats cruised past, seagulls fought for food and the mud flat would appear and then disappear with each changing tide. The northeast aspect would capture the sun all year round, making it a warm spot to absorb its rays.

When I wasn't watching the activity outside our window, I was glued to the TV, which was a means of escaping from the real world. I would go to Gilligan's Island, the Korean war in MASH, then immerse myself in I Dream of Jeannie, Here's Lucy, The Brady Bunch, The Beverly Hillbillies, The Bionic Woman, The Six Million Dollar Man, and plenty of cartoons.

Dad didn't like Matthew and me watching TV as he said it, "dulls the brain." He also had an aversion to American TV shows, his voice frequently booming from the next room,

"Turn that rubbish off."

Mum loved MASH as she was in love with Alan Alda, making her our allies. After school I would rush home to my position on the beige fabric

THE TV ROOM

lounge. Its worn arm rests, covered in matching fabric to hide the fraying edges. It was a well-loved couch and my happy place.

It was another stifling hot summer day at school, and I couldn't wait to get home for a lemonade icy pole. I wondered if we had any in the fridge or if Matthew had finished them off. There was always an argument about equal shares. With ten in the box, I calculated there were five each, but somehow Matthew would lose count and take extra to my annoyance.

I didn't sweat easily, but on this day, trickles of perspiration dripped down my flat chest and the back of my neck. Pierre, our French poodle was at the door with his over excited greeting. I didn't have time to give him any attention as I made a beeline to the fridge. Last one! An icy pole was calling me. I plonked myself on the lounge tearing at the wrapper frantically as if my life depended on it. The cold ice soothed with its sweet tang of lemon. I sank deeper into the couch ready to enjoy my afternoon sitcom.

I didn't notice him entering the room until he was sitting next to me.

Brother Dave wiggled closer until his leg was against mine. It felt too close for comfort. I felt his hot breath on my cheek as he drew nearer to speak to me. He spoke softly, asking about my day at school.

"Did you play skipping ropes at school today?" he murmured.

My school tunic rested an inch above my knee. His hand maneuvered slowly pushing it up enough to slip his fingers into the front of my panties. My body froze in horror, yet his calm reassurance kept me very still and quiet.

He continued to fondle as my mind tried to make sense of what he was doing to me - again! I didn't like it nor understand it.

Why was he doing this unthinkable thing to me?

Trust was being violated yet again, sending mixed messages into the depths of my being. This man was a man of God. He was like an 'uncle' or a family friend. Confusion swept through my mind spinning around and around. He finally stopped. Nowhere was safe. My happy place, my beige lounge, the sanctuary of my home, my childhood innocence all taken from me like a thief in the night.

He comes to steal, kill, and destroy. There was an enemy in my home. Fear grew into terror, as panic engulfed me. My heart was pounding at a speed unfamiliar to me, so fast I thought it would explode. I couldn't breathe. Was I dying?

"Help, help," I screamed in silence, no sound able to escape my frozen self.

"Where was my mother?"

The large two-story family home with its many rooms was not safe. Brother Dave could violate me and go unnoticed. Was my mother in the music room at the other end of the house? Had she popped up to the local shops for some dinner supplies? I didn't think to call out to her. What would I tell her? I had no words to describe what had happened to me and why suddenly Brother Dave was touching me. I didn't like it. It felt 'yukkie'.

He left the room as quietly as he entered, slivering like a snake past the couch.

The TV continued to blare its content, complete with 'canned' laughter as my sitcom remained oblivious of the crime that had just been committed before it. I stared at the screen, mentally vacant. Hearing but not hearing. Seeing but not seeing. Time stood still. My panicked breathing began to slow. My racing heart quietened, slowing, as if the race had now finished and it could find a normal rhythm. A sudden sickening in my stomach, I ran quickly to the bathroom to vomit up my lemonade icy pole.

Brother Dave had gone.

Chapter 11
The Royal Princess

As a young girl I was hypnotised by the fairy tale stories of becoming a princess. An ordinary girl would be noticed by a prince and saved out of her average miserable world. She would be carried to a world of royalty. This fantastical place would transport her from a dark grey muddy mire to a sparkling glistening palace. She would enter a kingdom, a place of provision, dance, and joy. My parents named me Sarah - a name meaning 'princess'. I believed I was destined for royalty.

Cinderella was my favourite. The injustice of her situation rang true to me. She was born into a world of abuse and control inflicted on her by her evil stepmother and wicked stepsisters. An orphan girl, trapped in a house being forced into slavery and silence. I too was trapped in my family home waiting for my prince to rescue me.

"Where was my fairy godmother?" I would often ponder.

"Where was God?"

As much as I did not enjoy church or the nightly Rosary ritual, I did like to pray to God. I would position myself on my knees and pray,

"Please God stop Matthew being so mean to me."

"Please make me do better at school."

"Please stop the teachers being mean to us kids."

"Please stop people hurting me."

But where was God? He had deserted me. He didn't care. How could he let me get hurt? Why didn't he protect me from the 'yukkie' touching?

I wanted a magic wand to be waved over me to set me free, but this seemed unlikely. Drowning in fantasy stories, I wished that someday my prince would come and rescue me.

Each school morning commenced with a stoic version of "God save the Queen." I wasn't sure what she needed to be saved from as she seemed quite comfortable in her elegant gowns, golden carriages and surrounded by noble servants. Even her two corgi dogs seemed to strut by her side, noses in the air with a defined arrogance. I yearned to be a royal, a princess in a kingdom surrounded and safe. A royal moat, filled with ferocious crocodiles or thousands of flesh-eating piranhas, to keep the evil out.

I would bury myself in children's picture books about royalty. I would never tire of their stories. It somehow seemed that if I kept myself buried in the illusion of these worlds, my mind would be wiped from the truth of my tormented reality.

On a warm Wednesday afternoon there was a knock on the door,

"Sarah, come and say hello to Brother Dave," Mum commanded with a shout.

I had not long arrived home from school and had been enjoying the sanctuary of my bedroom. My single bed was in the centre of the room surrounded by lolly pink wallpaper saturated with pink and white flowers in a neat striped row. I didn't like pink, even though it had been selected on my behalf when my room was decorated.

Numerous stuffed toys covered my bed. Snoopy and Pandy had the leadership positions in the middle of the pillows as my faithful favourites. Pandy was a panda bear, my first teddy after I was born. He was the standard black and white, as panda bears are and was always my chosen cuddle toy. I spent notable time at my dark wooden antique desk, drawing pictures I would copy from books. I would first trace them using fine see through baking paper from the kitchen then copy exactly every detail. Perfection was always the aim not allowing any variation from the original. The desk matched the other dark wooden antique pieces in my room along with a tall two door wardrobe and a dressing table with a large mirror. Dad loved collecting antiques, so every room in the house was filled with his prized collection.

Matthew's room also had a striped theme - Mum chose a blend of brown and orange. We had been upgraded into our own bedrooms after some home extensions, which added three new bedrooms. My room was larger than Matthew's, which added to his annoyance with my existence. No longer sharing a room with my brother was a relief. Puberty was around the corner, and I would need my own female space. I was fourteen years old when I finally got my period, being one of the last in my class to menstruate.

"Come and say hello to Brother Dave," Mum called out again.

Brother Dave stood quietly in the hallway just outside the kitchen door. The kitchen was the heart of our home, and he was waiting to be invited into its pulsating chambers. Mum walked through the door beckoning Brother Dave to follow.

I stepped out gingerly from my bedroom and walked slowly into the kitchen, my heart beating at a rate that concerned me. The adrenaline rush increased, and calls of desperation to run back to my bedroom for protection were increasing. I could retreat and crawl under my bed making myself small and invisible.

Mum was proudly aware of the fondness Brother Dave had for me, embracing it like a certificate of merit. I was her show pony, and I dare not leave the performance. My hair was in its usual high ponytail, which

Mum had pulled back tight, not a hair out of place. A tension headache had gripped me most of the day, but I was too afraid to relieve the elastic. Image was everything to my mother and I was her trophy. My petite figure, pretty face, long blonde hair, and blue eyes were the perfect formula for her dysfunctional display of pride. Whether I liked it or not, I was expected to present myself to visitors in a respectable manner. Speaking was only to be accepted by invitation with short, formulated responses delivered.

"Yes, I had a lovely day at school", "I want to be a nurse when I grow up" and "I love ballet lessons," were typical responses.

Brother Dave seemed a bit sheepish. He quietly maneuvered his lean body into the breakfast nook sliding gently along the bench. I followed him sliding along the faux red leather seat keeping as much distance as possible. We were both facing Mum who was in the kitchen prancing back and forth chatting and performing in her element before us, her audience. She was always very animated, and Brother Dave seemed to be captivated by the essence of her vibrant energy. I tried to make my body smaller and smaller somehow by breathing in as far as I could so that the distance between myself and my abuser would increase.

Matthew entered the kitchen throwing down his school bag on the kitchen bench with a commanding bang.

"Matthew, take your bag into your room," Mum said in a cross tone.

The rude interruption to her performance was not welcomed as her audience's eyes were now fixed on Matthew.

"I'm hungry! Hello Brother Dave," he added knowing this was expected.

"Hello, Matthew, how was your day at school?" Brother Dave asked lightly.

"It was ok. My lunch got squashed in my bag and I had to throw it in the bin," Matthew said.

Matthew had a way of being present but at the same time was not present. You could see that he hadn't even noticed me in the room, and I wasn't about to draw his attention to myself. I was as small and quiet as I could be, hoping to disappear.

The terror of my secret had no words. How could I articulate what was happening to me when 'paedophile' nor its meaning were not in my vocabulary or understanding?

I sat in silence.

Chapter 12

Friends

Ruth was my best friend. We met in kindergarten at Villa Maria, and it was love at first sight. She was bright and electric with a sweetness that was magnetic. We were inseparable, sticking together like glue. Childhood giggles were a daily dose of glee as we sucked on toffee made of pure boiled treacle poured into cupcake paper cups, hardened ready for consumption. These delicacies were a popular sale item at school fundraisers along with chocolate crackles made from coco pops and toffee apples. These apples, smothered in artificially coloured toffee, usually green or red, were poised on a stick, a total contradiction to health. Perhaps disguising a healthy apple in poisoned coloured sugar would be enticing. It worked. This assortment of fundraiser food items were so laced with refined sugar that all the children would be instantly buzzing around the school grounds on a crazed high. The teachers would be frantically trying to find order. This endeavour was unobtainable until the children's digestive systems had processed the sugar overload that resulted in a sudden crash. The volunteering mothers selling from the stalls seemed oblivious to the crazed behaviour. They were quite happy with the children's purchases; eagerly taking the five cents per item.

FRIENDS

We began our school day on the asphalt quadrangle with a few announcements from the headmistress before we were all ordered to march around in a large square. A tune from an old war movie blared over the loudspeakers mounted high on poles above us.

"Left, left, left right left."

It was important to coordinate the steps as any lapse in concentration would cause a missed step - suddenly putting you out of sync. A couple of shuffles would bring you back in rhythm with the continuing chant of "left, left, left right left." This military style parade would attempt to bring control over the mass group of primary-aged children. This tactic was successful for the scheduled 15 minutes as the children marched in a circle around the playground. Then it was time to go to class.

The worst day in my seven-year-old life arrived. Ruth's father had decided to move the family to Melbourne.

"Move away," I shouted. "No."

How could he be so cruel. My life is over. Ruth and I sobbed and sobbed in each other's tight grasp - never to let go. They would have to ply us apart as we refused to accept our fate. Melbourne? Where was that?

A city a long way from Sydney I was to learn. It might as well have been Africa. Distance was distance and in the 1960's with no internet and only expensive timed paid phone calls, we were doomed.

This is when Jean suddenly appeared in my life, shining like a light in my darkness. I would have sleep overs at her place and Jean would reciprocate by staying at my house. Her 3-bedroom red brick single story home in Ryde seemed small in comparison to my two-story large waterfront home in Hunters Hill. Her parents were divorced, and she had three sisters at the ready to listen to our secret chat. We concluded that the Hunters Hill residence was a better choice. My house was big enough to find refuge and hiding spots, so we could tuck away and find privacy. My dinghy and outboard engine also offered an escape into a fantasy world. Here our childlike imaginations could run wild, conjuring up stories of being captured by aliens never to be located again. Our escapism was an essential part of my survival.

At the end of Grade four, aged 9, it was my time to leave Villa Maria. My parents had decided a private education at an elite all-girls school would be to my advantage. Instead of a five-minute drive to Villa Maria Primary School I would now be travelling to Kirribilli, a 10-minute drive to the local wharf, a 20-minute ferry ride followed by a steep walk to school. In a new stiff school uniform complete with blazer and hat, I started my time at Loreto Convent Kirribilli.

Victoria Daniels became my new bestie at my new school. She was also a doctor's daughter and reminded me of Ruth. I often wondered if Ruth was happy in Melbourne and if I would ever get an opportunity to visit her, but I never did. Victoria 'Vicki' had a similar sweetness to Ruth, and she was a joy to be around. I still saw Jean at the weekends as my local buddy when my parents allowed me to have her over for a play date. The secrets in my home life had become an anticipated torment etched into my soul. The vibrant spark in my spirit began to dull. The twinkle in my eyes became dim. My deep inner sadness was difficult to cover up. I would find myself drifting off in class losing the attention of my teacher only to find myself in trouble.

"Sarah doesn't pay attention in class," was a common description of me on my report cards.

Emily, a new girl, arrived at Loreto with her cheeky smile and high energy. She was instantly accepted into our group. I soon discovered that Emily was also from a divorced family. Divorce was rare at the time, yet two of my friends had now succumbed to the consequences of divorce. There was a stigma attached to children of divorced parents at my school, and they were made to feel they were different. Often a group of girls would snigger as they passed, whispering behind their hands with unkind gossip.

My lack of understanding about anything sex related, including sexual abuse, muted my voice. Growing up, we were never supposed to mention 'those' words that described our private parts, so how could I explain what I didn't have permission to explain. It was therefore best to keep silent, even with my friends. This was the only choice I had.

Brother Dave's weekly home visits continued for four years. His Datsun Sedan would be waiting for me in our driveway, forcing me to my hiding place, the wood pile. The carefully placed wood resting against the wall of the house began to welcome me into a familiar state of terror. The spider webs laughing in my face. Shame and confusion trapped me in silence. An inability to mutter a word of the abuse began the 'Silencing Syndrome'. Symptoms of fear, shame, guilt, low self-esteem, isolation, anxiety, and numbing all correlating to form this disorder that I had put a name to. A syndrome that would be a part of my identity from childhood to adulthood.

Chapter 13

The Lie

Concentrating at school had become more and more difficult. I would sit at my desk, gazing out of the classroom window, my mind vacant. The teacher's voice would become a soft distant hum while my mind wandered, creating images of the fairy tales I wished were my reality. My Fairy God Mother would fly through the window, her sparkling wand waving in the air, sending magic dust all around me. The golden powder would gently fall onto my skin, illuminating an iridescent glow. Her smile was radiant, her eyes kind as if she knew my pain. She had come to take me to another land, a land flowing with milk and honey. All I could feel was her acceptance and love.

"Sarah, pay attention!" an abrupt shout from the teacher disturbed my fantasy.

Homework was always a challenge. My scattered thoughts would attempt to remember the parrot learning of my mathematical times tables. Mum would read a list of spelling words, while I sat at the kitchen table. As hard as I tried, I would struggle to remember the patterns of letters and their correct order. My frontal lobe had been damaged from Brother

Dave's abuse, causing a persistent sense of feeling overwhelmed. Any new information would overload my system, causing it to shut down.

Mum loved to write. Her childhood accolades in song and story writing were a merit she enjoyed reminding me of. The trauma had caused me to lose my self-esteem and self-confidence. This was reflected in my studies. Mum decided to engage a family friend, Doreen, to help me with my schoolwork. Good results were important to Mum, as image was everything. Doreen was in her early twenties, a bright young woman studying an Arts degree at university. Mum began to pay Doreen to coach me, which soon resulted in Doreen doing my English and Art schoolwork for me. She began to undermine any natural talent I may have had and introduced me to cheating.

"I can't do it," I would plead with Doreen.

Fear of getting it wrong struck hard. Children of abuse, in a desperate quest for control, can turn to perfectionism. The belief is that if they can do everything right, then perhaps they won't be blamed. I needed to be perfect to feel safe. The only way to avoid failure was to avoid starting the task altogether. Internally my mind was scrambled, therefore my external world needed to be perfect.

Already confused and broken from the ongoing abuse being inflicted on me by Brother Dave, I soon became a shadow behind Doreen's and my mother's control. Any ability I may have had academically, was pushed down, squashed to a pulp. This disregarding of my ability spoke a deafening roar,

"You are not capable."

As my mother's trophy, I was to be presented to the world as a 'clever child', reflecting her own self-image and social status. Her desire to elevate herself in the doctor's wives circle, only revealed her narcissistic tendencies. A personal gain, even if the price was her daughter's self-esteem. My unique gifts and skills were never discovered nor given a chance to be birthed. Children were not to be heard; I therefore had no choice but to submit to the manipulation. Too immature to understand the lie I had been forced into; I became passive and meek.

"Did all children experience this?" I quietly asked myself.

Doreen's status as 'family friend' meant she was to be trusted. Through my childhood lenses, she was like a big sister. Why did she agree to be a co-conspirator in my mother's deceitful plan? I realised later it must have been the money. As a struggling university student, any extra income was a bonus. Doreen was being paid to pretend to be me, a 10-year-old girl.

Doreen was excellent at drawing. My reports began to show 'A's in both my English and Art subjects. I couldn't understand why the opportunity to do my own schoolwork had been taken away from me. My lack of confidence needed to be supported with encouragement. Intense emotional problems began to escalate as I was unable to keep up the lie in the classroom. When the teacher asked me to draw in class, I froze. I was terrified that the lie would be discovered when I was unable to replicate Doreen's standard. I was a cheat, a liar, a deceiver, a bad girl. Terror and confusion oscillated as I tried to figure out how this scam had begun. I had not asked for it. This lie seemed to belong to me, yet I had nothing to do with its creation. It seemed to be placed on me in a scheming background plan without consultation. I began to shrink into a void of nothingness.

Mum began to brag to Brother Dave.

"Sarah is so clever, she got an 'A' in essay writing."

"She is such a special girl," Brother Dave replied, looking intently in my direction.

I didn't feel special, I felt stupid. I had lost all self-esteem and self-confidence. I was vulnerable, the sexual abuse deepening my vulnerability. I now believe that perpetrators know their victims. Just as a wolf identifies the weak lamb, the one who is falling away from the pack, the one who is lost, the enemy comes to kill, steal, and destroy. I was a living sacrifice for their gain. A lamb led to the slaughterhouse over and over. My life was sacrificed for the gain of others. My identity stolen.

Doreen continued in the lie throughout my schooling to the Year 12 HSC. She completed my Art Major Work. I was voiceless in my mother's convoluted scheme, having no means of escape. Another secret to remain silenced.

Chapter 14

The Numbing

I was a young lost soul in a big house. Whenever panic or fear struck, which it often did, I wanted to escape.

But where could I go?

Dad had a well-stocked bar on the ground floor of our house in the style of an English pub. Many nights, his bar was filled with the laughter of drunken friends, including doctors and their wives who were offered an array of possibilities - brandy alexanders, scotch and dry, gin and tonic, beers, and wines. It was all available. Both Mum and Dad enjoyed a drink, especially socially. There was always an abundance with glasses being topped up before they were empty. Mum and Dad also enjoyed a glass of wine with the evening meal, which Dad often had alone, late on Wednesday nights. This was his allocated night on duty for the surgery, so a 9pm dinner was usual for him on Wednesdays.

I had never been offered alcohol, but somehow, I knew it would take away pain. Thoughts of what had happened to me, being touched in a way I didn't invite, nor wanted, brought disgust to my mind. Had I caused this? Was it my fault? Why had he picked me?

THE NUMBING

One night, while everyone was asleep, I snuck downstairs searching through the vast array of bottles that lined the shelf underneath the round oak bar. The bottle with the clear spirit didn't smell at all. Perhaps this wouldn't taste so bad, I thought.

Loosening the lid, I pursed my lips over the opening, blocking my nose and taking a big swig as large as my small mouth could contain.

"Uhh." I grimaced as the sharp, burning liquid ran down the back of my throat. Three swigs would do it. I put the lid back on and carefully replaced the bottle in the exact position so as not to be noticed. Dad would never know.

A comforting warmth flooded my belly, followed by a lightness in my head. Slightly giddy, I ventured back up the stairs tiptoeing carefully so as not to creak any floorboards. I flushed the toilet to cover up my reason for being out of my bed.

Once back in my bedroom, headphones plugged into my faithful record player, I blasted the sounds of Pink Floyd's 'Comfortably Numb'. The melody swept me away into an emotional sea of crashing waves, whitewashes blending tears with numbness. This escape became a habitual blanket covering my loneliness extending from late primary school into high school. A secret liquid indulgence to numb the pain.

Chapter 15
The Reporting

My favourite part of the school day was the ride home on the ferry from the Kirribilli wharf to Alexander Street Wharf, Hunters Hill. Precariously walking down the swaying gangway, held in place by the young deckhand, was scary yet thrilling.

"What if I slipped, falling into the water?" I regularly imagined.

With a smile and a nod, the deckhand would usher the next child to take a wide step making the crossing from the land to the vessel. The red and yellow Rosman ferries had cruised Sydney Harbour for many decades. The wood was old and worn, thick layers of coated paint weathered and peeling. Once on board, I would head straight to the bow allowing the water lapping on the hull to captivate me. The ferry would pull away from the wharf tooting its horn at departure.

"Go inside and sit down," the deckhand would yell in his tiresome daily request.

We were under way bouncing over the choppy waters, leaving the memories of school behind. My favourite place for the ride home was on the back deck where the Aloysius boys would congregate. The boys' raucous

THE REPORTING

behaviour was a delight to watch, a contrast from my day at an all-girls school.

One boy caught my attention. Charlie had thick brown hair, a well-proportioned body and a smile that lit up his face stretching from ear to ear. We would sit together on the back deck, taking off our school shoes and socks to dangle our legs in the water. The splashing of the whitewash was cooling to our sweaty feet. The ferry would make its 20-minute journey towards the Lane Cove River, the Jacaranda trees a blanket of mauve on the shoreline. Charlie and I would smirk at each other as the ferry chugged along. I liked being in his company.

Charlie had an older sister, Rebecca. She was two years ahead of me at school and would sit quietly inside the ferry reading a book. She was studious, carrying an air of maturity. I thought she was so grown-up. Her jet-black hair was cut short, shining like silk. Thin rimmed glasses sat poised on her nose as her eyes scanned the pages.

The secret of my abuse was an anchor around my neck, dragging me to the depths of the ocean. I was drowning in confusion and trauma. But on this day, I found myself sitting next to Rebecca. Her gentle smile enticed me to move closer to her on the hard ferry bench. The ferry rocked from side to side lulling me into a sense of safety.

I broke my silence.

The words came slowly at first, my face blushing red as my sentences formed.

"He visits my house and touches me ...... down there," I said in a soft whisper.

"It's usually after school, when Dad is a work."

The story of my perpetrators inappropriate touching, the home visits, his position in the church poured out, the flood gates had opened. Rebecca sat silently listening, her concern evident in her furrowing brows.

"Don't tell anyone," I concluded.

The following week, I was sitting in the classroom when Sister Anne walked in. She approached my English teacher, whispering in her ear. Sister Anne, alias 'Gigantor' was the nun in charge of all the year 7 girls. This title was suitably given to her by the pupils. 'Gigantor' was a TV cartoon series introduced to Australia in 1968. The main character, Gigantor was a huge steel, remote-controlled Space Aged Robot, lacking in intelligence. Sister Anne stood six feet tall, her foreboding presence getting everyone's attention. Her face was stern, always scanning for mischief makers. Her eyes fixed on me, motioning me to follow her out of the classroom. Fear and dread engulfed me like a kick in the guts. Any call to leave the classroom sent alarm bells. Had something happened at home? Was there some kind of medical emergency? Was I in trouble? My chest tightened as I followed her like a meek little lamb into her cold office. Her office was minimal, not unlike most of the places I had seen associated with the nuns. It was as though anything aesthetically pleasing was not Godly, an education in worldliness was not Godliness.

Sister Anne sat behind a solid wooden desk, her arms crossed, and a strange smirk curled on her face. She sat in silence for what seemed like an extraordinary length of time.

"Do I speak? No of course, not," my thoughts swirled into a panic.

The strange look continued as her head moved from side to side. She sat back so deeply into her wooden throne that it rocked up onto two of its four legs.

"So, what's this about you and Brother Dave?" the words finally came forth from her pursed lips.

My heart seized. How did she know? No No No! Had Rebecca broken my trust? How could she tell and not only tell but tell 'Gigantor'? My life was over. The secret I had held for years that was never to be spoken of was

THE REPORTING

now out in the open. I felt a vulnerability wash over me weakening my core. A nausea forced bile into my throat as I struggled not to faint.

In terrified obedience I recounted my confession. With reluctance, I told her about the abuse, the sexual touching, and the sordid details. I told the truth. As I was speaking, she maintained a strange smirk curling upwards into a snarl.

"Are you sure?" she sniggered.

My mind was spinning. My face pounding red with the heat of embarrassment. I sat emotionless, too terrified to cry. She didn't believe me. I had been betrayed and now I was on the stand to be judged, portrayed as a liar.

Weeks later, I found out that Rebecca had spoken to Mrs Manns, fondly referred to as 'Mummy Manns'. She held the position of supervisor for all the girls in the school. Rebecca could not keep my secret. The weight of my confession was too much for her to commit to my promise of, "don't tell anyone."

The story that was passed on to me by childhood Chinese whispers was that Mummy Manns was also overwhelmed by the confession and immediately contacted the Marist Father's Presbytery anonymously to report Brother Dave's sin. I was not included in further discussions after my session with Sister Anne. The abuse was never to be spoken of again.

* * * * *

In the 70's, sex education took place in year 6. I was 10 years old when we were all gathered for the lesson. As Loreto was an all-girls school, the giggles in the room were high pitched. I had heard that some of the girls had already got their 'period' with some being as young as nine years old. I had not developed breasts or had a single extra hair in sight. My nipples became slightly engorged and tender but that was it. Some of the girls in my class had full breasts and were wearing bras. I was way behind, being one of the youngest in the class. I would be a late bloomer.

The sex education talk was about boys and girls; their changing bodies and where babies came from. The nuns were not too specific on the sexual intercourse part of the story as maybe they had no experience to share such details.

Sexual feelings and masturbation were not a part of the Catholic sex education that day. We were given a booklet that I read over and over every night as my curiosity told me this was vital information. My inquisitiveness superseded my interest in the lessons we were having in Geography on the Serengeti.

Education on sexual predators and paedophiles was not in the Catholic school curriculum.

Chapter 16
The Wooden Bench

After the interrogation with Sister 'Gigantor', I continued as a year 7 student. The shame and embarrassment of that day never left me. A mask, a necessary disguise, was adorned daily, hiding my pain from the world.

One lunchtime I was enjoying playing a game of elastics with Victoria and Emily. This was a popular game at the time where a piece of elastic was stretched between the ankles of two girls. The third girl would then have to jump in and out of the elastic in an orchestrated sequence.

As the game progresses, the elastic is moved up the body of the two girls. First to their knees, then hips, waist, and the last stop: the back of their necks. Each stage made the game more difficult as the person carrying out the sequence had to jump higher and higher each time.

I loved this game as I was very flexible, which gave me an advantage. We would all squeal for joy as each of us took turns to see who could complete the game. Today was no different to any other lunchtime and it was my turn. I was up to the hardest challenge: the elastic at neck level. My small stature stood ready. As the second smallest girl in my class, I took a deep breath, bent my knees in preparation and I was away.

Jumping high, swinging my legs to reach the elastic, I made the first leap. The sequence needed to be completed like a delicate dance of movements in and out of the elastic, pulling it down with each move, while the tension forced it to bounce back to position.

"Go Sarah," the girls cheered.

I did it! Panting heavily, my face beetroot red I glanced up smiling with success.

Then I froze.

Brother Dave was walking through the school gate only five metres from our game. My already pounding heart pumped harder and my stomach plummeted. This was completely out of context. He had never come to this school, my senior school miles away from his presbytery in Hunters Hill. His visits to the gate at Villa Maria were common but why was he here at Loreto? He walked through the gate in his familiar manner, sheepishly pushing the heavy wooden gate with both hands. He seemed lost as he caught my eye. Panic flooded me and my already red face flushed a deeper shade of crimson.

He didn't stop to extend the glance but kept walking past.

"What on earth was he doing here?" my thoughts contorted in confusion.

Emily and Victoria had paused wondering why I had disengaged from the game. They knew nothing of my relationship with the man at the gate. I somehow knew he had been summoned to the school for questioning. Perhaps Sister Anne had called him in for a chat? I was in the dark.

I wondered if my mother had received a phone call to be informed, if so, she never spoke of it. Her way of dealing with problems was to pretend they never happened. Forget and move on. Remain silent. What would the neighbours think? What would the doctors and their wives think? This secret if revealed would bring shame to our family, our 'perfect' family. Silence was already a familiar practice in our home. Children only spoke when spoken to and were seen and not heard. An inconvenience like this would be treated as if it never happened. The problem for me was that it did happen and I would never forget. My father never spoke of it either. My later conclusion was that he was never told.

Abuse not only steals from you in the moment or the moments afterwards, but continues to steal portions of your being, all your life. It takes away the essence of who you would have been if this had not been 'done' to you.

Victim is a word that was etched on my forehead like a banner. This banner only served to alert other abusers that I was weak, broken, fair game. A beacon flashing, 'I'm a victim pick me.' I never told any of my friends at the time because of deep shame. I was not believed by Sister Anne, so why would anyone believe me? I was not heard so why waste my breath? Brother Dave's choice to violate my body for his selfish pleasure was to remain a private pain.

Not long after the Loreto school sighting of Brother Dave, I was at Villa Maria Sunday Mass, fulfilling my duty to attend. Mum was feeling unwell this Sunday, so Dad had dropped me to the church. Matthew had decided to go to Edward's place after Mass, which was in the next street.

The long hour finally ended, and I quickly bolted for the side door to make a getaway, but Brother Dave was waiting for me. I shuddered in disbelief thinking that even after the uncovering of his 'sin' he might continue the abuse.

"Oh no!!!!" I screamed inside.

He walked over to me, stooped down, and whispered in my ear,

"Come with me." His tone was soft displaying no emotion.

Knowing the enemy, your abuser and yet remaining locked in his spell is something now as an adult I can't even fathom.

Why didn't I run?

Why didn't I say, "no"?

Like a lamb going to the slaughter, I took in a deep breath, my eyes down and followed half a step behind his pace. He led me to the back of the church grounds walking down a long grassy hill lined with tall well-established trees. These trees had been on this church land for over a hundred years witnessing many unspoken secrets - whispering in the wind to the birds while the leaves blew across the soil. I had never been to this forbidden place. Where he was leading me was 'out of bounds', a special site reserved for the priests who resided on the property.

The walk seemed endless, my terror increasing with each step. The veins on my neck puffed out like thick worms. Fight or flight response began to surface, but the commanding power of this man was too strong, demanding obedience, I had no choice but to obey. We came to a wooden bench, and he motioned me to sit. We sat quietly for a few moments, my tension increasing as I awaited another 'touching up.'

He cleared his throat and began to speak,

"Sarah, I know this must be very confusing for you and I don't expect you to understand. I am asking you not to think about what has happened and to put it out of your mind. When you turn 20, then you can think about it, and you will understand." His voice was measured as if he had been planning this statement thoughtfully.

I sighed with great relief; this was only to be a talk.

"Ok," I agreed.

I had no understanding of what he meant. Silenced, afraid, and confused, I walked back to the church. I was to never lay eyes on him again.

I honoured this request, burying the disgusting thoughts of his abuse until my 20th birthday. But in the meantime, I suffered symptoms of his abuse - anxiety, flash backs, panic attacks, drug and alcohol abuse, relationship issues and more. The symptoms of the Silencing Syndrome had embedded into the core of my mental health.

Chapter 17
Under the Bridge

My world remained silent. The abuse was never mentioned again. The unspoken message was, "It never happened" and that "I didn't matter." When you speak words of encouragement to a person you watch them expand and grow. When you silence a person, you watch them shrink and die. Like un-watered plants, they wither, drying up until all life is sucked out of them.

Looking back over my yearly school photos, I can see a little girl full of joy in grade 5, who then gradually sinks into despair. Her face becomes sallow, her eyes empty, her posture hunched.

Only now, through adult eyes, can I identify with the deep sadness of this silent child.

But life went on, summer came after the winter, and the cycle repeated over and over.

One evening, my parents were getting ready to head off on their usual Thursday night out to dinner in a restaurant. This was a weekly ritual to give Mum a night off from standing in front of the deep fryer. Some weeks it included friends, but other weeks it was just Mum and Dad. Matthew and I were now old enough not to need a babysitter, so Mum and Dad were happy to leave us alone together. I was not always happy with this arrangement as a babysitter could protect me from my brother's incessant desire to torment and tease me.

Matthew's friend Edward was staying over this night. They had both headed off on their bikes up the hill to the local fish and chips shop. The juicy potato scallops were my favourite. The oil would ooze out with each bite dripping the hot fluid down my chin. I wouldn't even stop to wipe the drips, eager to move on quickly to the second scallop. The fish was delicious too, fried in bite size pieces with a choice of tartare or tomato sauce.

"Mum, they went without me," I whined.

The boys never waited for me, leaving me to feel left out.

"Don't worry we will drive you and you can walk back with them," Mum said as she sprayed a shot of hairspray over her massive beehive.

She always looked glamorous and took great pride in her make up application and choice of outfit. A lifetime in show business made her appearance particularly important and she certainly did a good job. Dad was so proud to be at her side, looking intently at her with gentle loving eyes.

When the car started, I was ready to jump into the back seat for the quick drive up our street. Out the front of the fish and chips shop was a bus stop, where Dad carefully pulled into the curb handing me a $10 note. This was way over what I would need for my dinner.

"Now go home with Matthew," he instructed.

I smiled at the $10 note and shut the door.

"OK," I replied.

The shop was bustling. In the line was a husband with his wife and their two small children placing a large order. There was a nurse or a care worker of some kind wearing long blue pants and a matching tunic top. A fob watch pinned on a short chain to the left side of her lapel glistened in the bright lights. A large man with a long scraggy beard was staring up at the menu board still deciding on what to order. His stomach bulged over his 'stubbies' (a favourite Australian brand of shorts), which his tank top wasn't long enough to hide.

I placed my order and waited patiently in the ever-growing queue.

I munched into my first potato scallop with delight. Now to find the boys. I scanned the area to see if I could spot their bikes.

"They must have already headed home," I concluded, licking my fingers.

In the fading afternoon light, I began to walk down Joubert Street, which ran parallel to my street. This was a short cut home down a steep hill via a path under Figtree Bridge. The familiar walk I used to take on my way home from primary school. A quick pace would only take me about 10 mins. Still focused on the hot goodies in my white bag, I leisurely began my journey, my ponytail swishing from side to side.

This was the street with the evil magpies, but with the sun now setting, they were tucked away in the treetops and would not bother me. Five minutes away from home, I noticed a car following me down the hill. I stopped looking closer, thinking it must have been someone I knew. But I didn't recognise the car, so I continued.

At the bottom of the hill the path turned under the bridge into a dark tunnel. The eerie sound the cars made above me quickened my steps.

Bang!

A man's hand snapped over my mouth. My already quickened heartbeat began to race into an uncontrollable panic. In an instinctive reaction I tried with all my strength to pull the hand off my face. Both my hands gripped his bony formidable force, prying each finger from my lips. But it was useless. The man's strength was overpowering, my efforts were fruitless. His hand slightly moved then quickly slapped back into place. Unable to breathe, I tried once more to move his hand, but again it slapped back with incredible pressure. The man's other arm reached around my shoulders to hold me in place as he pushed me up against a sandstone wall that lined the path.

It was as though he was trying to squeeze life out of me. I managed to wiggle my arms free, placing the palms of both my hands onto the rough wall surface. I tried to scream, but only muffled whimpers emerged through the gaps in his fingers. Struggling to take another needed breath, the reality of what was happening hit me. Beads of sweat dripped down my back as the icy chill of terror manifested. Fear began to flood every cell in my being. My mind was swimming in a deepening whirlpool. I miraculously gained supernatural strength as I locked my elbows into solid rods holding back my attacker's power.

My breathing was rapid and audible with a painful sigh on each outward breath. He released the grip from my shoulders and began to run his hand up and down my chest. I had not developed any breasts yet, but he continued to rub my flat chest. There was a moment of stillness allowing me to hold my thoughts and for some reason I had a strong desire to look at him.

Mustering all the strength I could, I swung my body around, just enough to see his face. The hand across my mouth remained heavily fixed. His eyes were wild, like a crazed animal. Although slightly built, I estimated he was in his early twenties giving him the strength needed to overpower a child.

"Do you know how old I am?" I shouted through the gaps in his fingers. His hands softened,

"I'm not going to rape you; I am just going to molest you," he said.

Catastrophic dread flooded me. *NO.*

I had never heard this word before and had no idea what it meant. My imagination ran riot as I envisioned my 12-year-old body being cut up into small pieces and put in a suitcase. Again, there was another moment of stillness with my eyes still fixed on his. Rage welled inside me overcoming any fear I had of death. Then suddenly he let go and ran.

I ran too, but in the opposite direction.

Terrified he might be following me; I ran past my home into the neighbour's yard and bolted full speed down the side of their garden, jumping the fence. My mind was spinning. *But what if he saw me?* I didn't want the 'molester' to know where I lived.

Panting and wheezing, I knocked on my neighbour's front door. It was a large wooden door beautifully carved in rich dark cedar. Mr. Clements answered the door. I wasn't aware that blood was streaming from my mouth a result of my braces cutting into my lips from the force of my attacker's hand clasping my face.

Mr. Clements looked at me and gasped. I opened my mouth to speak but I was unable to utter a sound.

"He…lp," I stammered.

"U-U Under the bridge," I was finally able to say.

With that Mr. Clements and another man in the house sprinted towards the bridge. I was relieved to be safe with Mrs. Clements who wrapped me in a blanket as we waited for the police to arrive.

The police questioning seemed to go on and on.

"Where did he touch you?" the police officer asked. "Did you say, he was going to molest you?"

The questions were repeated many times until I felt exhausted and frustrated. Mum and Dad finally arrived thanking everyone for caring for me and then ushered me home. Not much was said as I walked up the carpeted staircase to my striped, pink bedroom, putting on my pajamas in a daze.

I didn't want to talk anymore, I quickly grabbed 'Pandy' who was perched on my bed and held him tight. My soft teddy always brings me much needed comfort.

UNDER THE BRIDGE

Lying quietly in my bed, tears rolling down my cheeks, Mum came in for a final tuck in. She pulled the covers up to my chin and leant over close to my ear.

Her voice was quiet yet firm.

"Now Sarah, we don't need to tell anyone what happened tonight. Do you understand? No one needs to know."

My attacker was never caught, and I did not speak another word about that night.

Chapter 18

The Tutor

The next two years at school continued with blurred sadness. Shortly after my 14th birthday, I got my first period. This event only added to my sultry moods and emotional distancing.

"Your fault, your fault, your fault," the taunting voice would accuse.

My grades were falling fast, my ability to concentrate deteriorating by the day. Mr Blackman was my math teacher who offered to tutor me. He lived a 30-minute drive from school and the tutoring was to be conducted in his home. On a bitterly cold July afternoon, Mr Blackman walked me to his car which was parked in the school staff parking area. I climbed into the front seat of his pale brown station wagon. It was a 'poo' colour and certainly not a car I was proud to get into. He chatted to me about my interests of which I had none. I found his questions annoying as I answered in short 3-word replies.

"Do you like to read, Sarah?" he asked.

"No, not really," I replied.

The tyres crunched on the rough asphalt driveway outside a red brick federation home signalling our arrival. Donned in a loose floral maxi dress to hide her heavily pregnant belly, Mrs Blackman stood in the doorway and smiled warmly as though we had met before. Her shy demeanour was evident as Mr Blackman with his towering six feet plus height bent over to gently kiss her cheek. This was their daily formality, an unspoken expectation. My eyes were fixed on her belly. I had never seen a woman this pregnant before and reasoned with myself that she could not possibly get any bigger.

I hated math and hated Mum for agreeing to this torture. It was bad enough that I had to spend a day at school, but now having additional math was a nightmare. As the winter sun began to set, Mr Blackman suggested we go for a walk while Mrs Blackman finished cooking the dinner. Anything to get me away from his desk and the confusing sums was a better option.

I could smell the sizzling sausages, the spitting fat popping in the distance.

"Please don't let there be any broccoli," I silently prayed.

We paused at the front door to put on our winter coats and Mr Blackman gave a quick shout to Mrs Blackman.

"Won't be long love."

Mr Blackman led me down the street. The wide pavements were flanked by a canopy of grand leafy trees. Roots forcing their way through the concrete path were a twisted obstacle course to be aware of.

"Watch you step," Mr Blackman said, pointing to the gnarly roots.

As the glowing sun dipped further into the horizon, the evening chill set in. I didn't like the cold; my slight body was devoid of any warming fat. Rubbing my hands together, I had wished I had brought my gloves. Mr Blackman suddenly reached for my hand,

"Oh, your hands are very cold Sarah," he said.

He quickly forced my hand deep into his pocket. A hard hot rod of flesh awaited. Mr Blackman pushed my hand onto his erect penis. It was pulsating with intensity. I instinctively formed my hand into a ball to repel his touch. His grip was firm, his hand large. I tried to pull my hand out of his pocket, but he forcefully held my hand in place. I began to panic. Why was he doing this to me? His wife was heavily pregnant. He was my teacher. I was a child. Disgust burnt my throat as bitterness of anger and terror regurgitated. I felt like I was going to pass out when he released his grip.

The walk back to the house was in silence. I couldn't look at Mrs Blackman over dinner nor eat the food placed in front of me. I didn't tell anyone about my walk with Mr Blackman. The harvesting of silence was deep rooted in my soul.

My drinking alcohol to numb my pain continued. One night I was going to a birthday party, and I carefully filled an empty 300mls bottle of tonic water with Dad's gin. I drank the entire contents in the garden before entering the party. Before long, I became very ill. I could not stop vomiting violently. I was discovered behind a bush by the birthday girl's mother, who put me in a taxi and shipped me home. In a drunken stumble I staggered up the stairs to my bedroom hoping not to be noticed. Mum was standing at the top of the stairs horrified at my state.

"Get to bed!" she grunted in a deep angry voice.

Great! That was exactly where I wanted to go. The vomiting didn't stop all night long. At 9am a shout woke me out of a deep sleep.

"Get up!" my mother's gruff tone commanded.

It was Saturday and I was to attend Saturday morning school detention. Each student had a 'Conduct Card' at Loreto Kirribilli, with five available points to be subtracted for unaccepted behaviour. If your five points were lost in one week, between Monday and Friday, the consequence was Saturday morning detention. This commenced at 10am at the school where tasks were assigned. These tasks were usually cleaning, such as the bathrooms or the 'tuck' shop, the place where you could purchase food, including

THE TUTOR

lunch items and snacks. Mothers volunteered to work in the tuck shop to maintain this service. I seemed to be required to attend most Saturdays as I would lose the five points, sometimes all by the end of Monday.

"Oh no," I thought with dread as I dragged my limp body out of bed hoping I would not be assigned to the tuck shop as the smell of food would only continue to make me vomit. I knew not to protest as Mum's fury was evident all over her face. Each frown line deepened by the second. I later questioned this form of punishment and wondered why Mum didn't suggest another consequence as this was obviously not working. I was at school scrubbing most Saturdays. The teachers all seemed to pick on me, blaming me for any disruption in the class. Both the nuns and the lay teachers seemed to have it in for me. It was always my fault. I was the child who reported Brother Dave.

Chapter 19

The Interrogation

The call went out for all year 10 girls to go to the D Room, a theatre-style room where we would go to watch films, usually documentaries of various kinds. The seating was rows of long wooden benches that were elevated like a cinema. I used to enjoy going to the D Room as this was a time to chill out and not have to listen to a teacher. The lights would go out and I could relax. No teacher to pick on me.

This fateful day I obeyed the command and marched to the D Room with the rest of the 14-year-old girls. On the whiteboard at the front of the room were written two questions in large writing:

Do you know anyone who has smoked marijuana?

Have you ever been offered marijuana?

We were all given paper and a pen to write our answers. Once I had recovered from the shock of the questions, I quickly wrote a large NO on my paper. I started to experiment with marijuana at the age of 14. Some boys from a local school had offered it to us girls and we were curious to try. I was not going to tell the nuns this information as I saw it as typical teenage experimentation.

THE INTERROGATION

My task was completed in two seconds. I waited as the silence tore through the room. A simultaneous holding of breath as each student took on the magnitude of these questions. We were eventually released to return to our classrooms to pack up ready to go home. It was now 3pm, 10 mins before the final bell.

An announcement came over the loudspeaker. This was a common occurrence as the principal and deputy principal would often have some final instructions at the end of the day. But today was the beginning of the end. The announcement bellowed from the classroom speaker,

"Would Sarah Cook come to the office."

As I gathered my books and packed my bag, I knew this was it. I couldn't even cast my eyes around the room, only to the floor. I gathered my thoughts somehow knowing I would be blamed. I was always blamed so why would this be any different? I thought back to the two questions on the whiteboard. Had some of the girls written, "yes" on their piece of paper? Deep down I knew I would be the scape goat.

Going to Sister Joan's office always meant trouble for me as I was targeted for wrong doings. I was the one to blame in every class setting. The one talking, the one causing trouble, I was simply 'the one'. The scape goat, the seductress, the child who had led the man of cloth astray. Sister Joan's stern plump face seemed to always seethe with hatred and on this occasion, she didn't fail me.

Sister Gigantor appeared around the corner,

"Follow me," she growled.

Her large foreboding frame led me down the staircase, along the corridor, across the playground towards two mammoth wooden doors into the nun's convent. The secret places no child's eye had seen. Out of bounds with no one in the history of our schoolgirl conversations ever having entered their sanctuary. It was terrifying to be approaching this place of mystery.

No words were spoken as I continued to follow her gloomy shadow down the long dark corridor. I walked with great trepidation, my heart sinking into dread, the unknown destiny was petrifying. Where was she taking me? To be tortured? To be hidden away never to be found? My mind could not think soundly as the immense fear increased with each step.

Finally, she stopped at an old iron door and gestured for me to go inside. It was a small stark room, damp and cold with a simple wooden chair.

"Wait here," she commanded, closing the door with a loud bang behind her.

I felt better to be away from her oppressive presence, but the reality of my situation dawned on me. It was 3pm when I was ordered to the principal's office but now, I was in this small room, trapped and wondering for how long. I had no idea.

I would have already missed my ferry home. My mother waiting at the wharf to collect me would be alarmed not to see me disembark from the vessel. I had no access to a phone, so I had no way of calling my Mum to inform her of my kidnapping.

Time passed slowly. The frigid air and the smell of mouldy ancient wood gave me chills. My body was vibrating with cold and dread. A trembling that was visible. I tried to subdue it, but my overthinking only exacerbated it. So much time seemed to pass but with no watch and no clock, I had no idea how long I had been in my dungeon. No explanation, no information, nothing. Just left alone, in solitary confinement with the fear of the unknown.

After what seemed like hours, which in fact was hours, the door finally squeaked open. Sister Gigantor ushered me out with no words spoken. My spirit was successfully crushed so I followed obediently. The narrow passage meandered through the old sandstone building to an opening with two huge pale green glass doors, each pane of glass lined in a gold painted

THE INTERROGATION

wood. The doors swung open to reveal a vast room surrounded by panelled glass windows with heavy cream curtains.

I instinctively knew this was an important room. I walked in, sheepishly glancing my eyes up from the floor where they had been locked since taking my walk to death row.

"Dead man walking," echoed in my head.

I took a quick look and to my amazement the room was full of people. Chairs had been arranged in a large semi-circle with one empty chair in the centre of the outer rim. I knew that this chair was for me. I walked slowly towards it, my eyes still cast down not really wanting to know what was ahead. When I went to sit on the only vacant chair, I looked up gulping at the disturbing site before me ... my parents were sitting on the two chairs either side of mine. A surge of nauseating nervousness arose as I sat down. Squeezing in my arms and legs, pulling in my body as tight as possible, I became the smallest me I could be. I could not look at them. The rest of the semi-circle of chairs were filled with all my teachers each carrying an angry look screaming, "she's guilty."

The front of the room had a desk where the principal sat. Sister Joan stood holding a clip board ready for the accusations to begin. The two questions from the D Room were revisited.

"Have you ever smoked marijuana?"

"No," I lied.

"Have you ever given marijuana to anyone?"

"No Sister," I answered respectfully.

"Well, that's not what I've been told," she scoffed.

She began to go through a pad of notes telling me who had said what and naming my friends and their disloyalty. Each accusation was like a knife going through my heart. My friends were everything to me and now they were all like Judas, especially Delia. Delia was a Hunters Hill girl who was very bright. The youngest of 10 children, she was the teachers' pet. The dux of the class was her badge of honour guaranteeing to give the school a good result in the HSC. The academic children seemed to be favoured, holding value for the future standards of the school. This was very vital for the up-and-coming wealthy parents looking for a school with results.

I had befriended an Alloysius boy, Oliver, who would babysit for a couple of marijuana dealers. One night he invited me to join him. His task, apart from putting the kids to bed, was to bag up mull, marijuana leaves into plastic sandwich bags. The stash was stored in large green garbage bags, of which there were multiple, stuffed to capacity.

I didn't ask any questions but watched as he carefully measured the amount into each bag with weighing scales like he knew what he was doing. Quite knowledgeable for a year 10 boy but I am sure they had trained him. One of the perks of this position was he could smoke as much as he wanted.

With such a large amount I am sure, no matter how much we smoked, they would not see a dent. Oliver rolled up a joint with about five tally-ho papers - the result was a spliff that looked like a trumpet. He was trying to impress me. We puffed away until we couldn't anymore. The massive joint was only half smoked before we both ended up like vegetables on the couch, unable to move. This was strong gear. I vaguely remember going home in a taxi with my head spinning.

Smoking pot had become another means of escape. A temporary numbing of my negative shameful thoughts.

Another time, we were at a party with a group of Loreto girls and Alloysius boys who gathered in the back yard and began puffing on a joint that was being passed around. We all eagerly took turns as it was the cool thing to do. I was later to find out that the mother of the party boy saw us and called Loreto to inform the school we were partaking in dope smoking. This was on a Saturday night and not on school grounds, but this mother

THE INTERROGATION

felt it was her duty to report us to our school. It was this call that instigated the D Room meeting.

Finally, the big question came.

"So, who gave YOU the marijuana?"

There was no way I was going to be a traitor like the others.

"You may have made all my friends dob me in, but I am not going to tell you that."

I was surprised at how calm I felt in the thick of my trial. The question was asked again but again, I had the same answer. I had a deep sense of loyalty to my friends even though I had been thrown under the bus.

As my mother and father walked with me to the car, there was an eerie silence. I was trying to embrace the shock of what had been inflicted on me when, to my surprise, my mother said,

"Well Sarah, at least you didn't put your friends in."

I knew Mum was furious and my punishment for her humiliation would be waiting for me when I got home, yet I knew this statement had a 'well done you' sentiment.

I was jailed in my bedroom for the next two weeks while we waited on the nuns' verdict. My only respite was visiting the bathroom. Meals were at my desk and no phone calls were permitted. It was a long two weeks as I questioned why it was taking so long to decide my future fate.

Finally, the jury had come to a verdict and my mother delivered a letter to my desk,

"We no longer require the presence of your daughter at our school," it read.

I was expelled two weeks out from the year 10 school certificate exam. The nuns had put the final nail in my coffin. The girl they believed had led poor Brother Dave astray had met her fate.

Chapter 20
The Holiday

Family holidays were not a part of my upbringing. I never questioned why other families would go to the snow each year or go away for school holidays, and we did not. My mother was happy in her Hunters Hill waterfront home, which was renovated to her perfection. It was her pride and joy.

"Why go away when we have everything here at home," she would say brightly.

Dad, on the other hand, loved adventure. His idea of a holiday was trekking in Nepal or an elephant safari in Thailand. Mum couldn't think of anything worse. Her only acceptable holiday was a five-star hotel, Dad's worst nightmare.

I do recall an attempt at camping in my primary school years. Dad had purchased a large heavy canvas tent. It was a deep kaki colour and I remember Dad and Matthew struggling to lift it out of the station wagon boot. The trip took us to the banks of the Hawkesbury River not too far out of Sydney. I have no idea how Dad convinced Mum to go, but he did. It would be the first and last camping trip my family would venture on.

THE HOLIDAY

Matthew was excited to be outdoors. Each night he took delight in pulling the bung out of my air mattress. I would wake up lying on hard ground every morning. He thought this was hilarious, especially when I cried. Our trip was shortly after Christmas, and I had been gifted with a butterfly net. I was overjoyed that the field we were camping on had hundreds of small white butterflies that loved to give me chase. Their tiny wings would flutter so fast until they would quietly settle on one of the hundreds of white daisies, waiting for me to pounce. As I approached, they would smile and fly off, beckoning me to follow. This butterfly play would entertain me for hours, an escape into a world of imagination. I was alone in nature lost in myself even though Mum and Dad were only metres away. But Mum was miserable.

The tension between Mum and Dad was palpable and I knew how to be quiet and to keep clear. After the camping holiday, the tent was packed up and stored in our attic until many years later it was taken to the tip after a rat had made a meal of it.

"We're going to New Caledonia," Dad announced one evening. I had recently celebrated my 14th birthday, and the mid-year school holidays were approaching. I was shocked but also delightfully surprised. I had no idea where this place was, but we were going on a plane! "Club Med Noumea," Dad replied when I asked for details.

"We are going to a French speaking island in the South Pacific," Dad said.

Growing up in the UK opened the door for Dad to travel on many trips to Europe. He loved practicing his French, remembering as a POW the French soldier who kept him warm and alive. He would ride on his motor bike through the countryside flirting with pretty girls. Somehow Dad had convinced Mum to leave her home palace and venture on a family holiday. I think the fact it was a resort convinced her to go.

"All meals and drinks are included," he told her.

"And it is very good value. You can practice your French, Sarah."

Dad was frugal, as he was brought up in The Depression. Here was an opportunity for a good value educational adventure. Mum would get her resort, so it was agreed.

I was not prepared for the education I would encounter.

The minibus arrived at the entrance of a large foyer surrounded by fragrant frangipani trees of yellows, pinks, and reds. A sea of extraordinarily good-looking people from many nations greeted us. With beaming smiles, they jumped with excitement singing and dancing all seeming to know the same steps and arm movements. I was mesmerised. Wow, what was this place?

The high energy pace had been set, and this was to continue for the next week. The staff known as GO's (Gracious Organisers) were to ensure that each guest known as GM's (Gracious Members) would have the best holiday experience possible. Club Med would source their GOs from a global staff pool, the staff moving from club to club each season. This made the offer very attractive for young adults to travel the world and work along the way. There were entertainers, watersports instructors, waiters, cooks, housekeepers, and managers filling every position at the resort. The food was displayed in smorgasbords, with endless culinary varieties to expand the imagination. Dad loved food, especially exotic international dishes. The all-inclusive menu, including beer and French wine, left him with a permanent contented grin.

Mum hated water. Any water really. She hated rain as it would spoil her beehive hairdo, she had painfully spent an hour creating each morning. She hated swimming pools, even though we had one at home. I never saw her go near it. Mum couldn't swim so water was to be feared. She didn't even like to drink it. I never saw her pour a glass of water. But here at Club

THE HOLIDAY

Med, she had positioned herself by the pool. A creamy cocktail, balancing a green and orange paper umbrella which pierced a pineapple slice, and a glazed cherry was poised in her hand. Her oversized sunglasses were a fashion statement complimenting her blue one-piece swimsuit and matching sarong. I knew this swimsuit would never actually get wet, but she blended nicely into the resort vibe. The pool was full of action, ball games and competitions creating wild splashing and laughter. Mum seemed to be happy sipping and watching. I was just happy that she was happy.

The resort was located on a white sandy beachfront. The humidity was high so getting wet regularly was a part of my coping strategy. I also enjoyed people watching as there were many multicultural varieties on display. Two men always caught my attention as they would walk up and down the beach each day. Their chests puffed out with their heads held high as if they were walking on a catwalk.

Andre and Didie both wore the smallest G-strings, their dark bronzed butt cheeks tensing with each strut. All the girls on the beach noticed them, and their egos knew they were being closely watched. They would stop at each beach towel that supported a pretty girl and with their thick French accents they would ooze out charm. Giggles of glee would come from the girls as the flirting began. I was fascinated as these two peacocks danced their daily mating performance.

Sunday was our last day before we were to fly back to Sydney. Mum and Dad had ventured to the beach much to my surprise as Mum not only hated water, but she also hated sand. I distanced myself further up the beach so as not to be seen with my parents. I wanted to be more grown up than my 14 years in this grown-up, exotic world. Right on queue Andre and Didie began their beach walk. I had overheard resort guests chatting, discovering that they were brothers who lived locally. They were known to spend most of their time at the beach in front of the resort.

Didie was the older brother, approximately 26 years old, whereas Andre was closer to 24. This Sunday, Didie had stopped at the towels of two Swedish girls. He was putting on an extra charm when Andre approached my towel.

"You, me, swim?" he asked in his limited English.

I was both surprised and delighted that he had selected my towel to stop at. He leant forward slightly offering me his right hand. I responded by taking his hand in mine to be assisted to my feet.

Without another word he led me down the beach away from the resort and into the water. The water was warm like a bath, yet it offered some relief from the intensive tropical heat. He led me slowly out into waist-deep water and then stopped. His face turned to face me as he placed his hands intentionally on my waist pulling me firmly towards him. I panicked briefly as I turned to see if my parents were watching. I could see them way down the beach still in the exact position I had last seen them. Mum was reading her book, and Dad was lying on his stomach, sunning his back.

Andre's grip became stronger as I turned back to face him. He was looking directly into my eyes as if he knew exactly what he was doing. He released one hand from my waist now that my body was hard against his. With a thrust he pushed his erect penis into my vagina while maneuvering my bikini pants to one side. In complete shock my breath was taken. Andre remained very still, quickly ejaculated, and then removed his penis.

It was all over within seconds. I stood weak at the knees wondering how this had happened. Did he realize I was only 14 years old? He then walked quietly back towards the beach leaving me alone in waist deep water.

I had been raped.

I walked back to my towel in a daze. How did that happen? So quickly? Did anyone see? Could I be pregnant?

THE HOLIDAY

I felt so dirty and disgusted in myself. Why did I take his hand? I sat in silence glancing at Mum and Dad in the distance. The overwhelming shame never allowed me to mention this incident to anyone. It must have been my fault. I was a victim again, a silent broken victim. Another secret to add to my growing shameful list, harvesting more silence. This man's crime was never spoken of.

The next day to my relief I got my period.

Chapter 21

The Nurse

I was Daddy's girl and his 'little nurse'. From as young as I can remember, he would ask me to assist in his home surgery. It made me feel grown up to hold such a valuable role.

Other adults in my world repeatedly asked me,

"What do you want to do when you grow up, Sarah? Who do you want to be?"

I continued to have no clue or capacity to even think about such a huge life decision. What do grown-ups do? In primary school I thought I might like to be a nun as they seemed so wholesome but now, I was against anything to do with religion. As far as I was concerned, priests, nuns, and brothers were all evil, a part of a depraved secret society.

A racing car driver?

A water ski champion?

These were my wishes but not likely options.

"What about nursing?" Dad suggested on more than one occasion.

"Yes," Mum agreed.

This career choice would suit the family status. I clawed my way through the HSC with last minute cramming; only just getting the required result

THE NURSE

for nursing. Dad was able to pull a few strings and get me into Royal North Shore Hospital (RNSH) even though I was only seventeen and the minimum age requirement was eighteen.

Vindin House was adjacent to the hospital. It was an old multistorey building that housed the new recruits for the compulsory three-month live-in requirement. I had never been to boarding school or lived away from home, so this forced situation was not attractive to me.

My room was tiny, only fitting a single bed and a small desk. A dormitory style bathroom to share with all the other girls on my floor was daunting. It was stark and cold. I hated it. All my friends who had decided on other career options and university degrees were going out on the town while I had a 9pm curfew to obey.

After the compulsory three months in Vindin House, I moved into a share house in Lane Cove, fondly named 'Barwon House', after its street name. My name was on the lease, so it was my responsibility to find other nurses to join me. I gathered my housemates, and we enjoyed the new freedom. We experimented with cooking, but our attempts were largely unsuccessful.

Dad was an exotic cook, always enjoying trying new recipes from around the world. Coquille Saint Jacques, a French dish with scallops in a creamy wine sauce, garlic snails served in special ceramic snail shells and fondues being his specialties. These dishes were a bit overly rich for my young palate.

With four young nurses away from the disciplines of home, this house became a popular hang for a group of local boys. Memories of my past traumas would come like the tides, ebbing, and flowing in relentless cycles. Chaos was stirring under a still surface as I struggled to understand the difference between love and sex. Pain and heartbreak swirled as the next cyclone approached.

I was infatuated with Noah, a handsome blue eyed third year nurse at RNSH. He captivated me with his friendly, warm disposition. I mistook his friendliness for interest and became increasingly more infatuated with him. His seven years of maturity beyond my 18 years, intrigued me. One day, I thought I'd turn up to his home and surprise him. That's when I found him in bed with my boss, Megan. Megan was in her mid-thirties, an experienced RN in charge of cardiology. I was heartbroken. How could I compete with this mature woman.

After the discovery of Noah and Megan's new forming relationship, they felt sorry for me (or so I believed) and invited me over for dinner. I met Noah's flat mate Jeremy who was so much fun to be around. So, Noah, Megan, Jeremy, and I quickly became two couples.

Jeremy was a 26-year-old dentist, a profession that would earn my parents' approval. A partner's job status was very important to my mother, an essential bragging tool to share with the doctors' wives in Hunters Hill.

"Oh, my daughter has married a neurosurgeon. He has a master's degree in blah blah blah and a double degree in blah blah. They are off skiing in Aspen, blah blah," Doctor Tate's wife would boast.

"Oh, how marvelous," my mother would reply.

"Sarah is studying nursing at RNSH the best training hospital in the country."

Jeremy and I decided to move in together. We found a lovely, bright unit on the top floor of an apartment in Manly, Sydney. The balconies wrapped from north to east showcasing the panoramic display of coastal perfection. I had to pinch myself to believe this was happening in my life. It was pure bliss. I was madly in love. I always had his undivided attention, with his bright eyes lighting up as he listened to my stories. He would tenderly wrap me in his arms and just hold me close. No sexual demands, no pressure to please him, no abuse, just kindness.

Our mornings would begin with the short stroll from our unit to the golden sand of Manly Beach. The two of us would walk hand in hand into the cool waters of the Pacific Ocean. I would sometimes begin to struggle breathing, hesitating to go further. My asthma inhaler, the friend in my bag was there to save me from my affliction of asthma. My heart would pound as the drug opened my airways; my sweet Jeremy was always there. His hand in mine, his beaming smile would lead me out through the rippling waves as they sparkled in the early morning sun. These moments should have been perfect, except that the memory of the New Caledonia holiday where I was raped would trigger an unwanted memory. It was always lurking in the background. Jeremy's gentle touch of encouragement promised to protect me. I never told him of the rape. I was too ashamed.

Breakfast was enjoyed on the balcony, soaking in the vast view of the Northern Beaches. I felt like the luckiest girl in the world as I devoured my bowl of colorful fresh fruits. Jeremy's blue eyes flashed love with his booming laughter contagious to all. Jeremy was a likeable, intelligent, fun-loving guy.

I said, "Yes!" as he proposed, and we were going to get married. It was a dream come true. I had met a man who loved me, a man I would start a family with. A man I would love until "death us do part". I instantly began to think about the perfect wedding. My dress would be classic white with a train embroidered with sparkling sequence. Frangipanis, yellow and white would be positioned in my hair, their fragrance tropically sweet. I decided that we would be married on the beach as a church would be out of the question. I was euphoric as I pictured myself as Jeremy's wife.

In 1982, Dad had a stroke. As I was training on the cardiology ward at the time, he was admitted onto my floor. This was a huge challenge for me, seeing him so terribly unwell. My Dad was my hero and the thought of losing him was too much to bear. I struggled daily on the ward questioning my choice of starting a nursing career.

Nursing in the early eighties involved three years of practical training in the wards, along with some classroom training. I found shift work grueling and dreaded the night duty shifts. The ten hours seemed to never end, and the lack of sleep made me nauseous. Sleeping during the day was something I never mastered, only increasing my sleep deprivation.

The senior nurses were cruel to the new recruits. They seemed to take pleasure in giving us the worst jobs to do.

"Nurse! Get down on your hands and knees and manually evacuate this patient," the senior nurse commanded.

The military style was harsh and often tyrannical. Doing the sputum rounds was also a struggle for me. There was a 'clean' nurse and a 'dirty' nurse. When it was my turn to be the 'dirty' nurse, I stood stiff, horrified at what was waiting ahead. The 'clean' nurse's role was to push a stainless steel trolly while manning a clip board ready to take notes. The 'dirty' nurse was to go to the bedside of each patient and pick up the paper cup, look inside and then describe in detail the findings. This cup was used by the patients to cough up their sputum and hence being in the cardiology ward these people had plenty to get off their chests.

"30mls, green mucus with brown lumps," I gagged my results.

My mother was horrified when I announced I had decided to leave the nursing profession only eight months into the course. She didn't speak to me for three months, her chosen punishment. She was a professional at the 'silent treatment'.

No longer training to be a general nurse I had landed myself a job as a nanny and a part time job as a 'Dial a Bubbly' girl. My job was to dress up in a French maid's costume, delivering champagne or sparkling wine and a message to an unsuspecting recipient who was celebrating a birthday or an anniversary. Dressed in a short black mini skirt, a white blouse and frilly apron, fish net stockings and black stiletto high heels, I would start my shift. Tottering through the busy streets of Sydney, I would seek out the 'lucky' person who was the recipient of my celebratory wishes.

Long blonde hair floating behind me, my face glowing with innocence, my slim figure fitting the costume perfectly. I was oblivious to the leering eyes on me.

My mother eventually forgave me for my career change, but her deep-down resentment never let go. The image of a doctor's daughter as a registered nurse from a prestigious hospital clung to her dreams.

Our family station wagon was traded in for a brand-new Mazda RX-7 sports car. The humming rotary engine showing off its power under the bonnet. Dad was not happy with my mother's sudden decision to make a significant change in her life during midlife.

"This is not a suitable car for a mature woman," Dad said.

Mum got her way, arriving home in her new car. I was permitted to take the wheel of her precious red sports car, even though I had only just passed the driver's test. Driving around Hunters Hill at high speeds, I was looking to show off to anyone who would look my way. I think Mum liked the attention I would get as this was a reflection on her. Her trophy daughter was on display in a prestigious car. This overpowered vehicle was a temptation for reckless behavior.

Victims of childhood sexual abuse have a predisposition to risky behaviours. A part of the brain is altered during development, which diminishes the fear of dangerous actions and their consequences. This becomes another way to deaden the reality of life, euphoric numbing through adrenaline. Drugs and alcohol added into the mix with the reckless behaviour, and you have a cocktail for potential disaster.

Mum's RX7 was a semi-automatic with a redlining feature, an alarm that sounded when the revs exceeded the limit. My ultimate challenge was to see how fast I could get this car to go. The goal was to work through the redlining sequence of the gears to reach the maximum speed possible. The M1 motorway north of Sydney was a perfect raceway for my mission. The screaming buzz of the engine as the rotary heated up gave me an incredible 'high'. The engine would jolt with the change to the next gear with a G-force planting my back into the driver's seat like a perfect fitting glove. The speed was intoxicating. It was another form of escape from my unpleasant earthly reality. Danger was not a consideration for me nor my passengers. I was the racing car driver I had dreamed of as a child. I was comfortably numb.

Then the tragedy struck. My world came completely undone. Only one week after Jeremy announced our engagement to his family, he had an episode. He hadn't come home from work this evening and I was worried. I called Noah, who had just come off shift and immediately came over to drive me to Jeremy's work. Jeremy was in the middle of a mental health episode locked in the bathroom. This was the first time I had seen him in this state. I panicked desperately trying to speak to him through the door,

"Come out Jeremy, its ok. It's Sarah here. Please, please come out," I begged.

Hours passed when he finally emerged shaken and pale.

"We need to get him to a hospital," Noah directed.

The doctors diagnosed him with, 'Hypermania' a heightened level of psychological mania resulting in delusion. I visited St John of God Hospital daily hoping he would come out of the trance and know my name.

"It's me, Sarah," I would repeat over and over, but it was as though he had never laid eyes on me.

THE NURSE

With each passing week my despair deepened. I moved back into my family home in Hunters Hill only to sit on the green plastic faux leather lounge in the bay window staring out at the Lane Cove River. All kinds of watercraft would pass, speed boats, wind surfers, canoes, and a rare ferry on a scenic tour. I sat mesmerised and detached most days until Dad's voice brought me into the present.

"Sarah, would you like some kidneys on toast?" he asked.

This food choice would horrify most of my friends, but this was one of Dad's favourite 'pommie' delicacies. Other English offerings were tripe and onion, kippers broiled in milk, pork pies with hot English mustard, but I had no appetite for anything. My stomach was knotted tight like a boa constrictor trying to kill me from the inside.

Eventually, Jeremy was released on medication with his family determined to blame me for his mental condition. His parents didn't like me. This was painfully obvious the night Jeremy told his family about our engagement. His mother's eyes widened in distaste responding with,

"Can you pass the salt?" Her words cut through my soul.

It was a sunny Sunday morning, but I was not aware of the sun. The bold bright light that used to entice me out onto the river in my dinghy was a distant, blurred memory. I trudged back upstairs into my childhood bedroom and lay down. My body was weighted. I had no desire to move. A dark cloud surrounded me, I drew the blinds hiding the day from the room.

"I'm going to church Sarah," Mum called out on her way to the carport.

I had stopped going to church and Mum no longer insisted that I go. I wondered if she knew what had happened to me with Brother Dave. There was still no mention.

Hours passed. I finally emerged only to flop onto my green plastic couch once again to continue staring out the window. I could see Dad dragging the netted scoop across the surface of the swimming pool in a slow rhythmic pattern. Occasionally, he would glance up and wave at a passing boat with his warm friendly smile. The people on the boats would frantically wave back as if they knew him. People on boats always seem to wave at each other. It is as if the joy of being on the water gives permission to greet others who have the same privilege. Living on a waterfront property also gives you the right to wave to strangers.

Later that morning, Dad came upstairs.

"I have something for you Sarah," he said handing me a white envelope.

I moved my glance slowly from the rippling water to catch his eyes. Their piercing blue flooded me with love. My father was a man I could always trust. He was consistent in every way. His daily rituals, preparing to go to work, his evening greeting as he walked up the stairs at the end of the day, sitting in his large chair in front of the TV reading the paper, all brought me comfort.

I took the crisp white paper into my hands and carefully unfolded the creases. Inside there was a plane ticket to London. I was speechless.

"What?" my thoughts sent me into apprehension.

He wants to send me to the other side of the world! What about Jeremy? I can't leave him.

Dad looked deep into my eyes and gently said,

"It's time to go."

The ticket was an 'Around the World' ticket allowing five stopovers as long as you kept flying in the same direction. The journey allowed twelve months for completion. I knew Dad was right, it was time to let go.

Chapter 22

Around the World

The 12-month adventure began flying me to the UK. Departing Sydney in July shortly after my 19th birthday, I sobbed tears of the unknown mixed with grief as I hugged my parents' goodbye. Dad's identical twin, Uncle John, would meet me at Heathrow Airport.

Shortly after arriving in the UK, I purchased a car. I loved my white Mini Metro and the freedom it gave me. Driving all over the countryside - Oxford, Cardiff, Bristol, Birmingham, Manchester, London, and Shrewsbury, I visited family and friends.

On one of my drives from London to Shrewsbury to get to a party, the engine started blowing smoke. The billowing white mass turned dark grey then to a thick black cloud. I decided to ignore it and pressed on.

"Bang!"

The engine came to a grinding halt. The radiator had overheated, blowing up the engine. Tragedy had struck when I had a party to get to. I wasn't going to let this stop me. I left the car on the side of the M1 freeway and started to hitchhike. Another risky behaviour that I thought nothing of. A huge semi-trailer stopped. The deep blue cabin reached high above me. I stretched my neck to see a ginger bearded man hosting a surprised look,

"You can't leave a car on the M1, lassie," he bellowed down at me in a thick Scottish accent.

"I have to get to Shrewsbury, it's an emergency," I pleaded with wide eyes.

My Australian accent caught his attention. He gestured for me to climb up into the cab, a stale smell of cigarette smoke overpowered my senses. With a grunt of a gear change, we were on our way. The exhilaration of being so high up off the road gave me goose bumps. I let out a squeal of delight forgetting my injured Mini Metro instantly. We flew past the 'tiny' cars which looked like toys from this height. My driver was on his way to Scotland and said he could drop me at Watford Junction. I smiled gratefully at his offer. This drop-off point would leave me with a remaining 2 ½ hours' drive to my party in Shrewsbury via the M6 motorway.

I convinced a grey-haired woman at the Watford Service Centre to call my cousin Donald. She had a grandmotherly appearance, her white hair carefully pulled into a bun. The floral A-line dress was loose fitting with a string of faux pearls lining her neck. I peered into her steel rimmed glasses which were perched on the end of her nose. With tears in my eyes I pleaded, "Please, it's an emergency. I need to use the phone."

The party was to start at 6pm. Cousin Donald didn't hesitate to offer to drive the five-hour return trip to pick me up. I was his young cousin all the way from Australia, behaving recklessly.

"You can't just leave a car on the M1 in the UK, Sarah," Donald confirmed what my Scottish truck driver had told me.

I got to my party just in time. I was impressed by my ingenuity.

The following day I made a few calls under Donald's instructions to find out that my Mini Metro had been towed to a delegated lock up. I was to face a large fine. The proper action in this situation was to always stay with the vehicle and wait for a tow. But I had a party to go to.

AROUND THE WORLD

My heart ached every day for Jeremy, the distance between us did not soften the pain. Each night I would cry myself to sleep, sobbing so deeply that I would choke on my secretions. I loved him dearly, a gut-wrenching guilt telling me I had abandoned him. For months I had waited for his recovery before Dad decided on my behalf that the wait was over. As a doctor he knew the prognosis was not good, and certainly not a future for his beloved daughter. His professional wisdom took command, removing me from a situation he deemed doomed. I trusted his judgement.

Six months into my overseas placement, my heart began to heal. The pain gradually weakened, the tightening clamp surrounding my heart, piecing its tender flesh began to lose its unrelenting grip. I would continue to love this man, as the pain became a past memory. Alcohol and parties became my distraction.

"Call from Australia," Cousin Donald shouted urgently.

Phone calls from Australia were very expensive so I rushed to the phone to hear the three beeps indicating a new pay cycle,

"Hello," I answered.

"It's your mother. I'm coming to visit."

Shocked that she was to leave her home comforts and fly to the UK, I laughed in disbelief.

"Really?" I replied, my voice's pitch inclining with intrigue.

Mum didn't like Dad's English relatives, especially Uncle John. I began to anticipate her arrival with curious excitement. My repaired Mini Metro and I proudly met her at Heathrow Airport. After a few days of recovering from jet lag at Cousin Donald's, we ventured to Europe. I was driving while Mum oversaw navigation. A huge fold out map (no GPS in the 80's!), was to be our guide. The map was so large that when fully unfolded it would fill the front two seats of the car.

Our first destination was to be Nice in the French Riviera. After crossing the English Channel on the car ferry, we arrived in Calais. The drive south began after two chocolate croissants at a local patisserie.

"Let's take this turn here Sarah, through Pue St Vincent," Mum directed in her best French accent.

"Sure, why not," I replied. She had been entrusted with the map.

I didn't realise that Pue St Vincent was a ski resort, and that we were about to climb the French Alps. My Mini Metro struggled up the steep winding roads, huffing and puffing at each turn. It reminded me of the billowing smoke episode on the M1, and I hoped her little engine wouldn't 'blow up' again. The drop off on the side of the road was so steep that I couldn't bring myself to look over the edge. A glimpse would make me nauseous from terror. I had never been this far up from sea level. The oncoming traffic stared at me, wondering which vehicle would inch slightly to let the other vehicle pass. The squeeze was tight on the narrow winding road, and I was tempted to close my eyes.

The French Alps continued to beckon us upwards. We had no choice as there was no opportunity to turn back. Huge pine trees of deep green increased in number and size. A dusting of white powder began to appear on the tips of the branches the higher we ascended, glistening in the sun's rays. I sighed in awe at the majesty of the scenic beauty before me.

"Is that snow?" Mum shrieked.

"I think so," I replied.

Laughter broke forth between us at the ludicrous situation unfolding.

I quickly returned my attention to the road.

We survived the two-day detour through the French Alps. Mum's poor map reading turned out to be a blessing. The topography had escaped her as map reading was not included in an opera scholarship. After enjoying the town of Pue St Vincent, we continued down the mountains to the Riviera.

AROUND THE WORLD

The seaside town of Nice buzzed with beautiful people, shining affluence of sparkling bling. Gucci handbags accompanied the scent of Chanel perfume wafting in the salty seaside air. This colourful cosmopolitan city, rich in history, culture, and fashion, was a polar opposite to the Australian culture back home. I watched in fascination as girls walked hand in hand and boys walked arms over each other's shoulders. An outward display of affection and friendship was on parade with no reflection of sexuality. A kiss on each cheek was the standard greeting as people met in the street, filling the air with a tangible love.

We chose the pretty seaside village Saint-Maxime for one of our night stops. The entrance to the hotel was welcoming, a high vaulted ceiling painted with naked bodies hypnotised me into a trance. The white, puffed, fatty flesh reminded me of my art history class at school. Seeing this display of nakedness towering above, forced me to stare.

"Sarah," Mum's voice directed my attention away from the ceiling to the woman behind the desk.

"Une Chambre pour la nuit, si vous plait," I asked the woman.

My school French lessons finally had some meaning.

"Oui, madam," she replied with a smile.

I was grateful she had understood my limited French. Mum returned a proud smile to the woman, chuffed that I had learnt something during my difficult traumatic school years. She led us down the side of the building, down three flights of stairs to a sliding door. Behind the door was a dark room perfectly square, featuring two single beds draped in dark brown corduroy covers. Mum quickly lost her smile as the woman bid farewell and took off. We stood momentarily trying to make out the shapes in this dark space, before grappling the walls in search of a light switch. With a click the awful room came to light. Other than the two uninviting beds there was a dark wooden wardrobe and a door to a tiny bathroom. With synchronised sighs, we concluded this was our resting place. Too tired to climb the stairs back to the welcoming foyer to insist on a room change, we accepted our den. The day had been filled with strolls along the sun-drenched promenade, coffee and croissants in a quaint café, multiple boutiques, a posh French restaurant serving 'frogs' legs' and a bottle of Beaujolais. We were ready to collapse on the brown beds. Shortly after retiring, I heard a strange buzzing around my ears. Mosquitos? I pulled the corduroy cover over my head and fell asleep.

Morning arrived late, as the dark blinds shut out all outside light delaying our rising. The thick springs of the bed had left an indentation on my right shoulder.

"Mum, are you awake?" She wasn't.

"MUM," I repeated.

She was lying flat on her back, her mouth slightly open and breathing a deep rhythmic sound. Not quite a snore but an indication that she was in a deep sleep. She stirred, then gradually came to consciousness. Pulling herself slowly to her feet she made her way to the bathroom.

"What's this on my face?" she yelped in horror.

Flying back into the room, she looked at me for an answer. I could see that her face was dotted with what seemed like hundreds of small red dots. I took a step towards her to examine the measle-like rash all over her face. 'Mosquitos!' I quickly determined.

She had not noticed the buzzing, laying victim to the swarm of flying blood suckers that lived in the dark wood wardrobe. We were to rename the hotel, 'Saint-Maxime Mosquitos', which brought us great laughter later in life when we recalled the stories of our overseas adventure.

Italy was next on our list with Mum eager to speak Italian, the language she had become fluent in when studying Italian Opera in Rome. I took over the role of navigator, carefully studying the map spread out on the bed in our hotel room. She could no longer be trusted with directions. My Mini

Metro was a perfect size for the tiny winding cobblestone streets. Wolf whistles from handsome Italian men echoed as we drove past.

"They are whistling at you Mum," I said.

"No, they are whistling at you, Sarah."

Two 'blondes' was enough to draw their attention, and attention we got. One night a group of young Italian men stood outside our hotel throwing rocks at the window insisting we come out and join them for a drink. I lay terrified on the floor pretending I wasn't there. Ignoring their pleas, they eventually went away.

My mother's month-long holiday soon came to an end. She waved goodbye with a tear in her eye at the departure gate at Heathrow Airport. I had never seen her cry, so a small drop of fluid encouraged me of her love. This time spent travelling together produced unspoken healing. Two adult women braving a European adventure. Her past control and silencing had put a wedge between us, creating a distance that seemed impossible to bridge. But, the English pubs, the French Alps, the French mosquitos, along with hilarious stories, ignited a spark in us. My mother, a carefree woman, took off the mask. 'The doctor's wife from Hunters Hill' let her hair down, dancing a new dance I loved witnessing.

There were no conversations about Brother Dave, this skeleton from the past was to remain in the closet. If the dark closet was opened, my mother may revert to overpowering control and I did not want that. The door was to remain firmly closed.

The twelve months on my Around the World ticket was coming to an end. The surprise visit to the French Alps with Mum, lured me to the heights of the Rocky Mountains in the United States. I worked in a child-minding centre at the base of the ski resort in Snowmass, Colorado, eight miles from Aspen. The snowfall was heavy, dropping a thick blanket on everything in its path. The mountain side blared a bright frosty white, a white whiter than the sand on the famous Australian Whitehaven Beach. The cold was bitter to my skin, each layer of my thermal clothing was not able to stand against the minus 30-degree Celsius wind blowing on me. I waded shin deep along the 1.5 kilometre steep path to work.

It was my 20th birthday. Suddenly, my subconscious mind awakened, obediently remembering what I had been instructed nine years earlier. Brother Dave's instructions were:

"Sarah, I know this must be very confusing for you and I don't expect you to understand. I am asking you to not think about what has happened and to put it out of your mind. When you turn 20, then you can think about it, and you will understand."

Shocking floods of memories from Brother Dave's abuse and the subsequent pain were too intense to manage. I fell to my knees, the snow soft enough to allow me to sink deep until I felt the solid rocks beneath me. A guttural sound emerged spontaneously from within, a sound that frightened me. I was launched into a cavern, a dark place of memories. I did not understand, even though his words told me I would. I was imploding violently as my physical body connected with my subconscious mind. The past was now in my face laughing at my stupidity and vulnerability.

"It was your fault, Sarah."

"No-one believed you."

"He got away with it."

A panic brought me to my feet as I ran through the deep snow as fast as I could, pushing the white mass in my strides. A pattern of numbing was now deep in my subconscious, a sequence I knew as 'my normal'. What substance could I find to dull down this memory? I knew that the guys at the ski hire had marijuana, I desperately needed to be comfortably numb.

"I don't understand."

"I don't understand."
"I don't understand."
I had to make these thoughts stop.

Broken and traumatised, even more now from this birthday surprise, I became a magnet for predatory narcissists. Dysfunctional relationships and drugs followed me into this frozen fairyland. The evil lurked in the alleyways, looking for that innocent light it could snuff out or feast upon. The repeating patterns in my life only confirmed that I was marked as a victim. Re-victimisation became another symptom in my Silencing Syndrome.

I refocused my mind on the birthday celebrations ahead later that day. Drinks with friends after work at the local bar. I would use 'tequila lay backs' to blur this new mental anguish that had suddenly slapped me in the face. This added trauma memory would only deepen the pain and lower my self-esteem further into the silenced victim I had become.

* * * * *

On returning to Sydney, I knew I had to rethink my career. I had left general nursing without completing the three required years. I didn't enjoy the military style of RNSH, but I did enjoy caring for others. Dad suggested I become a Mothercraft Nurse. I had not heard of this kind of nursing but as a specialised nursing for Mothers and Babies I was curious, so I enrolled.

Two years of on-the-job training commenced, and I was in my element. Having a baby was always a priority for me, so being around other people's babies was a perfect interim until I met my future husband and started my family. The traineeship offered a distraction, as I buried myself in study and more shift work. A year of maturity along with world travel helped me to cope better in a nursing role. My new coping did not stop me from weekends of partying and recreational drugs. A familiar escape in search of comfort.

Chapter 23

Bobby Dazzler

The foyer of the lavish high-rise apartment building in Sydney's CBD was 20 feet of towering glass reflecting lights from all directions. I was in awe as I fixated my eyes on its beauty. The mirrored glass ceiling captured the decadence of the gilded furniture placed strategically on shiny marble floors. Looking up I caught a glimpse of my reflection, a young fresh face, a reminder that I did not look 20 years old.

At the centre of this architectural feast was a large gold fountain cascading with an abundance of pure clear water from an unknown source. I took several moments to absorb the majesty of this building's entrance and what may lie behind this splendor.

All the girls from the earlier opulent dinner in Kings Cross, Sydney's notorious red-light district, had been invited back to Bobby's apartment. Bobby was infamously known as, 'Bobby Dazzler'. A local Sydney identity who famously wore a heavy gold chain around his thick neck to match his gold capped tooth. Bobby Dazzler was the Harvey Weinstein of Sydney in the eighties. He was a self-proclaimed celebrity, well into his forties, who had gained his position by waving cocaine and cash in excessive amounts to gain influence and power, which he successfully achieved. The Sydney 'in crowd' would step aside to allow his huge presence, physically and notably, to march directly to the front of any nightclub line. His thick set deep black beard matched the thick curled locks flowing below his shirt collar. His arrogance oozed a scent thicker than treacle, sickly in its drips yet enticing in its invitation. His entourage of beautiful super models, one under each arm and others following like new puppies, was his signature entrance. There was something intriguing about this man but also repulsing.

I felt so honored to be included in the invitation after dinner to come back to Bobby's apartment in the city. One of the girls in his entourage warmed towards me at the bar and had invited me to join them for dinner. A sweet aroma of temptation and intoxication told me I was accepted. This inclusivity was palatable as I was now a part of this exclusive, elite, selected group of girls, Bobby's girls. I was chosen.

My breathing rate quickened as I was drawn from the foyer's splendour towards the lifts. Up up I went finally reaching one of the top floors.

The apartment was spacious, adorned with couches of deep green velvets and satin fabrics. As the other girls arrived, they quickly settled into the soft couches sinking deeply into the opulence, kicking off their shoes with giggling thrills. A pile of tall stiletto heels seemed at home cushioned on the cream shag pile carpet, no longer needed. Long slender legs emerging from short skirts showcased smooth tanned skin. Lacy knickers made an appearance as legs were crossed and uncrossed and crossed again.

I found my place on the couch sinking into its softness, taking a moment to inhale the perfumes, while observing valuable art works on every wall. They were modern, exotic, colourful - in complete contrast to the art in my family home. Dad's art depicted landscapes, somber renaissance scenes in muted browns and ochres, to tie in with the dark wood paneling and antique furniture. These vibrant colours excited me. Abstract lines creating chaos, wild disorder fashioned by artists with expression to challenge the norm. The culture of the early eighties had an affluence, a sophistication that I yearned to be a part of.

Laughter billowed across the room as Bobby began to spread the pile of white powder on the glass coffee table into neat lines chopping the small lumps with his Amex credit card. The regular girls seemed familiar with this drill and the excitement in the room was building into a buzz like bees around honey. All eyes were fixed on Bobby, his smile flashing gold as his tooth caught the light.

Once the table was covered in carefully manicured straight lines, the consumption began. The girls were handed a rolled-up hundred-dollar note to place into their nostril to sniff in the white fluffy line of powder. Laughter broke out as the first girl took her position quickly consuming the first line and then placing the note into the other nostril to consume a second line in one inhaling swoop. The next girl was eager for her turn as she grabbed the note ready to consume her lines. As the drug disappeared, Bobby poured more powder onto the table while his Amex credit card furiously chopped endless powder into perfect straight lines.

My turn came.

The girls who had already participated in this familiar activity seemed so relaxed and confident. A couple of other older men who had also come to the apartment after the dinner led the girls outside to a large deck with a spa bath. I could see through the glass internal windows the girls giggling and flirting. They removed their clothes one piece at a time effortlessly with a confidence while the men watched with lustful attention. Their slender feminine bodies climbed into the bubbling water, the girls kissing each other passionately.

I inserted the note into my right nostril. After observing the others, I knew I had to inhale the white powder in one go. I took a deep breath and with an inward sniff I removed every white trace before me. Instantly, the back of my sinuses felt hot and irritated. I sniffed again while rubbing the top of my nose with my thumb and index finger directly under my watering eyes. My head swaying from the champagne consumed earlier, I was now flooded by an energy that was subtle but acceptable. An elation spoke to me saying I had passed the initiation. I was 'cool', and I felt cool. Valued, grown up and now accepted into the 'Sydney Supermodel Gorgeous Girl Club'.

I was not a model. My 5 foot 2 inches was far from the required height for a catwalk. I had a slender body, long blonde hair, a pretty face, and a vulnerability that made me easy game.

Time stood still, the pulsating beats of the music assisting me to get lost in its rhythm. This drug induced world was peaceful, and I was comfortably numb. The music changed to a more upbeat tune, grabbing my attention as I transitioned into consciousness. The girls and their mature male companions had left the apartment.

I was alone.

I thought Bobby, who was the leader of the pack, would escort me to the door and tell me the party was over, but instead he presented me with a small white pill.

"This will help you to feel much better," he suggested.

He had introduced me to the elite crowd, paid for a lavish dinner, indulged me with endless French champagne and invited me to his exclusive party in his apartment with as much high-quality cocaine I could consume. So now in my heightened state of delusion, the white pill offer seemed enticing and trustworthy. I took the pill.

Almost instantly, I felt a wave of heaviness engulf me. Not like the gentle intoxication of alcohol or the subtle stimulation of cocaine, this was like an overpowering blanket that weighed heavily from my head to my toes. Still deep in the couch's cushions, I took to my feet somehow knowing I had to test my sobriety. I staggered from side-to-side; grappling to grab furniture or some solid object to secure my body that was uncontrollably falling. With all my strength I tried to control my physical self, but my body was failing me, no longer my own as the drug took over. I fought and fought a losing battle, my mind confused and woozy as it tried to make sense of its failing commands.

Bobby calmly guided me to the next room assuring me that I would be okay. Swooping my limp body into his arms, his sweaty hairy physique carried me to his bed. I was thankful to be lying down and no longer fighting the powerful force that was taking over my ability to stay vertical. I lay on the bed trying to make sense of the incredible heaviness that had caused my legs to stop functioning and the new 'drunkenness' of my mind. Bobby's large grotesque body moved on top of me, pinning me under his weight. The stench of musky aftershave mixed with foul body odor oozed from his open pours. His eyes were wide, flickering an evil lust.

I wanted to push him off but as hard as I tried, I couldn't move my arms. I was physically paralyzed. Flooded with terror, the same terror I had experienced by the wood pile, I knew I was powerless against this evil presence breathing heavily into my face. His stale breath reeked of alcohol - my nostrils were unable to defend themselves from the attack.

My heart was now racing uncontrollably as I ordered my brain to find the remaining strength to break free from paralysis and escape. The panic seemed to only heighten the cocaine in my blood, bringing a new alertness to my mind. I was fully aware that I was physically pinned to the bed unable to move any part of my body. My arms were heavy as lead and my only defense was heavy pillars by my side. Bobby began to remove his pants and pull my panties down. My internal panic escalated as I realized what was about to happen.

"No!" I cried out.

"I have a boyfriend. STOP. NO."

Bobby continued to force his erect penis into my lifeless body. I had no ability to resist or push away. As he raped me, I continued to say, "No, No!" He ignored my pleas and ejaculated.

I had always thought of rape being a violent act. I pictured a girl being grabbed and forced to the ground while she kicked and screamed using all her power and effort to fight off her attacker. Just as I had tried to fight off the man who had grabbed me under the Figtree Bridge as a 12-year-old, she would fight for her life to stop a rape. Andre's rape in Noumea was a subtle attack. It happened so quickly, there was no time to fight. Bobby's rape was trickery. How could I fight my attacker after he had drugged me?

I continued to lie motionless and in shock, waiting for the drug to wear off so I could escape. Bobby had fallen asleep. As soon as I had command of my body again, I rose from the bed gathering my belongings in a daze of disbelief. I pressed the 'G' button in the lift to deliver me back to the ground level. The doors slowly opened, inviting me back into the glass filled foyer now filled with natural light. I walked out to the street squinting, my eyes paining against the sun that was beginning to rise. My heart thumped with anger as I began to berate myself.

"How did I let this happen?" I asked myself over and over.

I don't remember the drive back to my parents' home in Hunters Hill, where I was living at the time. I was in a daze of delusion trying to isolate fact from fiction. The drugs gradually letting go of their paralysing grip more and more.

Did that really happen to me?

Was I drugged and raped?

But I willfully took the champagne, the cocaine and agreed to the 'little white tablet that will make you feel good'. I later realised that I had been given a 'date rape drug' called Quaalude. I felt stupid and ashamed. Shame knew me, it knew me by name.

"You asked for this Sarah," a creepy voice whispered with a hiss inside my head.

I arrived back at my parents' home at 6am, the morning sun breaking into amber light, erasing the darkness of the night before. A greasy residue of Bobby's sweat and semen coated my skin. I went straight to the shower and turned on the cold water to wash away the filth I felt. The chilling flow shook me into present reality. I stood there for what seemed an eternity, it could have easily been 30 minutes. I thought of the boyfriend I was currently dating, knowing I could never tell him. I thought of my parents, knowing I could never tell them either. I knew I could never tell anyone, and I never did.

Silenced into another secret.

The conditioning of silence was embedded from my past. Brother Dave planted the seeds all those years before, seeds to be watered, harvesting silence. The Marist Fathers and the Loreto nuns continued the conditioning by brushing my abuse under the carpet. My mother added fertiliser by conditioning the silence with her quiet 'hush'. I had been shown by adults' actions and inactions, that to speak up was fruitless. Silence was safe. It didn't enter my head to tell anyone about the night in Bobby Dazzler's apartment nor report it to the police.

Raped and silenced again.

Chapter 24

Speed

Hatred is like a weeping sore that never heals and mine was oozing deep below the surface. Say the wrong thing or hit the wrong button and the wound would fester with contempt. Like rubbing sandpaper into an open lesion, the torture of hatred scrapes at the soul.

I blamed my abrasions on the church. They were the cause of all the destruction in my life.

A man training in a religious institution had pierced my heart. A religious institution had covered up my truth making me a target - vulnerable, quiet, silenced, and unable to discern danger. Abusers could now identify me as easy game. The church was at fault, and I hated everyone and everything to do with it.

"A Bundy and coke thanks mate," I barked at the bar tender to be heard above the booming beat of the band.

'Then the boys light up,' a popular rock song boomed from the stage as James Reyne strutted back and forth in his skintight jeans. It was 1985, a humid summer's night, 'Aussi Crawl', the fond name given the 80's iconic band Australian Crawl, was cranking up a beat. So often I had learned to drink away my feelings, singing familiar songs, never absorbing the truth of the words.

'The Boys Light Up', a song about a prostitute, a prostitute to government MP's. I was joyfully screaming in unison with the intoxicated crowd. Wedged in, tight bodies against mine, strangers touching me as we swayed and jumped to the pound of the drum. Each jump would spill my Bundy carelessly onto the drunken dude next to me who would smile in agreement as we slurred out the chorus.

What were we agreeing to? Our political leaders getting prostitutes? 'She's got 15 ways to lead that boy astray' and then the chorus again over and over repeating, 'Then the boys light up'.

The words meant nothing to me, they were not considered. How often do we sing words to songs that go against our beliefs? What are we instilling into our subconscious by parroting off words without thought or care? How many times did I cry in my bedroom alone and confused as a young girl to 'Pink Floyds Comfortably Numb' blaring on my record player? It was a song about injecting heroin, 'just a little pin prick' … 'there is no pain you are receding.' I wasn't one to pour out my emotions in a journal, too fearful it may be discovered, and the secrets released. A troubled thought would revisit me from my past and my solution was to extinguish it with alcohol and drugs.

"I'm going outside for a ciggy," I told Jean.

We continued our friendship past our days at Villa Maria Primary School. A group of smokers were gathered on the verandah lighting up and drawing the smoke deep into their lungs with a sigh of relief. Nicotine addiction had control over me, yet I felt accepted and even privileged to be a part of this 'accepted' group of addicts.

"Did you know that girl over there goes to church?" I heard a man with a mullet hair style say.

I had been triggered.

"Church!" I scoffed.

"Anyone who goes to a church just needs a crutch. What a loser."

I had made a vow never to set foot in a church again. The seething hatred I had towards an institution that bred paedophiles, would be triggered into an eruption of rage.

A violation of a child in any way is unacceptable. When men clothe themselves in robes wearing holy ornaments and claim to be followers of Jesus, while secretly sexually molesting young girls and boys, then surely there is something wrong. The Catholic Church was a law unto themselves. The Canon Law and the Pontifical Secret offering a safe place for paedophiles to hide and be protected. I wanted nothing to do with any church and promised myself to keep away.

The beat of the band was calling me back, hopefully to subdue my swirling anger.

Reckless behaviour was my normal; an avenue to release the anger. Strangely, I did not recognise my behaviour as different, it was simply me - the me I had become. Have I always had this tendency? Was I created reckless or were my behaviours a product of circumstances? An adventurous child who had her spirit crushed, violated, abused and who now embarked in crazy, dangerous behaviours. Reckless behaviour was one of my means of escaping.

My escapades continued to include trips up the Lane Cove River in my dinghy, visits to my father's bar, plane trips to anywhere, loud music through headphones, and driving fast in my mother's red RX-7.

The RX-7 was my favourite danger zone. Jumping into the low bucket seat, my petite body low and close to the road, I would continue to pretend to be the racing car driver I had always hoped to be. Speed promising to wipe memories, if only for a moment. Imminent danger and traumatic memories cannot be present in the mind at the same time.

One cool spring evening as the sky darkened into a royal blue velvet littered with thousands of stars, Marcus agreed to join me on a joy ride.

I met Marcus at QB1, a top Sydney nightclub where I was holding my 21st birthday. The negotiations for the night led to us dating for the next 12 months. He was 10 years older than me; his Peter Pan boyishness enticed him to be my RX-7 passenger. His tall lanky body had to curl into the passenger seat, his spiky short blonde hair tight against the roof of the car.

I pushed a CD into the player in the dash.

'I'm free to do whatever I want any ol time', The Soup Dragons tune began to play.

"I'm free," I thought as I dialled up the volume.

Driving fast was a way I could show I had control over my life. The controls of my past, the forced rollers in my hair, the nuns sending me to Saturday detentions, the starving before Mass, the hiding from visitors in my home, Brother Dave's grooming, all vanished in a blur of speed. My reckless confidence empowered me, alienating me from my world of confusion and pain. Hitting speeds more than 150 kms per hour, the adrenaline rushed through my veins like a pure drug. My eyes fixed on the road, the red-light alarms at each gear change directing me to shift the semi-automatic gears. With each gear shift, a new serge of speed would force me back into the seat ready for the next acceleration. The euphoric rush would light up my face like a beacon.

On one escapade, a car suddenly appeared out of nowhere and was headed straight towards the passenger side of my car. Marcus went white as he gripped the sides of his seat, wide eyed in fear. My instinctive response to avoid a high-speed collision was to jerk the steering wheel to the right violently changing my direction. This sent the RX-7 into a spin.

Time stood still, as the slow-motion spin took control. Marcus' hand gripped harder to stop the force on his body, which was desperately trying to come towards me. The car spun a full circle and a half, the G-force pushing my body hard against the driver's door, a force too strong to resist.

SPEED

What seemed like an eternity the RX-7 came to a stop. The three north bound lanes were miraculously empty as the red car rested facing the opposite direction to the potential oncoming traffic.

A man was frantically running towards me. I panicked, awaiting his fury, expecting him to take a piece out of me for my high-speed reckless driving. His face now at my driver's window was screaming,

"Are you alright. I'm so sorry," he cried.

"He was sorry," I questioned.

I was to discover that he was transporting his very pregnant wife to hospital. She was in labour and hysterical; he had shot the red light. Once he was reassured that we were safe, he continued his journey to the hospital. I slowly steered the car, turning it to face the right direction, amazed that we were alive.

In my quiet reflection I realised I had sensed an angelic-like being in the car with us as we were spinning. A strange calm, peace that surpassed understanding had filled the car.

"Was this a supernatural encounter with an angel protecting me?" I pondered.

On my 22nd birthday, Marcus had an affair with my nursing buddy Margaret. Betrayal cuts deep, an abuse of the body, soul, and spirit. On confrontation, he lied then left me. Margaret never answered any of my calls. The pain of betrayal from a woman penetrates to the marrow. The unspoken sisterhood, a knowing of trust, a 'bestie' you have let into your world and into your heart, has betrayed you.

I flashed back to my school friends at Loreto. The betrayal, the lack of loyalty, the dobbing me in for their own protection. I concluded that women could not be trusted nor could men.

* * * * *

The Sydney nightclub scene continued to entice me. An underbelly world of bright lights, loud music, dancing, and escapism. 'Rogues' was the club to be seen at. Hidden down a back lane off Oxford Street, a secret entrance exclusive for the elite members stood under soft glowing lights. A huge bouncer guarded the door, his gruff face, and bulging muscles warning off any uninvited partiers. Because I held my 21st birthday party at QB1 nightclub, I had been issued with a Diamond Membership keyring. This coveted item gave me VIP status entrance into any nightclub in Sydney, including Rogues. My key ring gained popularity with my friends as two others were always welcome to join my entourage. There was no queuing at the entrance, my entitlement allowed me to pass to the front, the gruff bouncer breaking into a beaming smile as he opened the door. I was 'somebody', or so he thought I was. It felt like I was somebody, as I was ushered to the VIP section. The bar offered a VIP only area behind two swinging glass doors with a large 'R' embossed into each panel. Moet Chandon champagne was flowing freely in this overcrowded space. Bodies were pressed against each other, making it necessary to shout into ears to be heard over the booming beats of the music. Every woman was beautiful, dressed in the highest of fashion. My friends nodded at me in approval before heading to the dance floor.

Standing at the bar was Sheila. A stunning blonde, a TV personality from a top rating show at the time. I was in awe being in her presence. She was surrounded by other TV stars - they were all glamorous and laughing. I sauntered to the bar to get a closer look at her, pinching myself to be in the same bar where she was drinking. A man approached me asking if I wanted a drink. I agreed for my glass to be topped up with champagne. He leaned close to tell me his name,

"Hello, I'm Davo."

His accent was exotic, his face square, and his eyes were soft. We talked and talked and talked, struggling to hear each other's responses over the music.

SPEED

"Come outside with me. I need to get something out of my car."

Without hesitation, I looked into his eyes and followed him to the door. An inner response of obedience to follow an older man at his command was on repeat. Davo appeared to be in his forties, his expensive clothes commanding a class my mother would approve of I thought. I walked two steps behind him as I tottered on my ridiculously high heels trying to keep up. After a short walk from the club, we came to a shiny black BMW, with cream leather seats. I climbed into the passenger seat engulfing the new car smell. Davo sat in the driver's seat and reached over to the glove box above my knees. He pulled out a bag the size of a shoe box stuffed full of white powder. A panic swept through my bones. This must be cocaine. I quickly reasoned that this was a huge amount, perhaps a jailable offence. Would I be an accomplice? I pictured a police officer tapping on my window then insisting I get out of the car, hands in the air. I sat frozen and speechless as Davo portioned an amount of the powder into a smaller bag and slipped it into his pocket. The large stash was returned to the glove box. I was relieved to get out of the car.

I tottered behind him back to the nightclub. Sheila saw us return and rushed to my side.

"Hello, what's your name?" she asked.

My heart still pounding from the car experience only escalated as I was being spoken to by Sheila, a famous person.

"I'm Sarah," I quivered a reply.

"You and Davo look so good together. You are a perfect match," she said.

"A perfect match, with a drug dealer?" I questioned.

The crazy celebrity world surrounded me in the Sydney darkness. I was a young woman desperately searching for my place in life, a place to find value. The predators could identify a vulnerable soul, a soul conditioned to silence.

Chapter 25

Island Life

The Sydney life of recreational drugs, alcohol and speed had a grip I knew I had to break from. I was on a path to self-destruction. I had completed my Mothercraft Nursing training and was now working for families as a private nurse. Supporting mothers with breastfeeding, settling their babies, introducing solids, colic support, reflux solutions and any other problems they may be struggling with. Surrounded by problems, the problems of others, my problems remained hidden. I desperately needed a change, a change of environment.

Searching the ads in the Herald newspaper, I found a position on Great Keppel Island in North Queensland as a House Maid. I was hoping for something a bit more glamorous, but this was the only "yes" reply after multiple applications. I saw the position as a foot in the door to island life, away from the sordid Kings Cross night life.

On a wet Sydney afternoon, I boarded a plane for Rockhampton, a large town in north Queensland. After a three-and-a-half-hour flight, the plane door opened, a blanket of heavy warm moist air engulfing the plane. It was not raining but the air felt wet. I peeled off my jacket quickly, tying it around my waist, dragged my backpack onto my back and proceeded down the stairs to the tarmac. A 30-minute bus ride to the coast past deep green acreage properties was a pleasure in the airconditioned comfort. A large boat was waiting at the Rosslyn Bay dock, a Fast Catamaran, a splendor of white with an ocean blue hull. At a speed of 20 knots, my vessel rose above the waves, bouncing and darting in a joyful dance of expectation.

Great Keppel Island was stunning. Her golden beach stretching the length of the bay welcoming me with open arms, a humid hug of tropical delight. Frangipani trees framed the path, their sweet fragrance intoxicating. A weather-beaten wooden sign, awaited in the distance, which seemed rustic and relaxed.

'Get Wrecked on Great Kepple', the white painted words beckoned. The resort was famous for 'getting wrecked', a subtle double meaning suggested. Either getting shipwrecked in this glorious getaway or getting wrecked on partying. This clientele certainly had the latter in mind. Boozy nights in the Wreck Bar went on until the early hours every night. My days were spent cleaning up the aftermath in the guests' rooms, which often included vomit.

But I was happy. This new island life was paradise to me. No drugs, no fast cars; I left my past behind. Alcohol was still readily available, but I convinced myself that this was the lesser of my evils. Somehow this seemed to be a safe choice and necessary for my survival. A familiar comfort, a numbing. I was in good company as the other island staff were eager partakers.

A small grass shack on the beachfront housed the watersports department. This was the hub for all water activities, paddle boards, snorkeling equipment, catamarans, water skiing and parasailing. Here you could also book scuba diving and jet skiing that were held at the other end of the point.

Drawn to the water and to the boats, my childhood passion resurfaced. I quickly noticed the handsome water ski instructor. Joe was slender in build, a head full of tight long ringlets sun kissed bright blonde. His skin was deep brown, bronzed golden, exaggerating a white inviting smile. We were soon boyfriend and girlfriend and waterskiing every afternoon after work.

It was time to move out of the housemaid role. Cleaning up after the 'wrecked' guests was becoming intolerable. I approached the Entertainment Manager, Andy, to ask if I could work in the Kids' Club. This was a service offered to entertain the resort kids, and I believed my Mothercraft Nursing training was a great credential. Unfortunately, he informed me, that the woman in the role had held the position for 12 years and had no plans of letting go of her tight grip. I had to think quickly and killing her off wasn't an option. I had to be creative.

'A Teen Club', I gleefully shouted across Andy's desk. He looked back at me with a confused look. Andy was a very talented man, taking pride in his roles as evening entertainer. Thick dark hair framed his boyish handsome features, facial hair was nonexistent. He could play a variety of musical instruments, dance, sing and was a hilarious comedian. Leading a team of gifted performers, they would present entertaining evening productions. Each Friday night Andy would perform the lead role, Dr Frank-n-Furter in 'The Rocky Horror Picture Show', a spectacular with fish net stockings and all.

I placed my Teens' Programme on Andy's desk, rattling off all the reasons I believed this was a great idea. Andy, tired of my persistence, agreed to allow me to run my programme during the next school holidays, which would run over six weeks. I was ecstatic.

"Thank you, Andy, it's going to be great!" I assured him.

One of my planned school holiday activities included convincing Jack, a middle-aged man with a scruffy stubble, to allow me to use his barge. Jack lived at the other end of the island at 'Woppaburra', the name for the

Aboriginal Australian people whose traditional lands are on Greater and South Keppel islands. I never saw one Aboriginal person on the island in the two years I lived there.

Jack ran the dive school, taking resort guests scuba diving and had a good-sized barge for this purpose.

"I need your barge Jack for my Teen Club programme. I need to take a group of teenagers to Middle Island on Saturday night, please," I asked with a sweet polite smile.

I had 30 teenagers already booked in for a trip to a neighboring island to take part in beach games. I knew Jack would say, "yes." The Watersports staff and the diving staff worked well together and as Joe's girlfriend I had favour.

Jack helped as we loaded the 30 teenagers onto the barge. The sun was beginning its descent, glowing a warm orange on the horizon. The trip to Middle Island would take us 20 minutes. The excitement was electric, as each kid huddled together to avoid the inevitable splashes breaking over the bow. The barge's top speed was six knots; therefore, it would be a slow and steady ride. The frantic arms of parents waving on the beach began to fade. They were all a little dubious about this arranged island departure into the oncoming darkness. I waved back, adding a reassuring smile that all would be well. It was a still night, the moon now appearing in its full round glory, lighting up the tips of the waves that the barge made in its wake.

One young teenager, Corey, was completely blind. His small stature and frail build did not allow him to appear his 12 years. His reluctant parents were on the beach, trying to hide the anxiety they were both feeling as we boarded the barge. Corey had pleaded managing to convince them he would be safe. He had his mind set on going on Sarah's teen adventure.

The games were a real hit, the favourite being a game called 'Spotto'. This is where all the kids run around on the beach with one kid holding a flashlight. If the kid with the flashlight shines on a moving kid, this kid must instantly freeze while the torch bearer shouts, 'spotto'. Once all the kids have frozen, the last one still running around is the winner and becomes the torch bearer for the next game. Corey loved this game as the dark of the night was not a disadvantage in his already dark world. The squeals of delight echoed across the bay with Corey's squeals louder than any other kids.

The time came for us to return to Great Keppel Island, much to great sadness from the teens who let out cries,

"No, not yet."

The moon was even brighter now with its shimmering silver glow high in the night sky, its face seeming to smile down in approval on my successful evening.

Jack started the engine. It ticked over, began a hum then suddenly stopped. He tried again and again… then once more.

"We ain't going nowhere," Jack mumbled in his thick Aussie accent.

"The engine is stuffed."

The engine seemed to smirk in its silence. We were stranded. Wrecked on Middle Island.

I knew the parents would be on the beach outside the front of the Great Keppel Island Resort waiting for their children to safely return at the promised time of 10pm. The kids watched Jack earnestly as he stared intently at the troubled engine. They all soon realised our fate and began to cheer a chant in perfect unison,

"Hip Hip hooray. We are staying the night on a deserted island."

The chant was repeated over and over as they danced and stomped in the cool night sand. A young teen couple appeared from behind a rock where they had been stealing their first kiss. "What's going on?" they questioned.

"Hip Hip hooray. We are staying the night on a deserted island," the chant continued.

ISLAND LIFE

I had to think fast. My job and reputation were at stake.

"Give me your two-way radio, Jack. I'll radio Watersports." I knew Joe would be listening to the radio as he waited for my return.

Joe was quick to respond. I told him of our plight with 30 kids and four adults stuck on Middle Island. Two other staff members had come along for the ride as my assistants. They were also caught up in the excitement, chanting along with the kids.

"I could come and pick you up in the Watersports ski boat," Joe offered without first checking with his boss. The ski boat was 16 foot long. I reasoned that five kids maximum in a load along with the driver would mean six trips, a seventh trip needed to include the staff, Jack, and me. The ski boat could travel a lot faster than the barge, so estimating 10 mins each way, I calculated approximately two and a half hours with the last drop off after midnight. This was our only option other than sleeping on the sand at Middle Island in the moonlight, a choice many of the kids would have preferred.

Corey insisted he go on the last trip with me. He wanted to savour every moment of this unfolding adventure, which lit up his world. His giggles were contagious as he chatted with his newfound island buddies. Joe was methodical as he loaded each teenager in the ski boat instructing them to crouch as low as possible to the floor.

Finally, it was the last load. Joe looked fatigued but remained calm and focused.

"Last trip, all aboard," he announced with a strained grin.

"Time to go, Corey. Take Joe's arm, sit on your bottom on the side of the boat and swing your legs over," I calmly instructed.

I was weary due to the night's unexpected events and the additional hours with the kids. Corey turned his head towards Middle Island in a final farewell and we were off at top speed.

I could see the stern silhouette of Corey's father on the beach as we approached. The grimace on his face, the burrows on his forehead becoming visible in the moonlight. A foreboding wrath awaited, expecting a plausible explanation. His wife stood still and meek, exhausted from the wait and worry. Corey remained oblivious to his parents' presence on the water line as the ski boat hit the sand.

"Let me help you out, Corey," Jack offered.

Two other kids saw themselves lucky to be on the last ride, their parents also glaring at watches as the clock struck 12:30am.

"I had the best time ever," Corey yelled in a near hysterical manner when he heard his father's voice shout, "Corey!"

I stood at Andy's desk the following morning listening as he bellowed at me his concerns and how he had to deal with 30 pairs of worried, stressed-out parents into the night. His face was a crimson red, his eyes blood shot and puffy. He looked terrible.

He went on to remind me, the veins in his neck bulging with each word, of another adventure trip I had designed the week before. I had taken a large group of teens in four-wheel drive vehicles to a cove on the other side of Great Keppel Island. We lit campfires and toasted marshmallows while telling ghost stories. Some of the girls were terrified and wanted to go back to the resort early. Our return pick-up was scheduled for a specific time and the driver was not reachable as our two-way radio was not working. I tried to calm the girls but to no avail as they were also getting bitten alive by midges. There were lots of tears as the girls threw themselves into the arms of their parents on return. The boys had a blast! Andy's recap included all the details again, adding the upset parents he had to deal with to the drama.

"But the kids had a great time, except for a couple of precious girls," I gently added, hoping to win back some credibility.

School holidays finished and it was time for me to leave Great Keppel Island. The infamous Great Keppel Teen Club that I pioneered continued for years after my departure. The adventures and the memory of Corey's squeals of delight would always bring a smile to my face.

The next stop was Hamilton Island in the Whitsunday Islands, further north on the Queensland Coast. Joe had been offered a position with Hamilton Island Watersports as a water ski instructor and a parasailing boat driver. I had passed my ski boat license test at Joe's recommendation and was also offered a job as a water ski instructor.

My childhood of racing up and down the Lane Cove River in my dinghy had not gone to waste. The complaints of my father telling me I was spending too much time on my boat and not enough at the books came to mind as I stepped into my dream job.

Dad was an avid reader. Every shelf in our house was full of books on every subject imaginable. There were so many that he built an attic in the roof to create a library. Art, science, religions, music, literature, poems, encyclopedias, national geographic magazines, medical journals, novels and more. He had a special cabinet with first edition books including Charles Dickens, DH Lawrence, and Mark Twain. My father loved me dearly, but I was haunted by inadequacy when I chose to be on the water rather than reading books.

After the abuse of Brother Dave, I found it extremely difficult to concentrate. I would read a line or two and then immediately forget what I had read. Known as 'trauma brain', a brain saturated with traumatic memories does not permit additional information to be uploaded. These memories, dwelling deep in the sub-conscience, blocked my mind. I could not understand why the space between my ears would go blank unable to retain the words I had just read.

"What was that I just read?" I often stopped asking myself.

I felt stupid. I must be a dummy. Dad was right when he said the TV would 'dull my brain', I wrongfully concluded.

My time practicing as a waterski driver for Joe, and other staff members on Great Keppel Island, was worth my while. Joe was a great water skier and a patient teacher. Now, on Hamilton Island, I developed confidence and a passion in my role. 'Hammo', Hamilton Island affectionately called by the staff, is where I learnt to instruct many Japanese tourists, mainly honeymooners. I could instruct water ski lessons in basic Japanese, instructing them to bend their knees, keep their arms straight and to let go of the rope when they fell off. Many a time the water ski student would forget to let go after a fall, only to be dragged through the water until I quickly brought the boat to a stop.

Hamilton Island, one of the 74 islands of the Whitsunday Island group, formed a part of the Great Barrier Reef. It offered some of the most spectacular reefs, and dive sites in the world.

The Great Barrier Reef, a seventh wonder of the world, never disappointed. Escaping the Bobby Dazzlers of my past, I found utopia in the reef, my underwater paradise of silence and beauty. Snorkelling was a solitude, the only sounds to absorb were the in and out rhythm of breath, a source of comfort and peace. This mesmerising chant numbed the chaos of my real world above the surface. A world I was trying constantly to escape from. I had found my solace in this magical underwater wonderland. Vibrant colours of darting fish put on a show, using the coral both hard and soft as their stage. The clown fish would perform hiding in the anemone, before making an appearance, being careful not to be eaten by a passing hungry fish. Huge sea turtles entered with grace, oozing a prideful arrogance as if they knew they had been alive far longer than I had been. Over one hundred years old, their wisdom was something I wanted, I would chase

ISLAND LIFE

them into the depths, having to give up when they went deeper than my breath would allow.

Sydney's underground world of flashing colourful lights illuminating lustful fame and fortune was far away. The sinister abusers, drugs and night life, a dulling memory. Yet an emptiness of shame still had a grip on me. A gripping tourniquet around my neck, that was relentlessly trying to take my life. The deep sadness of 'victim' formed my identity, a secret, silent identity. No matter where I went, or how far I travelled, even to the depths under the sea, it would find me, hunt me down like a wounded animal.

"You are a victim, damaged, dirty," the dark voice would chant in my ear.

I imagined a man with hot, foul breath on top of me pinning me down, to remind me of this truth. But I was alone. No one knew my past, no one knew my pain, no one knew my secrets. The reef beckoned me to come deeper.

Island life was simple. Living in staff quarters, walking to work, driving boats, water skiing, snorkelling, beach picnics, sailing, and going to the pub.

Most evenings the island offered a sunset cruise. I would be the deck hand on the catamaran, named 'The War Canoe', a Tahitian style brown wooden vessel unique in so many ways.

My duties included untying the vessel, throwing the ropes at the dock, serving drinks and nibbles to the guests, and generally having fun. All this time on the water was added into my logbook that Joe insisted I get to log my hours.

Hamilton Island Race Week, an annual yacht race hosted by Hamilton Island, is a much-anticipated event. Yachties from all over the world come to race and party. Daily races around the Whitsunday Islands are followed by presentations and celebrations. Bars are packed full, and restaurants pump out culinary delicacies while copious amounts of alcohol are consumed.

When the weeks' festivities are over, many of the exclusive yachts and power boats that have travelled to the event need to be delivered back to their ports of residence. The owners, too tired or wealthy to complete the homeward delivery, would jump on a flight. This meant that the return delivery required crew, a task which offered generous payment. It was a joy for me to be able to take time to do these deliveries whilst clocking up many sea hours for my logbook. Sailing off the east coast of Australia, days of nothing but deep blue ocean below and vast skies above, was a pure detraction from a 'real' world.

On most of these trips the dolphins would join us. These majestic creatures would frolic alongside the boat dancing back and forth - always with one eye fixed on mine. They seemed to smile as if they were offering me an invitation to their freedom. I would sit on the deck watching for as long as they would grace me with their company. If I banged my hand against the side of the boat, they seemed to get more excited, and this would often attract more from the pod. Riding along with us they were getting a free ride in our slip stream, which I was happy to provide. Escapism had become something I longed for. A 'normal' life back on the mainland was unfathomable.

Joe and I broke up, his deep depressions and sudden outbursts of anger becoming intolerable. He pushed me violently against a wall in a rage one evening, which terrified me.

I called my parents in Sydney. Somehow hearing their voices reconnected me to a sense of family and comfort.

"How is everything going up on the islands?" Dad asked.

"Fine," I replied knowing to keep the dramas in my world silent.

The Whitsunday Islands continued to nurture my love of the water and my deep need to escape. Escapism being the mechanism I used to try and extinguish my sense of victimhood.

ISLAND LIFE

The nature of water, its ever-changing form taking instruction from a greater force, was a fascination to me. I would watch the storms approaching from a distance, sheets of rain, grey and foreboding as a gift from above. The wind whipped up ripples into waves, a chaotic, choppy dance bringing a beauty of unpredictable change. The tides would ebb and flow at different times each day, yet their consistent regularity had a reliable pattern - a soothing comfort of prediction. Still mornings, the waterways would appear as glass, not a ripple, no movement giving the illusion of a solid surface. I imagined I could step out of the boat and walk on water. The wind would often whisper,

"All is well," in a still small voice.

Chapter 26

The Top End

A stunning white launch entered Hamilton Harbour. Her elegance was apparent, a classic Halvorsen Cruiser, named 'MV Victor'. Her smooth hull glided effortlessly into her pen on the second arm of the marina. The Halvorsen family, originally from Norway, came to settle in Australia in the 1920's. A family of renowned boat builders, building over 1500 handcrafted wooden boats, of great quality and style. During World War II, they built more than 250 boats for the American, Netherlands, and Australian armed forces employing a staff of 350 tradesmen at a shipyard in a suburb of Ryde, in Sydney, New South Wales.

After World War II the family company acquired a lease at Bobbin Head located north of Sydney in the Ku-Ring-Gai Chase National Park. They built a fleet of approximately two hundred hire boats. The hire boat operation was the world's largest privately owned fleet of its time. In 1962, Lars Halvorsen Sons Pty. Ltd. built *Gretel* the first Australian challenger for the America's Cup.

In 1975 the family formed a joint venture between Lars Halvorsen Sons Pty. Ltd. and Joseph Kong, former General Manager of American Marine Company, in Hong Kong to design, build and market a new range of pleasure boats worldwide. The company was called Kong and Halvorsen Marine and Engineering Company Ltd. Over the next two decades, hundreds of craft ranging from 30 to 134 ft (9.1metres to 40.8 metres) were built under the Kong and Halvorsen, Island Gypsy, and Halvorsen brand names. These wooden boats were certainly noticed and MV Victor with the stunningly beautiful stewardess, Simone on board, was to be noticed.

During my childhood, my father owned a 25-foot Halverson cruiser, named 'Petalia'. Slow and steady she would putt up and down the Lane Cove River, with Dad at the helm smiling from ear to ear. She was his pride and joy. It has always interested me that boats are referred to as 'female'. This long-time maritime tradition may have come to fruition, due to a boat's curves necessary to allow the hull to delicately glide through the water. Or perhaps it is because men seem to love their boats more than their women?

The crew on Hamilton Island Marina always noticed any newcomers and 'MV Victor' was a beauty to behold; and so was Stewardess Simone.

Simone was breathtaking. An English rose, skin smooth and glowing, gently curving in the right places. Her hair, silky brown blended with golden hues of soft flowing curls, bouncing effortlessly below her shoulders. Her locks were a crown of glory, a royal display commanding attention from all her subjects. Simone's command was instant as she leaned carefully over the bow rail ready to launch the starboard line to the young man assisting with the docking. Long slender legs emerged from brief navy shorts, while her white polo shirt proudly stated the name, MV Victor, embroidered in gold letters. MV representing 'Motor Vessel'. All male eyes were fixated on this newcomer.

"Hello," I yelled from the dock, eager to make a new female friend.

A rare jewel in my male dominated world.

"Hello," she responded in a posh refined English accent.

I liked her straight away.

Simone was travelling around Australia on a 12-month visa seeking adventures while seeing as much of the country as possible. We both shared a love of the ocean and very quickly became best friends. She was looking for a change from the vessel she was currently working on and was excited when I told her about a job out of Cairns in far north Queensland for stewardesses on a cruise boat that paid very well. I convinced Simone to come with me. We both completed the application form for the MV Holiday Hopper. It was a 25-metre catamaran with 16 cabins, hosting 35 guests travelling north out of Cairns on a seven-day journey to Thursday Island and back. Simone loved the idea of seeing this remote coastline and so did I.

Thursday Island is a part of the Torres Strait Islands located 39 kms north of Cape York Peninsula at the very top of Australia. A population of approximately 2,000 people, mainly Kaurareg Aboriginal people, the traditional people of this archipelago. The lucrative pearl industry dominated in the 80's on this small 3.5 km square island.

The cruise was due to set sail in a weeks' time, beckoning me and Simone. We waited with anticipated excitement for our acceptance. I had packed a small bag when I left Hamilton Island consisting of a few fashionable outfits, ones I felt would be suitable for a north coast cruise. Uniforms would be provided for the stewardesses on board, and we would have time in Cairns to go out on the town. The heat would be stifling so cotton dresses would be best. I packed three in total along with a light jacket to combat the air-conditioned cabins, a few basic toiletries, and a hair dryer. Space was limited in crews' quarters on the MV Holiday Hopper therefore packing light in a small soft bag was preferred.

My acceptance letter arrived in a crisp white envelope at the front desk of the backpackers' hostel, Simone and I were staying in. I was elated as I tore the glued paper to reveal my start date and time. I quickly glanced towards Simone who was holding her open letter. Her face sullen, her soft beauty twisting as if there had been a death in the family.

"I haven't been accepted," her words finally arrived through pursed lips holding back tears.

"What?" I cried.

Not for one minute did we think this possible. We had both applied together at the cruise office, the woman dressed in a perfectly pressed uniform taking our forms, her welcoming smile indicating we would be accepted without question. We were to find out that there was only one stewardess position available, I was the ONE chosen.

But I didn't want to go without Simone!

A torrent of tears flooded the foyer, our sobs heard all through the hostel. Then, I had an idea. We would both go to the dock when it was time to board and at the last minute, Simone would sneak on board. Once on the vessel, she could wear one of my uniforms as I was to be issued with two. Everyone who met Simone loved her and I was sure the captain and crew would soon be delighted with her radiant presence. The stowaway would be accepted with open arms. I convinced Simone that my idea was brilliant, and she reluctantly agreed.

The morning of departure didn't disappoint. Cairns in its 'true to form' glory, lit up under a vibrant sun, so bright to the eyes that dark glasses strained to hold back its glare. The rays bit the skin with a hot sting.

The lady in the well-pressed uniform who took my application was holding a bright green clipboard, with pen poised to tick off her well-constructed list. Her military style precision caught my attention as I held back a strong urge to salute her. She was the owner of the business and had a job to do. No one should dare to get in her way.

I walked directly to the boarding ramp, eyes fixed ahead, my feet skipping automatically into a march, and my only free arm swinging at my side.

"Left, left, left right left," I could hear in my head. The obedient five-year-old marching around the Villa Maria school playground was being called to action.

The orientation of the ship was brief. I was shown to my quarters, my two allocated uniforms hanging in a small built-in robe, then walked around each deck to get acquainted with the ship's layout. The Galley where the chef prepares the meals, the Fly Bridge where the captain and the first mate attend to steering and navigating the ship, the Saloon for dining, the Passengers' Cabins, and the Purser's Office. I soon discovered that the purser, Brendon, was the son of the company's owner.

Introductions to the crew completed, it was time to welcome the passengers. I was carefully scoping out the situation noting an entrance on the starboard side where the engineer could enter and leave the vessel without encountering the guests. Dressed in overalls, at times grease stained, he could go straight to the engine room unnoticed. This entrance was also being used to load the supplies for the trip, boxes of dry goods, loaded on trollies that rolled up the gang plank into the hull. This was a perfect entrance for our stowaway I concluded.

Hiding behind a bush past the cruise office, Simone was awaiting my signal. I sauntered precariously along the lower deck, waiting for a moment where she could board with the staff who were loading supplies. The coast was clear.

"Now," I indicated with the pre-planned signal as I waved both arms above my head in a birdlike flap.

Simone emerged from her hiding spot, darting in a flash to the entrance. On approach she slowed to a pace matching the other staff slipping into the slip stream to board unnoticed.

THE TOP END

Mission accomplished - she was onboard. I quickly grabbed her arm dragging her to my cabin where she could hide under my bunk until after departure.

My uniform was blue. Not a royal blue nor a navy blue, but an electric blue harsh to the eye. The upper collarless shirt was a block blue, the lower skirt was a kaleidoscope of pink, mustard, blue and white. The hemline fell to mid-calf, a length that made me look stumpy. I preferred to wear a length of just above the knee or to the floor, this in-between was not flattering for my height. A scarf matching the colourful skirt was styled into a knot around the neck sitting like a low-lying collar. White deck shoes finished off the uniform.

All onboard were called to the upper deck for the safety briefing; life jackets worn so we could practice an event of 'abandon ship'. Most of the passengers were in their seventies or older, I observed, their life jackets weighing heavily on their frail frames. Life rafts were positioned high above the decks on ropes ready to be launched should the ship sink. The pre-sail drill was a depressing discussion before a lovely cruise but a necessary requirement before each trip. Simone, stiff and still, lay under my bunk waiting for the long-prolonged blast from the ship's horn to indicate the vessel was leaving the dock.

At last, the horn sounded its blast, all lines were cast, we were underway. With the passengers on the upper deck waving to anyone and everyone left behind on the dock, it was time to release the stowaway. My spare uniform fitted her perfectly, with her extra height suiting its length better than me.

"Simone would look stunning in a potato sack," I pondered while we both stood in front of the mirror glued inside the wardrobe door.

"Perfect," we said in unison followed by a giggle.

The two of us in our electric blue entered the saloon to set the tables for lunch. Flowing through the tables placing knives and forks, Simone was a natural. Her experience as a stewardess was evident as she glided without instruction. I wondered how long it would take until she was noticed, and I could make the introduction. I pictured the crew delighted when they finally got to meet my friend Simone who was willing to work for free on this weeklong cruise.

Brendon entered the saloon. A look of horror stripped all colour from his already pale complexion. Tall in statue, his unhealthy lifestyle was evident by the puffy fat he carried around his middle. I estimated him to be in his early thirties, given the powerful position as the purser due to family connections. His reaction surprised me.

"Who is this?" he ordered in a low guttural growl.

"I'm Simone," she said in a sweet as treacle reply - the English rose in full bloom.

Brendon's scowl softened waiting for an explanation.

"Come into my office," he commanded turning abruptly.

Simone followed like a little lamb, head dipped, eyes to the floor.

I watched the two of them disappear wondering if I should follow but I was frozen, a fork still poised in my right hand waiting to be positioned next to the knife.

I had been playing out this scene many times in my mind over and over and this was not the outcome I had envisioned. The welcoming smiles of joy meeting the glamorous newcomer, with comments of,

"You should have been given a position too, welcome aboard young lady," were pure fabrication, a fantasy I had created, wishful thinking, completely wrong.

Simone had been taken to the captain. Captain Chris Porter, a man in his mid-fifties was serious yet calm. An ex-navy officer, he had many years of experience at sea, and I wondered if this was his first stowaway. He concluded that the ship would not turn around and return to port, but

Simone would stay onboard and work for her keep. We were both relieved to get the outcome we had hoped for.

Settling into work at sea, Brendon started to see Simone in a new light, stunningly beautiful. Every man who encountered her aura would be captivated and fall in love. They would be love-struck as if shot with an arrow between the eyes. I saw this many times while travelling with Simone, and Brendon had been struck. The angry scowl from day one at sea had turned into a puppy dog pant quite pathetic to be a witness to. An unattractive man in many ways, it was his arrogance that was the most unappealing.

His onslaught was relentless, following Simone closely in a swamy manner, trying to make light conversation.

"Where in England are you from? How long are you in Australia? Where have you been so far?" he gushed.

"I'm from the Channel Islands, but my family lives in France part of the year," she spoke in a voice that had its own melody.

A well-defined tone singing of education and refinement. Beauty and brains. I checked to see if Brendon was drooling.

"What am I going to do? I think Brendon likes me," Simone questioned in desperation.

"Every guy likes you, Simone," I replied, rolling my eyes to indicate she must already be aware of this.

We were on the ship for another five days and Brendon was our boss. Simone became dismissive of Brendon's advances, which he didn't take favorably. That grey snarl began to reappear, revealing the real core of who he was, a spoilt brat.

A storm was on the horizon. Huge cumulonimbus clouds towering high, puffing like cauliflower as far as you could see. The ominous blackening indicated that it was going to get rough. The sea began to swell, the wind whipping up waves that slammed into the bow with a mighty force.

A high-pitched sound haunted the ship as the wind whistled around the decks. The elderly guests began to fall, unable to stand against the swaying as the ship thrashed about in the wild weather. One down, and then another, bleeding bodies on the saloon carpet moaning with pain and fear.

"Where is the first aid kit?" Simone cried, a terror on her face that frightened me.

"I don't know," I replied in a panic.

I had not been shown where the first aid kit was in the safety briefing, and I was so consumed with hiding a stowaway I didn't think to ask. Frantic, I opened every cupboard in a desperate search. Brendon entered the room, bracing himself on chairs with each lurch.

"They're bleeding, where is the first aid kit, Brendon?" the panic evident in my quivering voice.

Brendon went into his office to retrieve the kit. Moans continued from the elderly now rolling on the floor as the ship swayed, having lost all control over the waves. Simone was on her knees cradling a white-haired head on her lap, blood gushing from a deep wound in the woman's leg. The blood was seeping into the cream flecked carpet, as if a tin of beetroot had been carelessly dropped.

"Stop the bleeding, Brendon," I cried as he held the first aid kit tight, his indecision petrifying him into inaction.

I leapt towards him, violently grabbing the first aid kit. Another fall, then another.

"Get down on the floor," I yelled to the remaining standing passengers.

Mr. Smith was a sweet old man. He had just celebrated his 80th birthday and was proud of his good health and sharp mind. He attributed it to doing the crossword every day from the newspaper and walking the two kms daily to fetch it. Mrs. Smith lay on the floor, the fall causing her to bump her head on the low-lying coffee table next to the lounge. She was still lying silent, and he was concerned. Brendon's face remained expressionless as he took in the carnage on his watch.

Wounds bandaged, pillows and blankets placed around the passengers all now lying on the Saloon floor, I sighed in relief that the stowaway was on board to assist in the storm.

The next day, the sea calmed down. Bruised bodies, sore and shocked, slowly moved to the tables as I offered warm sweet tea with Arrowroot biscuits. Grateful smiles spoke volumes in silent thanks. Words were not needed as we were just doing our job. My deep disappointment in Brendon's leadership, or lack of, was hard to hide, my dark eyes glaring as he entered the Saloon.

"Is everyone ok?" he spoke so softly.

I'm sure no one heard him even with their hearing aids switched on. His sheepish countenance a dead giveaway to his incompetence in an emergency.

The first mate, Dereck, walked briskly towards Simone and me,

"The captain wants to see you girls straight away," he spoke in a thick Aussie accent.

A quiet man, wallowing in the captain's shadow, this was the first time I had heard him speak. We did not hesitate to obey.

The Bridge was a place that inspired awe. The hundreds of dials and switches were flashing lights with purpose. A large wheel, the helm to steer, directed a small rudder to keep the ship on course. Captain Porter looked exhausted as he had stood at the helm all night battling the waves.

"Hello girls," he greeted in a kind soft voice, his lips barely moving behind his thick white beard.

"I hear you did a great job last night with the passengers," he commended us.

Brendon must have told him we were mopping up blood everywhere. I wondered if Brendon was more concerned about the carpet than the passengers.

"Brendon has reported Simone to the authorities as a stowaway, they will be on the dock at Thursday Island first thing tomorrow morning to arrest her," Captain Porter continued in a steady soleum voice.

"Oh no!!!!" I screamed silently to myself, my eyes fixed on Captain Porter.

"I am going to pull into the dock early, I want you girls off the ship. Be packed and ready by 5am."

Captain Porter liked us and didn't want to see Simone behind bars. Stowing away on a ship is a serious crime.

Neither of us slept a wink that night, anticipating our escape. There was the glow of the morning sun, and a deep orange lighting up both sky and sea in the approaching bay. I had crammed my few clothes, toiletries, and hair dryer into my small bag, laying out the electric blue dresses neatly on the bunk as a sign of respect. It was time to go. The ship docked against the old wooden wharf, broken pylons in disrepair looking weak and brittle. Simone and I clambered off, Dereck offering a strong arm of support as we jumped the small gap between ship and wharf. Captain Porter was on the Bridge, a gentle nod indicating we were safe. A quick dash into the nearby bushes was required, my heart pounding loudly in my ears.

Two men dressed in uniform arrived shortly after our disembarkation. The words, Port Authority in white bold letters stood out on their tailored navy shirts.

"Wow, they are up early," I thought. I suppose 'the early bird catches the worm', but these two worms had outsmarted them, with the help of our captain.

THE TOP END

The Holiday Hopper eventually sailed out into the bay to anchor, the authorities leaving empty handed. The coast was clear, so Simone and I came out of hiding only to realise that we were on an island with no means of getting back to the mainland or the 800 kms back to Cairns.

Thursday Island was sparce and basic. A few dwellings ran along the foreshore with makeshift walls and corrugated iron roofs. A large square dwelling, with a thatched straw roof looked inviting. We entered to find a group of Torres Strait Island women preparing breakfast, young semi naked children at their feet. They seemed elated to see us, calling us in with beckoning waves and radiant white smiles.

"Where you gals come from then?" one indigenous woman curiously asked in her broken English - the surprise of our arrival bringing excitement to her morning.

"It's a long story," I moaned, too exhausted to start an explanation.

"Come have something to eat. You gals hungry?"

Yes, we were. The hospitality was much appreciated as we enjoyed sweetened bananas in coconut milk and cooked yam with hot tea. Four large crayfish sat in the corner still slightly moving a leg or two.

"Can you tell us how we can get back to the mainland? We need to get back to Cairns," I finally asked.

The women all laughed hard and loud as if I had told a hilarious joke. Their joy was contagious, so I joined in laughing loud and hard. Simone did not find our predicament amusing; it had been my idea for her to stowaway. I noticed a gold cross on the wall for the first time as one of the women pointed to it.

"You better start praying, miss," she strongly suggested.

"Ol Bill may be heading to the mainland," one woman spoke up.

Bill lived on a large ketch, a two-masted sailboat on an anchor in the bay. An 'old salt' he was referred to as he had spent a lifetime on the water.

His white skin was so darkened by the sun it took on a crusty appearance, so lined and dry it could be mistaken for leather. He carried himself with confidence, his long white hair pulled back into a ponytail, a thick beard, strong defined arms, and a determined stare as if he knew something you didn't know but wished you did.

Bill was on the shore gathering supplies into a small aluminum dinghy about to cast off and row out to his ketch.

"Hi, I'm Sarah and this is my friend Simone," I politely introduced us.

"We've been told that you may be going to the mainland. We were hoping you could give us a ride."

A puzzled look came over his face adding extra frowns to his already aged face.

"You're kidding me," he chuckled.

"NO, please, please, please help us. We have been stranded."

I quickly told Bill the stowaway story highlighting the awful experience on the Holiday Hopper and how Simone was going to be arrested.

He agreed to help but would not be leaving until the following day. Our new Thursday Island lady friends showed us to a room with two single beds where we could bunk down for the night. There was no linen or pillows, but we were so grateful for their generosity and willingness to help. Exhausted, we collapsed.

The heat of the early morning sun blew a steam of humidity through the glassless windows. I awoke wet, sweat dripping down my chest. Mosquito bites on my ankles began to irritate with an intense itch, my flesh being a meal to the pests throughout the night.

"Get up," I called to Simone. I didn't want Bill to change his mind.

The beach was deserted, and I could see Bill in the distance, attending to ropes on the deck. I waved my arms frantically as if my life depended on him seeing me. His white head tilted up as he heard my cries.

Soon we were on board, Bill instructing us on where to sit with a bossy authority I knew I had to adhere to. He pulled up the anchor, motoring slowly out of the bay towards the Australian mainland. A deep sense of relief flooded over me as I grabbed Simone's hand, squeezing it tightly.

The gentle roll of the ocean had lulled me into nodding in and out of a light sleep. Sitting upright on the deck, the waters below had comfort, a lullaby of rocking as if it knew how to instinctively rock a baby to sleep. In and out of my relaxed nodding I felt a sudden jolt in my ribs. Simone's fingers were pressing hard, the pain catapulting me to my feet. Three hours had passed.

"What," I cried in a semi stupa.

"Land," she screamed in a pitch that made the blood shiver in my veins.

Rubbing my eyes to assist them to focus, I could see the shore. A distant line of white sand, and a long stretch of glorious beach. Bill slowed the ketch, instructing us to gather our belongings to disembark.

"Ok girls, all the best," he said as he gestured us to jump overboard.

We were still 50 metres from the shore. I looked at him thinking he was joking when he waved a hand signal to jump.

Bill's ketch was unable to go any closer to the shore, so this was our destination. I looked at Simone with a fake smile, pretending this was a 'normal' Australian custom to reassure her that all was well. I was wondering how I was going to keep my belongings dry and how deep the water was that I was about to launch myself into.

I lowered myself gingerly off the side of the ketch, bag held high above my head with both hands, into neck-deep water. Wading carefully, I desperately concentrated on keeping my precious hair dryer away from the water. Thankfully the water was kind to us remaining calm and still while we waded slowly to shore. Once on the beach, we both sighed a deep relieved breath.

"Oh my God, we made it," Simone puffed in surprise.

Bill was quick to turn his ketch and disappeared into the distance with no additional goodbyes or message of good luck. I think he was happy to be rid of the 'crazy young travellers'.

For a moment or two, Simone and I stood silently on the long white deserted beach, taking in its beauty and isolation. Where were we?

Lowering my bag to the hot, pale sand, I pulled out one of my cotton dresses to attempt to dry off the salty sea. The steamy moist air kept me damp even after a rigorous rub, the dress looking like a sad rag. We began to walk along the beach hoping to find civilisation, or a human being would be enough. We had no food, and only a small amount of water. Simone had a water bottle she had wisely brought along in her ruck sack.

"What else have you got in your bag?" I pleaded in hope of a muesli bar miraculously appearing.

"Not much," Simone replied digging deep into her bag's pockets.

She pulled out a pink plastic Bic shaver and we both broke into spontaneous laughter. I didn't know whether to laugh or cry.

After what seemed like hours of walking in the scorching afternoon heat, we decided to rest. Meandering up to where the vegetation met the sand, we began to make our beds. I pulled out another cotton dress for a bed and rolled two T-shirts into a pillow. Simone lay directly on the sand using her ruck sack as her pillow. The sounds of the night bush were haunting. Crickets clicked a repetitive hum, owls hooted (I thought it might be an owl), twigs cracked.... Eventually we nodded into an uneasy sleep.

A glowing heat poured over my sweating face as the sun rose on the Eastern horizon. Without a word, I made a beeline to the water, hoping to find some relief in the wet invitation. I still had my bikini on from the day before when I made my leap from Bill's boat. The water was as warm as my blood, but I was grateful it was wet. Simone soon followed, jumping over the gentle lapping waves and joining me in full submersion in the Pacific Ocean. With sweat washed from our bodies, we began to walk back to our makeshift camp site.

I noticed a figure walking up the beach slowly towards us. Squealing with delight, my heart beating faster at the thought of being rescued and hopefully fed. Hunger pains were cramping my middle with strange groanings.

The man approaching wore a khaki shirt, the top three buttons unbuttoned. Thick hairy arms protruded from the short sleeves. His face was rugged, but not scary. Matching khaki shorts made me wonder if he was some kind of ranger - his sneakers were so dirty I couldn't determine what colour they used to be.

"Youse girls didn't go swimming in that there water, did youse?" he questioned in a serious Aussie drawl.

Both Simone and I were still wet in our bikinis so I think he already knew the answer to his question, but he was somehow hoping we would give a different answer.

"Yeeeees," I answered slowly, looking deep into his questioning eyes.

Our 'ranger' glanced at our bags on the beach - my cotton dress and T-shirts still trying to look like a bed.

"And youse didn't sleep the night there did youse?" he asked a second question with trouble in his eyes shaking his head from side to side.

"Yes," I responded with a nod.

"Well, I'm surprised the sharks didn't get you in that there water or the crocs didn't get youse. The crocs roam up and down this beach at night."

His local knowledge was so shocking I began to dry reach.

"Is there a town nearby?" Simone pleaded with puppy dog eyes.

"Nope, just a campground about 5 kms. north, how on earth did you girls end up here?" our ranger hero asked, notably puzzled.

Simone and I took turns blurting out the details of our trip on the Holiday Hopper, the stowaway, the storm, the wounded, the near arrest, Thursday Island, Ol Bill and now the deserted dangerous beach. The look on his face showed pure disbelief but how else would two girls in their twenties be standing in front of him in wet bikinis.

The camp site was a welcoming vision. An oasis of redemption. Half a dozen tents spread out in thick bush about 50 metres from the ocean. Campfires smoked a smoky haze, the wafting aroma of cooking bacon nearly causing me to pass out with its intoxicating fragrance. Deep relief consumed me, we were going to survive.

Far north Queensland is the epitome of isolation. The only road up the Cape York peninsula in the 80's was treacherous. A rugged dirt road crossing gullies and crocodile infested creeks, meandering for over 1,000 kms. The Old Telegraph Road, and crossing the Jardine River, would require a four-wheel drive and an adventurous spirit. The crossings would often be cut off after rain, so preparation and local knowledge was a must.

Our new camp friends were delighted to invite us to breakfast, staring in fascination as they listened intently to our unbelievable story.

"Any idea how we can get to Cairns?" Simone asked the group once she had consumed two fried eggs, and three large strips of bacon wrapped in white bread with tomato ketchup.

We were to learn that this group of travellers had arrived via a four-wheel drive adventure holiday tour and would be continuing to Thursday Island in a few days on a tour boat. Our only hope of getting safely back to Cairns was to wait a few days for Matty. Matthew Bryant was a tour guide who was due to arrive with the rest of their group in a few days. They would join this group for the boat tour. Matty would be returning to Cairns and may agree to take us with him.

"Hallelujah," I cried out loud.

THE TOP END

Matty didn't seem impressed when we shared our plight and pleaded to be taken back with him. He was concerned that the insurance with his tour company would not cover these two damsels in distress and he was reluctant to agree. After much pleading, and the prospect of us dying on the peninsular, Matty agreed to take us at a cost of 250 dollars each. Simone and I agreed with promises of going to a bank to get the money as soon as we got to Cairns.

Matty knew the treacherous track like the professional tour guide he was. The trip would take us five days, and it would prove to be one of the best adventures of my life. I was to learn that not all the creeks had crocodiles, as we swam in crystal clear cool waters. One day we ventured into flowing rapids, gliding over smooth rocks into a deep blue pool at the end of our nature ride. Matty seemed to enjoy showing us his favourite spots once he had accepted our company. His four-wheel drive vehicle was equipped with all the camp gear we needed along with ample supplies of food and water.

Breaking out of the deep green rainforest, our road turned into a vast landscape of towering ant hills in uncountable numbers. The majestic display of reds and ochers expanding into an unseeable distance. Kangaroos surrounded us, with Matty taking care not to hit a sudden bounding stray with his big black roo bar. The Australian icon did not seem to have any road sense, even though we were a rare vehicle on this dusty red road.

The lights of Cairns sparkled in the distance, a sign of civilisation. I had a strong yearning to turn around and head back into the wilderness to continue our escapade. I did not want to reenter a worldly life after experiencing a new freedom in remoteness. Freedom, immersed in nature and beauty, that was the true essence of escape. I loved my accidental discovery.

The bank would not be open until the following morning, so we agreed to meet Matty at the jetty with his cash for our rescue mission. Falling into the bunks in the backpackers' hostel, Simone and I grinned. Who would believe the tale of our past crazy weeks.

Simone decided to continue her trip to see Australia, heading off to pick fruit in rural Queensland, a popular activity for young overseas travellers. Free board and meals were on offer. We hugged tight and long, not wanting to let go of any memories.

"Goodbye my friend," Simone's refined voice sang for the last time.

Chapter 27

Three men and a baby

My time on the islands had enabled me to accrue enough sea hours from boat deliveries and sun set cruises to study a Master Class Five Skippers Ticket. This was a qualification, a requirement to captain boats, a monumental challenge I desired to conquer. Men had always conquered me, had the last laugh, abused me, and got away with it. This was my opportunity to show the world, my family, and myself that I was a strong capable woman.

My life had become engulfed in a male dominated industry, and now I was being called to the front line. A battleground for the brave, a courageous position in the trenches facing blood and gore. A life on the line with flesh being torn from the bone in a new level of defense. I would not only be defending myself, but the entire global female gender I represented. I was to enter a war for womankind to make a stand in the Australian boating industry. The 80's and 90's were uncharted territory that few women had ever battled.

I took a few deep breaths, then boarded a plane to Sydney to commence a TAFE course to complete the required studies. This would be another adventure into the unknown.

Women were usually positioned below decks, making bunks, cleaning 'heads' (the name given to toilets on boats), cooking and cleaning in general. An arrogance wafted like a septic cloud over the men onboard as they dominated the Bridge, the elite area where the captain commanded HIS ship. The captain's authority was not to be questioned as his role included 'going down with the ship' should it come to a sinking situation. The captains I had met so far were not the 'I'll die for my job' types.

My first TAFE class proved my belief in male dominance as I was the only female in a class of twenty students. Young men entering the water police, mature men endeavoring to captain barges and small ships, game fishing commercial crew and me. I sat eyes cast to the floor, hesitating to answer my name when called,

"Sarah Cook."

"Here," I gasped, the word getting stuck in my throat like dry toast.

All eyes turned to my small female frame. I could sense the sniggers being passed between the mate-ship that I did not belong to. I knew this was going to be a battle I would fight alone. A lone ranger.

"Hey, she missed the turn to the Home Economics Course," one of the budding police men laughed silently to his mate, loud enough for me to hear.

I blushed while pinching myself hard on my left arm hoping the self-inflicted pain would disguise the real pain I was feeling deep in the core of my being.

Why am I here? I don't belong here. Who am I kidding?

Doubt had been entrenched into me the moment Sister Anne had swung back on her chair in that stark office. Her questioning snarl doubting my character, my truth, my word, as my voice trembled recalling the perpetration I had endured yet not understood. Brother Dave's abuse had ripped friendships and education from under me, rocked my boat and brought a torrent of high seas bashing ceaselessly against my shores.

A sudden calm came upon me as I realised I was the only one left in the classroom. The teacher, a weather hardened seaman who had braved oceans like a pirate, stood behind a large oak desk, motionless, his eyes fixed on me. I raised my eyes to catch his stare, thick bushy eyebrows sheltering his eyelids. A sincerity that need not be spoken glared back at me. He dipped his chin in a nod to bid me well. I turned towards the door. This would not be the last of his many accepting nods that I would receive in the coming weeks.

In 1992, at 28 years of age, I was one of eight women in Australia to achieve a Master Class Five Skippers Ticket with an MED 3, Marine Engine Driving Engineer's Iertificate. I also achieved a Fire Fighting Certificate, a Radio Operators Certificate and Coastal Navigation qualifications. My new title, 'Captain Cook', was passed around the class. My male classmates held a new respect as I had topped all subjects.

Soon after I had my Captains ticket, a position became available on a newly built super yacht, 'MV Magic Times'. She was about to be launched for her maiden voyage out of Sydney, all 105 feet of shining glory. The owner needed a crew member onboard with the required qualifications, so I joined Danny. At 19 years of age, Danny had extraordinary engineering skills and could steer the ship beautifully. A highly capable young man. I quickly fell for him; we became lovers and best friends. We lived on the boat together full time, just the two of us.

His father was a doctor, devoted to his work and his mother a ballet dancer, physically strong with a soft nature. I admired his parents, a solid rock relationship, balanced yet with defined contrast. Danny's father was part Indian, blending Asian features into Danny's eyes that displayed Indian heritage from his ancestry. He showed me unfamiliar kindness, a gentle spirit that I embraced. This was the first man since Jeremy, before his mental breakdown, who had showed me something other than abuse. My heart had been shielded in steel, hard, cold, and rigid to protect a little girl hiding beside the wood pile. It was now softening in this newfound relationship.

Danny had an intelligence well beyond his years. He had already been an engineer in the building of MV Magic Times. His marine capabilities and expertise in maintaining large motor vessels made him an esteemed person in the boating industry. He could put his hand to any repair with problem-solving patience.

The owner of MV Magic Times requested us to base the boat on Hamilton Island for the summer. I was overjoyed to be going back to my favourite place, a place of waterways, sunsets, and reefs. The boat was berthed on the main arm in the marina, within walking distance of all the action. Danny and I would launch the ski boat off the top deck using the remote-controlled electric davit and race over to Gulnar Inlet at sunrise to waterski. The water would be like glass, perfect waterskiing conditions. Danny shared my love of water, and we enjoyed life together.

When Danny was offered a position to join a team to build top-class vessels overseas, I told him he had to take it. As a young talented man this was an opportunity of a lifetime. My heart was shattered. I wanted to tell him to stay with me, but I insisted he go. Deep sadness tortured my heart.

"Why did I let him go?" I later questioned, even though I knew our 10-year age difference held weight.

I didn't really believe I was worthy of true love. All I had ever known was abuse, rejection, and betrayal. Past adverse experiences create new neural pathways, and new brain passages that seem comfortable, and familiar, even if they are destructive. A man showing kindness and love, was an unfamiliar pathway and foreign to me. It terrified me and I felt undeserving. I had to let him go.

Damien, a tall, handsome, vibrant holiday maker arrived on Hamilton Island, and he soon noticed me. After Danny's departure I took a position on another superyacht 'MV Whisky'. She was a deep metallic grey with a large inviting rear deck. Damien walked along the dock, his long light brown hair falling into perfect ringlets. He came aboard with his appealing charm. It was lovely to have male company again and we were both swept away in electric chemistry. He had an adoration for both me and the jet ski I had access to on the top deck.

Jet ski rides, sunset drinks, and intense passion with Damien filled the painful void in my heart since Danny's departure. But my handsome holiday affair soon returned to his homeland of New Zealand, only deepening my sadness.

A few weeks went by, and the memory of Damien continued to pound in my heart. His professing of his love for me as he held me close was followed by a goodbye promise of reuniting soon.

A few weeks later, I called him.

"Hey, Damien. How are you? I hope you are well. I have decided to fly to New Zealand to see you," I blurted out with a nervous love-struck energy.

The phone went silent.

"Oh, really? Umm," he stammered.

The hesitation in his voice was not expected. I reeled back in surprise. A heavy dread brought an anticipation of the next words he was to speak,

"I have a girlfriend," he uttered.

"Her Dad is my employer. I have been working in his company for the past five years."

This was vital information that he had chosen to withhold from me. A familiar violation suddenly slapped hard against my face, a deep seething bile rising out of my stomach, burning, then burning again. How can passionate love turn 360 degrees in a split second into a newfound hatred. Another betrayal. He had invited me to visit him with an empty invitation. He was a liar. Not only to me but to his girlfriend as well.

"Sorry," he pathetically concluded.

I left my job on MV Whisky rejected, lost, and confused.

* * * * *

The game fishing season had begun. 'MV Paradise' was the creme de la crème in the game fishing world attracting wealthy fishermen from all over the world. Thomas, 'Tom' the skipper, had become a friend of mine, a 'boatie' buddy living on the Hamilton Island Marina. He was kind of goofy, in a big brotherly way. The paid captains of the other privately owned boats coming in and out of Hamilton Island Marina all congregated each evening on the back deck of one of the boats. We would take turns hosting sunset drinks with cheese and biscuits. Boat crews shared a comradery. We were like a family; our own families were miles away. There was an instant acceptance with people who a day before were complete strangers. The shared love of boating, and living on the water, created a passionate unity.

Tom had two Americans booked in for a week of Charter Fishing onboard MV Paradise, hoping to tag and release a big marlin. He needed a cook, and I was available.

Admittedly, cooking was not my strength, as my mother had never taught me how to cook but I didn't want to miss the opportunity to go on this incredible adventure. We headed up to the Ribbon Reefs not far off Lizard Island. The days were steaming hot as the sun blared down on the deep blue waters below us.

Fishing requires great patience. I love this sport. You can be simply doing 'nothing', but you are doing something, fishing! I was delighted to be given a turn to fish. Strapped into the large white leather chair on the rear deck, the rod firmly in the holster, I waited with anticipation. Even in nothingness, my heart was skipping beats just at the thought of a fish grabbing my flashing lure. Kyle and Wayne were the paying guests onboard. At the cost of 1000 Australian dollars per day per person, I was hopeful that the Marlin would be obliging. So far, no luck.

Suddenly my rod jolted. The deckhand, Russel was quick to his feet. He was unassuming, a quiet addition to the crew, rigging rods, fixing lures and generally being Tom's right hand man. It was now 'battle stations'. Tom was positioned at the tower steering station, high above the deck with the best visibility. He instinctively pulled off on the throttle, allowing the boat to bob patiently in the swell.

"Was there a fish on?" I asked.

"ZEEEEEEEE," a screaming whine came from the line as it rapidly flew from the reel. Everyone was shouting now,

"Fish on! Fish on!"

I was instructed to slowly wind the handle on the reel towards me, a great force met my attempts yet inch by inch I managed to draw my catch closer. The Americans were reaching for cameras and squealing in delight.

"Is it a Marlin?" Kyle cried.

All eyes turned to Tom who had a much better vantage point.

"YES," he shouted.

I was in the chair, so it was my catch. This was the rule of engagement. Adrenalin was pulsing through my veins at a level I had never experienced before. My heart was pounding so hard, yet I knew that all my focus was to be on one thing and one thing only, to pull in the fish.

As a water-skier my arms were reasonably strong, and my small frame was surprisingly fit. Time paused as I was taken into another world, game fishing. Eventually my catch tired, violently launching out of the water in a last attempt to break free from the lure deep in its gills. The fight was over. Russel grabbed a long pole in a familiar swoop, hooking my catch with precise accuracy. He tagged the Marlin then pulled it onto the back deck with the help of Kyle and Wayne. This moment was to be photographed. My fish stood taller than my five-foot two height, but I was told it was a baby Marlin. I later found out that Tom was reversing the boat onto the fish to assist me with reeling it in. This practice was illegal in a fishing competition, but we were just sports fishing. My baby Marlin was very happy to be thrown back into the ocean, although momentarily dazed he soon swam away. Celebratory beers were had on deck that evening and I was now the local hero.

Kyle and Wayne were both large, solid men with typical American builds. Wayne was a retired police detective and Kyle was a banker, based in New York City. Kyle seemed extra pleased with my fishing efforts, flooding me with attention. His eyes would follow me like a lost puppy dog, grinning wide when I caught his eye.

When we arrived back at the marina, Kyle invited me to join him and Wayne on the Gold Coast for a concert. In my spontaneous adventurous spirit I said,

"Yes."

The American guests had become my new buddies after our fishing adventure. I felt safe with them, especially with Wayne being an ex-police man. His six-foot six body towered over me; I was sheltered in his shadow. These men became my bodyguards, and I loved my entourage. Walking the streets, Wayne on one side, Kyle on the other I was the meat in a delicious sandwich.

Kyle had a boyish charm and an appealing face. His eyes were electric, a reflection of an exciting life in an exciting city. I had not been to New York but could only imagine his rapid pace in this financial kingdom. My laid-back island life was in complete contrast.

THREE MEN AND A BABY

The attention he gushed on me while on the boat continued. This handsome successful New Yorker was drawn to me, and I to him. The Gold Coast magic had me fall into his arms and into his bed.

Kyle and Wayne's Australian vacation came to an end, Wayne heading back to California and Kyle travelling back to New York. Big bear hugs sealed our goodbyes with promises to meet again. I was in love. Kyle was my dream man, and I couldn't wait to get to New York and be with him. My thirtieth birthday was just around the corner, and I was ready to settle down. My mother had been engaged to a doctor from New York and here I was now heart struck by a New Yorker.

* * * * *

I travelled to Sydney, moving back into the family home with Mum and Dad to plan my trip to New York. My heart yearned for Kyle so as soon as I had the funds, I would be on a Qantas flight and back into his strong arms. The charter boat industry was booming over the summer, offering plenty of work on various boats on Sydney Harbour. The funds would be in my bank in no time.

My period was late. As the days passed, I thought back to my three passionate partners of the last few months. Counting the weeks and the encounters, a rush of blood sent a pulsating red into my cheeks.

Was I pregnant?

I counted again. Oh no! Whose baby would it be? I rushed to the local chemist to buy a testing kit.

Positive.

I searched the numbers on the calendar attached to the fridge over and over. A growing baby was in my belly, and I didn't know whose sperm was responsible. A desperate panic began to manifest.

What was the date of my last period? When did I have sex with Danny before he left? What was the date of the 'fling' with Damien? The date of the love encounter with my American stud, Kyle? This unknown brought unceasing torment. How could I be so stupid.

Victims of childhood sexual abuse have a tendency towards sexual love. It is as though the awakening of sexuality so young distorts the brain. For me sex was love. This distorted belief brought confusion when men showed me this was not the case. It was a lie fooling me into hurtful sexual, loveless encounters. But I had loved these three men, in the only way I knew how to love.

Mum was sitting in the TV room on the beige lounge, an episode of MASH about to conclude. The Lane Cove River was still, an occasional gentle breeze sending soft ripples towards the shoreline. I would often sit in the bay window staring up the river, yearning to be in its embrace.

"Mum, I have something I need to tell you," I said shaking with internal terror.

After a long pause I announced,

"I'm pregnant."

The weight of the words stuck in my throat, causing me to cough violently. An announcement of a new life should be wonderful news but not knowing who fathered the child was deeply disturbing to me. An unplanned pregnancy from one of three men. I had wanted to have a baby, to be a Mum for as long as I could remember. Playing with my dolls in my bedroom as a small child, creating loving families in my pretend world was a joy. But it was not supposed to be like this. My insides knotted in a pain of personal disgust. I felt dirty.

Mum jumped to her feet. A silenced child had spoken. A secret had been released like a bird being set free from its cage. The magnitude of my confession was apparent in the fiery glare upon me.

"Well, there is only one thing you can do Sarah," she said through a stony face.

Fighting back nausea, tears welled, my racing thoughts gathered to contemplate raising this baby as a single Mum. My mother's Catholic conviction would surely insist I have the baby. I simply wanted to be swept up in her arms and told,

"It's going to be ok."

After a long pause her words finally came, "You must get an abortion."

The icy words washed over me as I drifted into a trance. A cold shudder of shock blinded my mind. Had I heard her correctly? Abortion? But what about God, my mother's God? I began to fall into a deep dark pit of despair. I had conjured up the same courage that I had used to confess Brother Dave's molestations. Why was I expecting a different result? My harvest was silence so I would inevitably be silenced again.

"Don't tell anyone, just get an abortion," was Mum's final solution.

Her control was as hard as a stone that could not be moved. I knew I could not face having this baby without her support. Lost in a new sense of aloneness, the decision was made for me. There was no other option.

Mum drove me to the clinic, to face the worst day of my life.

A middle-aged woman, in a crisp white nurse's tunic gestured for me to sit on the steel framed chair opposite her behind a clear glass desk. The room was cold and clinical, only softened by the pink box of tissues on the desk. Her role was to take my details and to discuss the procedure, before getting my consent via a signature on the bottom of a piece of paper. Her words were a blur that I did not wish to hear. My hidden internal sobs made my body shudder spontaneously, a cold sweat breaking on my forehead. I looked at the paper over and over but could not read a word. My signature, an unrecognisable squiggle, sat in the bottom right corner.

Trauma, shock, and pain were followed by deep regret. The horrific procedure was over.

"Would my baby end up in a jar in a doctor's surgery on display, like the baby in the bottle I grew up with?" my tormented thoughts envisioned.

Deep internal post abortion cramps were a constant reminder of my mother's control. Why didn't I have the strength to say, "no." Why wasn't I able to stand up for myself? The cramps subsided but the consuming internal agony of loss never left me. I was trapped in 'arrested development'. This is where emotional or psychological growth stops or slows down before adulthood due to factors such as trauma, stress, or lack of a supportive environment. When trauma, for example abuse, happens at a certain age, a person can become stuck at that age. I was an obedient eight-year-old child, saying "yes" to my mother's direction to abort my first child.

I named my baby 'Joshua'. I somehow knew he was a boy, he would always be loved and never forgotten. He was in heaven waiting to meet me.

Fast forward to 2008, the Abba story 'Mama Mia' was released. I had been living in this story in my real life for 15 years. I attended the musical romantic comedy Mama Mia with a friend at a local Sydney cinema. The story unfolded of a young woman who had sexual relations with three different men in a short space of time while travelling. The shock sent me cold. That was me. An uninvited trauma flooded every cell in my body, as I sat frozen in time. My friend leant towards me at the conclusion of the show, as the credits rolled on the screen,

"What an unbelievable story. As if that would happen in real life," she scoffed.

I cringed, sinking deeper into my seat keeping yet another secret silent.

Shortly after the termination, I began to plan my trip to New York. I would stop in Hawaii on the way to break up the journey and to visit a family friend, Christina. My father had befriended her father at a War

THREE MEN AND A BABY

Vets' function in Sydney, becoming instant lifetime buddies. War had this effect on people, comradery embedded in their souls even if they had never met before. Christina had married a multi-millionaire who had one of his holiday homes in Hawaii. I would then fly into LA to catch up with Wayne before flying across the country to New York and into Kyle's loving arms. I could never tell Kyle of the baby, he would see me through different eyes, as a promiscuous woman with no morals. How could a woman be pregnant and not know the father? A secret was to remain silent.

The Boeing 747 flight from Sydney to Honolulu was a joy. I loved being on a plane as it usually meant I was escaping something. The second flight was on a small aircraft, a short flight for the final leg to The Big Island, 'Hawaii' where Christina and Malcolm would be waiting to welcome me. I had planned a few days stop-over with them before I would continue to LA then on to New York.

"Have you heard the news?" Malcom announced in his thick south American drawl.

"A magnitude 6.7 earthquake has hit LA."

The 1994 Northridge earthquake was massive; causing the Golden State Freeway to collapse. The footage on the TV was shocking as fires were burning all over the city. It looked like a scene from an apocalyptic movie. We were all glued to the TV, watching the devastation from this destructive force. This smoking chaos was where I was supposed to be heading in the next couple of days.

All flights into LA were cancelled. I was not going anywhere. Hawaii was to be my resting place for another three weeks! I didn't want to rest. I wanted to be with Kyle.

Finally, flights resumed after a colossal clean up. The evidence of the disaster would remain displaying a deep scar on the city for many months to come. Wayne had given me detailed instructions on where he would be at the airport when I arrived. He would drive me to his place where I would stay for a couple of days. I felt safe with Wayne as my local tour guide. His towering presence and warm smile, a friendly reminder of the fishing adventure we shared a few months prior. I was exploding with questions as we drove at high speed down the freeway.

"Did you feel the quake? What was it like? Was it scary? How is Kyle? Have you heard from him? Does he know I am delayed in coming?"

I was unable to contact Kyle. The number he gave me was not answering and I was very concerned. Was he ok? Wayne was very hesitant to speak of Kyle. Did he know something I didn't know? A few days passed and I became more determined to contact Kyle. I had last spoken to him when I first arrived in Hawaii and now nothing. I didn't understand. He seemed so keen on me visiting him. Wayne broke the news.

"Kyle has met a girl. He has a girlfriend now in New York," Wayne reluctantly spoke.

His face was sombre as he knew I would not welcome this information. I fell back a few steps as I absorbed the words. Pale and weak, the gravity of the situation drew my aching body to my knees.

"What?" I uttered in a shocked whisper.

Kyle had 'ghosted' me. I was in California, on my knees, crying, heartbroken again.

The more I tried to understand the men in my life, the more confused I became. My distorted victimised brain, topped with a naive vulnerability, led me down many dark paths. Foolish decisions erased all the trust I had in myself. Again and again, more pain, more rejection, more abuse.

We all have an inner desire to be loved. To love and be loved. Was I making wrong choices or were the wrong choices choosing me? What role was I playing in creating my reality? An inner childhood belief, a narrative that all men will deceive me was silently ticking inside my head. That little girl hiding behind the wood pile knew this truth. Where was I safe in this cruel world?

I changed my travel plans, leaving the USA and heading to the UK to be with Dad's family. There I could hide in the pub scene behind drunken laughter and live music. I was alone in a crowd. Loneliness doesn't mean you are on your own. You can be lonely while surrounded by people. The more people the more alone you can be. Loneliness is a condition of the heart. Watching couples holding hands, new parents pushing prams, and groups of friends sharing stories were all catalysts for my loneliness. I would walk the streets at 4am, already alight with the early daybreak. The gentle sounds of the cool mornings washed over my soul. Swans calling each other by the canal, orange autumn leaves scrunching beneath my feet, rabbits scurrying behind the hedges, but the pain was always there needing to be soothed.

"You killed your baby," the dark incessant reminder echoed within.

My 30th birthday was days away. Contemplating the fact that my 20's were nearly over, and I was alone, I decided to head home. The pints of lager were no longer able to numb the sadness. I cried until the tears had dried up, a weeping and gnashing of teeth, a sorrow now turning to self-hatred.

Chapter 28
Salvation

The sleepless flight back to Australia was long and bumpy. Each hour that passed I reflected on my foolishness. I could not believe I had been so stupid to believe a man loved me.

"A dumb girl chasing false love," I told myself.

The descent into Sydney had begun.

"Would you please put your seats back into the upright position, secure your tables and fasten your seat belts," came the familiar instruction through the intercom system.

It was a pleasant female voice, easily obeyed by the passengers who already seemed to know the drill. Excitement welled up inside me as I looked out of the window. Bright diamonds bounced across Sydney Harbour while the sun joyfully captured the waves. The white tiled sails of the Opera House stood strong and bold, dominating Circular Quay. The harbour was calling out to me,

"I'm still here Sarah, welcome home."

Tears flooded my eyes as my heart pounded in anticipation of being home. I loved my country and felt comforted to be back on Australian soil.

Dad was at the airport, his warm gentle smile, a permanent fixture as he waited. Patience is a virtue, and my father was virtuous. His high moral standards accompanied by emotional composure held him in good stead. My love for him only deepened after such a long absence.

"Welcome home sweetheart," he beamed with outstretched arms, an embrace I wanted to dive deep into - to be washed in his protective warmth.

My father loved me. I knew by the way he lit up when I entered a room, the way he listened to my stories. He was often absent due to working long dutiful hours, yet when he was present, he was fully present. I would follow him around the garden, like a small shadow just wanting to be in his company. The hose would move slowly from each plant as he nurtured it with watering love, the same love he would show the people in his care. As a doctor he was immensely loved. He would deliver a baby then when that baby grew into an adult, he would deliver their baby. A generational GP who was greatly respected in the community. Visiting the local shops with my father was a social event. Every shopkeeper would greet us, every one of them was his patient.

"Dr Cook, my elbow is much better now, thank you," the butcher would gush.

Dad would smile and engage in a conversation with each one giving his time and expertise with every step.

Being back on Sydney soil was an adjustment. I was penniless and jobless. My relationship with my mother darkened each day, the unspoken sins of the past hidden, brushed under a carpet. The dirt piling up like a junk draw, where all the useless bits and pieces are discarded. I remembered my mother joyfully singing while Brother Dave played the piano, while he was planning to interfere with her young prepubescent daughter. I remembered the kiss, a kiss I saw them exchange on the driveway, a long passionate kiss. An abuser often grooms the mother, preparing the way for him to get to the child. This common strategy is deeply entrenched in an evil mind. Who are these creatures who have sexual desires for our young? The small innocent ones, twisting their words into silence.

Narcissists have an unreasonably high sense of self-importance while requiring constant and excessive admiration. My mother seemed to have narcissistic traits upon reflection. She led a privileged life, and no one was going to burst her bubble. On the stage, her gifted voice was a constant source of admiration and praise. She had been born into a world where she could be worshipped, even envied for her perfection in talent, beauty, and lifestyle. The mink coats and the diamond rings, adorning her outward show of wealth and prestige. A dirty sin had no place on her pedestal. The pretty blonde daughter, the reflection she would see in her mirror would be silenced into submission. Wear the clothes she was told to wear, put the roller in her hair, speak only the words she was told to speak and have the abortion she was told to have.

I was cranky. A mood of bitterness, loathing myself and my mother. My piercing glances her way spoke volumes of a hatred I was not permitted to have. I became an expert at pretence, everything was fine, yet the seething sticky black mess in the core of my being was slowly killing me. I had nothing to lose.

"Do you remember Brother Dave?" I casually asked her one day.

These thoughts had been festering for years, like a pimple ready to pop, the puss ready to spurt.

She was standing at the stove, her hair perfectly teased into its beehive form, each strand sprayed stiff into place. A freshly ironed apricot cotton shirt was hidden under a green floral apron, protection against the liquid fat heating on the cook top.

"Oh yes, he was very fond of you," was her nonchalant reply.

Fond!! I screamed loudly in my head. *Are you kidding me?* Noting her blank look, I huffed and walked away. There was no point in opening a can of worms. The past was the past. Secrets were never to be released, and I believed that she would cover for him. Protect him. Was he her secret love, my troubled mind pondered?

I needed work. A position became available at the hospital where I had trained as a Mothercraft nurse. I returned to a double life - working during the week, partying, and taking drugs on the weekends.

My destructive lifestyle was well hidden. Secrets had become my specialty, my past experiences teaching me the necessary skills of deception and falsehood. My outside shell could appear bright and confident while my internal chaos was darker than black. Drugs were a familiar friend, temporarily holding my hand and wiping away the pain. Mood swings were put down to shift work, a pendulum of highs and lows, the drugs coming and going from the blood stream. Days swirled into nights, weeks into months of more nothingness. My 30th birthday passed, uneventfully.

Dad suggested I join him on a trip to Nepal. He had visited the country years before and had a strong desire to return. For Mum, to visit a developing country was out of the question, so I was to be Dad's companion. I saw this as another opportunity to escape and Dad would be paying.

Kathmandu greeted us with chaotic fervor. Cars, motor bikes and buses crowded the dusty streets, tooting horns as they narrowly missed each other in a survival of the bravest. Beggars sat in the dirt, holding out metal bowls, desperately hoping to gather coins from passing strangers. Some had missing limbs and leprosy sores. The sounds and smells reeked of poverty, yet the people had joy in their eyes. I was consumed by the vast differences from the comfort of my Hunters Hill home; the thick polluted air of this city requiring face masks while at home I was surrounded by orderly cleanliness. The Nepalese dirt seeped into my pours, forming a sweaty paste. The water in the hotel was yellow and I was warned not to drink it. In fact, I was told not even to clean my teeth in it. Disease was rampant, dysentery a common infliction.

We took a flight to a town called Pokhara. The small 12-seater plane looked disheveled, and I was glad Mum was not with us. There would be no chance of her getting onboard. I was concerned when I read the sign on the seat in front of me, *'Your life jacket is under your seat'*. We would be flying above 26,000 feet over the tallest mountains in the world, a life jacket would be no use in the event of a crash. The Himalayan Mountains did not disappoint me. Their spectacular beauty was hypnotic, clearly indicating Dad's reason for this return visit. The pilot held the plane on course as the strong wind gusts jolted us in all directions. The terrifying flight was dissipated as the breathtaking scenery grew into a magnitude of magnificence.

Relieved to have my feet back on the ground, I was swamped by dozens of taxi drivers, all wanting my attention. This was a new terror for me. Dad took over selecting one driver to take us to our hotel. After a cool drink of sickly-sweet orange cordial, we ventured to the famous Pokhara Lake. The huge body of water was a perfect mirror reflecting the towering Annapurna Mountain range above. Colourful wooden boats lined the shoreline, inviting tourists for a ride. Ladies selling peanuts in brown paper cups waved, beckoning us to try. There was a peacefulness that was quite different from the hustle and bustle in Kathmandu.

The main street was filled with shops selling clothes and trinkets as souvenirs. Bright coloured dyed felts caught my attention, as they were crafted into a variety of goods including toys, mats, and decorations. The richness of the culture matched the richness of the people's spirits even in the absence of material wealth.

Tamding's shop was simple and different. We were to discover he was Tibetan. Living as a refugee, he told us the story of his escape from Tibet, fleeing from the Chinese invasion. He had climbed the mountains with his wife, eating roots to prevent altitude sickness to save their lives. I was fascinated by this story of struggle and survival. Tamding and Cheodon Metok were survivors. Their shop was filled with Tibetan antiques that Tamding had managed to bring into Nepal. He proudly showed me a photograph of their four young sons. Their poverty and their courage touched deep into the core of my soul. We exchanged contact details with the promise to keep in touch. I was later to discover that Tamding had died suddenly from liver cancer leaving his wife and four small sons in a very difficult situation. Education was not affordable for this family and a cry for help gave me no choice. I adopted these boys into my heart and into my family. I financially supported them to get an education and live a better life. They call me 'Mom' and I continue to be in communication today. I have had the privilege of selecting names for two of my Tibetan grandsons.

The following day, after visiting Tamding's shop, we were to go on a trek. Dad had organised a guide to lead us up the mountain to Sarangkot. We were to take a small backpack for the day with plenty of water. The high altitude was a challenge especially as we had travelled from the Australian sea level. The slow climb took us through small villages, the homes made from mud bricks and straw. Filthy children ran across the path, semi naked with their hands held high in the air asking for coins or sweets. Mothers sat on the dirt breast feeding while young girls prepared basic food. One mother held a new baby on her lap, its naked body revealed that it had no genitals. The sight shocked the air out of my lungs. Dad approached asking the mother if he could look at the child stating that he was a doctor. The woman was overjoyed to have a doctor in her presence. Dad carefully examined the baby listening to its heart. He glanced towards me and shook his head.

"This baby has a hole in the heart," he said.

"It won't survive."

I looked at the mother's pleading eyes as she hoped for an answer. Why was her baby born neither girl nor boy?

I had to look away, the knowledge of this child's pending death was too much for me to absorb. The loss of my own baby wrenched in my gut with a compassionate sigh.

We continued up the mountain to the lookout. Emotionally and physically exhausted, I sat on the ground to sip some water. A wooden shelter with a table stood in the distance. I could see a long line of people queueing behind the table. I wondered what they were waiting for. A man ran to us, grabbing Dad firmly by the arm to drag him to the people. They were all lined up to see the doctor, my dad.

Word had got out on the mountain that there was a doctor. These people were too poor to see a doctor, so this was a wonderful opportunity they were not going to let pass. Dad was surprised but could not disappoint them. He removed his backpack, emptying its contents onto the table. A handkerchief, a packet of band aids, a camera, a few Panadol and a near empty bottle of water. That was it. Without hesitation he got to work. One patient at a time, Dad carefully examined each person with loving kindness.

"You have scabies," he told one young man.

The endless line was finally exhausted. Our guide, whose role had morphed into the doctor's interpreter, led us back down the mountain. Halfway down a man came running at us, frantically waving in a panic. We followed him to where a 14-year-old girl was lying on the ground having a fit of some kind. Dad quickly went to her side, onto his knees to take her pulse.

"We need to get this girl to a hospital," he said.

The man, who was her uncle, swooped her up into his arms to join us for the rest of the descent down the mountain.

SALVATION

The Pokhara Hospital had a line of ill patients at the entrance that extended into the far distance. People had been waiting for hours in the hot sun to see a doctor. The man carrying the girl rushed to the front of the queue yelling something to an official managing the crowd. He pointed to Dad and got the go ahead to enter the hospital. A white foreigner escorting a local Nepalese girl meant the bill would be paid and priority was given. The girl had epilepsy and would need ongoing medication. Dad paid for her treatment and the medication.

The trip to Nepal was life changing for me. My problems seemed to fade into insignificance now that I had been a witness to real life struggles. I lived in an affluent country with clean water and access to free medical care. I wasn't living as a refugee nor wondering if I would eat that day. Australian children have access to education and health care, where many Nepalese children do not. I had seen my father spring into action in an hour of need, no supplies, no medical bag, just a few band aids, a couple of Panadols and buckets of love.

* * * * *

A still small voice began to whisper to me,

"Find a church."

How ridiculous, I thought in response. I had made a vow never to set foot in a church ever again. The church and its clergy had abused me. I ignored it.

"Find a church," it whispered again.

Who is that? A voice in my head? It certainly wasn't my voice as I would never have suggested such a thing. As if on a persistent repeat loop, it continued, still, gentle, and soft.

The Yellow Pages were the source of information before Google existed. A thick, large book listing in alphabetical order, names, addresses, and phone numbers was perched on my lap. Its weight left a dent in my bare legs. Each page was yellow, hence the name 'The Yellow Pages'. Hundreds of churches were listed, page after page. I closed the book.

I decided to consult with Julie, one of the nurses at work. A quiet woman, a wholesome woman, and a church goer I believed. When all the nurses sat together in the lunchroom gossiping, Julie chose not to join in. Her righteous separation annoyed yet intrigued me. She was a 'goodie two shoes', who always followed the rules and was known as a 'do-gooder'. She would know about churches.

"Hey, if someone you know, say a friend or someone wanted to find a church, how would they go about it?" I asked Julie casually one lunchtime, as we sat in the lunchroom munching on sandwiches. That someone was not me of course, I thought loudly.

Julie seemed surprised, perhaps because I was the least likely person to ask such a question. My continued distaste for anything religious was evident to most people who knew me.

"I go to a lovely church," she softly responded.

"You and your *friend* could come with me some time," she added, flashing a warm inviting smile.

My disguise didn't fool her. She knew it was me!

The invitations began.

"Would you like to come to church with me this Sunday, Sarah? There is an excellent guest speaker I know you will enjoy."

Oh no, what had I started?

"Sorry Julie I'm busy this Sunday," I politely refused, thinking to myself I would be busy every Sunday.

SALVATION

"Hi Sarah, this Sunday is the opening of our new church building, the Prime Minister is coming. It will be a wonderful event with entertainment and food. Why don't you join us?" Julie insisted.

A colleague, Maria, another Christian nurse was at her side for backup. Both girls were beaming their sweet smiles at me waiting for a response.

"Ah Ah no, I'm sorry…," I stuttered while my mind searched for an excuse. My mother was sick, I must clean the house, my budgie died…

"I'm already going out with friends," I replied. I was safe once more.

But this would not be the end of it. I started to regret my 'finding a church' question and tried to avoid the two girls at work.

"Sarah." Oh no, I was spotted.

"Hello Julie," I replied sheepishly, knowing what was coming.

"Would you like to come to church with me this Sunday?"

I had run out of excuses and so I reluctantly answered, "yes" with a deep sigh.

"Great. It starts at 10am. I'll meet you in the foyer," she said smiling.

Writing the address on a piece of paper, she placed it in my hand and dashed off to a crying baby we could hear in the distance.

My alarm clock sounded its usual loud annoying bells, but today they seemed louder and more annoying. I chose to sleep in on Sunday mornings, but today I was going to church. A dread came over me as I dragged my failing body to the bathroom. The mirror didn't lie as it shouted at me, "You look like shit."

Why had I said, "yes?" Julie's persistence had got the better of me.

What would I wear? Sunday best? Mum used to insist on us dressing our best for church. Are jeans, ok?

The beige slacks I bought for job interviews screamed, 'pick me'. A white shirt with cream court shoes completed the outfit. Mum would approve.

Munching on a piece of vegemite toast, I contemplated whether this was still a sin? Eating an hour before communion was not permitted before a Catholic Mass, a memory of stomach groans flashed to the forefront on my mind.

"Oh well," I brushed the thought away while swallowing another mouthful.

I wasn't a Catholic. I had committed far greater sins than eating toast before church.

The car park was packed as I slowly navigated the rows of cars searching for where I could park. I could tell Julie I couldn't find a parking spot; I told myself as a last-minute excuse to escape. I had made a vow to myself, "I will never step foot in a church again." But here I was, pulling into a vacant spot at the front of a church.

The building before me did not have the appearance of a typical church. It was large and modern, more like a theatre or a college.

There were no religious signs, no crosses, no stained glass, no dead man on a cross, nothing. I tentatively got out of my car and began to walk towards the entrance. I instantly became aware of a force, a heavy presence descending over my body. With each step forward this oppressive load began to pull at my body, trying to force me backwards.

Engulfed as if in a tangible weighted blanket, I felt like a dog being dragged by the collar, all four legs locked against its will. Pounding deep within my chest, my heart was sending a deafening beat echoing panic. I could see the glass doors of the church entrance in the distance - fixing my eyes, I placed one foot in front of the other, fighting the resistance.

The foyer was buzzing with people, all laughing and talking, and hugging, and greeting one another with a kiss. As my body pushed through the doors, the weighted assault instantly lifted.

"Welcome to church," an over friendly face met mine.

I smiled gingerly, scanning for Julie.

SALVATION

"Sarah," she squealed when she saw me, perhaps slightly shocked that I had turned up. Person after person came up to Julie. They were all too happy and sickly sweet in my opinion. "Why are these people so happy?" I silently questioned this strange foreign phenomenon; it was a building full of genuinely contented people.

"Let me introduce you to Sarah. We work together," Julie said.

Julie proudly announced my arrival to her many friends as if I was a visiting dignitary. Everyone seemed so delighted to meet me. We took our seats towards the back of the huge auditorium already filled with expectant people. The joy was palpable as I estimated at least 2,000 beaming faces.

Exquisitely blended sounds began to flow from the band on the stage before us. It was unlike anything I had ever heard before, seeming to carry a spiritual presence. I was swept away in a sea of melodious sounds. Guitars gliding into effortless riffs, keyboards creating soul-stirring tones, voices in angelic harmony while the drums kept a meditative beat. Everyone was on their feet, swaying and singing with gusto. The enthusiasm was electric, the joy contagious.

After numerous songs, we sat for a message from the pastor. He was introduced as Pastor Bill, not Father Bill as in the Catholic church. He was dressed in cool jeans, an untucked pale blue shirt, and groovy sneakers. His piercing blue eyes looked straight at me; his words melting my hard shell as if he somehow knew my pain.

"Someone is here for the first time; you were hesitant in coming today. Life has been challenging - however you need to meet Jesus. Come forward," his words vibrated in my ears.

It was as if he could read my mail. My heart was exploding with each beat, booming until that was all I could hear. Uncontrollable tears transformed into gasping sobs. I wasn't sad, I wasn't in pain, these tears were from deep within flooding me with an inner healing glow.

"Will you come with me?" I blubbered to Julie, wiping away the stream of hot tears with the back of my hand. I somehow knew that the still small voice that was telling me to find a church, was now drawing me to the front of the church.

Julie smiled, a knowing soft smile and nodded. The walk to the front stage was light and easy as I glided forward as if on a cloud. The heavy resistance I had encountered earlier outside the church no longer had a hold on me. It was as though I was safe in this sanctuary. I had a sense of urgency, wanting to run to the front, to the pastor, to meet Jesus.

Julie's grip on my hand tightened, as she led the way. It surprised me to see at least 15 people already up the front in a line wanting to meet Jesus too. Pastor Bill kept repeating,

"Come, come."

I noticed that the people who had joined me at the front were also crying. There was a young man next to me who looked around 18 years old, on his knees weeping.

Pastor Bill commenced a simple prayer saying,

"Repeat after me. 'Dear Father in heaven, I repent of my sins. Please forgive me, make me your child. I accept Jesus Christ as my Lord and Savior. Come and dwell in my heart. Amen.'"

A presence covered me like a warm wave starting at my head then flowing to my toes. Every hair on my arms was standing to attention, goose bumps protruding with an extraordinarily delightful tingling sensation. I closed my eyes as that still small voice whispered,

"I love you, Sarah."

I woke the following morning to the kookaburras laughing in the distance. Their joyful cries announcing the new day. The sun's beams poured through the cracks in my venetian blinds, creating a pattern of golden lines on my green and white bedspread. I was sleeping in the downstairs room

SALVATION

by the pool. My old childhood bedroom with pink striped wallpaper, had become mum's bedroom as soon as I moved into the dorms at Royal North Shore Hospital. I never saw mum showing dad any intimacy and concluded that separate bedrooms were her preference. Reaching for the Bible that I had been gifted at the church, I began to read Genesis chapter one,

"In the beginning God created the heavens and the earth." Did I encounter God yesterday? Did God create me?

I felt different. A new awareness filled my mind with freedom and light. Looking outside the trees glowed a deeper green, the flowers smiled brighter. I never touched drugs again.

"Thank you, Jesus," I repeated over and over and over.

Chapter 29
New Beginning

As the days passed, I began to struggle with the concept of a relationship with the church.

I knew God had directed me to this place, but my past wounds continued to fester. The memories of Villa Maria, Brother Dave and the Marist Fathers seethed hatred in my heart. I decided to write Pastor Bill a letter, telling my story and expressing my concerns. I wrote with a rawness and a reality, detailing my past and highlighting the confusion I was facing. His reply came quickly with great compassion and concern. He suggested I contact a woman in the church called Millie who was a counsellor. Her details were in the letter. Eventually I had the courage to call her.

Millie was a quietly spoken woman with mousy brown hair and not a lick of makeup. She was plain yet beautiful. It was spiritually beautiful, radiating skin, moist lips, sensitive eyes that dipped to the floor and up again to meet your eyes at the precise moments. I immediately warmed to her and looked forward to our sessions. We met every week in a small room hidden away at the back of the church offices. As each session began, she would invite me to sit on a basic chair in the middle of the room. There was another chair and a small desk in the corner away from the door, and a pleasant green pot plant placed on the floor in a large cane basket. A beautiful original painting in dazzling acrylic colours covered the entire wall in front of me. A spectacular display catching my attention and my admiration. I was later to discover that Pastor Bill was a brilliant artist.

"I'm going to ask the Holy Spirit to come and minister to you," Millie said in her soft gentle voice.

"Ok," I replied, having no idea what she meant.

After a short prayer she was quiet. I sat on the chair with my hands resting on my thighs, palms facing upwards as an expression of surrender and invitation. Millie had instructed me to close my eyes and take a deep breath.

Within seconds a presence filled the room that had a heaviness so strong that I found it difficult to stay on the chair. Not the same heaviness that was trying to force me from entering the church, not a drug induced heaviness, but a warm heaviness like when you are tired and peacefully ready for sleep.

I felt my body sway sidewards into a distinctive angle as I sunk deep into the chair. I was completely at peace and relaxed. A healing balm soothed every part of my being as this presence continued for at least an hour. Millie sat silently. When my time was over, Millie smiled and said,

"See you same time next week."

I slowly drifted back into the room, gathered my bag and jacket, and left. I had stepped from the darkness into the light, I had accepted Jesus, but that evil force that had gripped me outside of church didn't want to let me go.

At night, after I had gone to bed, a creature would manifest in the corner of my ceiling high up above me. It had a bat-like appearance, with big, pointed ears and piercing red, illuminated eyes. Its cold glances towards me would turn into an evil stare sending terror through my nervous system. This creature reminded me of the statues of gargoyles I had seen on my trips to Bali that fronted every temple. I was told they were to ward off the evil spirits, and I now understood they *were* the evil spirits.

As a new believer, I had been told that evil had to flee in the name of Jesus. Alone in my room I would shout out,

"In Jesus name, Go!"

The creature would hiss at me and vanish. One time, I awoke from a deep sleep, with a feeling of heaviness on my chest affecting my ability to breathe. I opened my eyes to see a hideous face, the shape of a ferocious wolf, with long white teeth dripping with saliva. It's hairy, massive paws were weighing down on my chest, pinning me to the bed. Its eyes were fixed trapping me with utter terror. When you are trapped in sleep yet unable to move, it is known as sleep paralyses. I was completely trapped under this hideous beast.

"In Jesus name, get off me," I rasped under its weight. Its weight instantly lifted, and the demonic creature vanished.

My weekly sessions with Millie and the Holy Spirit continued for six months. Each session went the same way, inviting the Holy Spirit in and letting Him do His thing. The Holy Spirit is the third person of the trinity, God the Father, the Son (Jesus) and the Holy Spirit. He is the counsellor, and He knew exactly the healing I needed from all my past traumas. Shame and silence held a grip on my life, a hidden vice upon my head tightening as triggers cruelly reminded me that I was a victim. I thought that I had attracted the abuse in my life.

My new age friends had told me about karma, manifesting destiny through thought and mantras, past lives, and the law of attraction. They informed me that I had to learn a life lesson before I could move on and into my higher self. I had to live many lives, be reincarnated until I learnt my lessons. Well, this life sucked. What lesson was I supposed to be learning through childhood sexual abuse and ongoing abuse? I discovered these were lies. The truth was that I had been created in the image of a loving God. It was never His intention for me to face abuse, rejection, or fear. He is a God of love. He was there at the wood pile, watching, knowing there would be justice. An eternal justice that I was beginning to understand. Everyone will be judged and held accountable before God. "For I, the Lord, love justice; I hate robbery and wrongdoing. I will faithfully reward my people for their suffering and make an everlasting covenant with them," Isaiah 61:8 NLT. And "For we must all appear before the judgement seat of Christ, that each one may receive what is due him for the things done while in the body, whether good or bad," 2 Corinthians 5:10. These are two scriptures in the Holy Bible that speak of a just God.

The day came when I knew, with an inner knowing, that the Holy Spirit had completed a healing in my life. The stronghold of past abuse had broken. I sensed a new freedom from the gripping claws of guilt and shame. My past was still my past, I could not change that, but I was no longer chained to my vow. The hatred of church and men of God had lost its grip on my life. I was able to begin to forgive, with the help of the Holy Spirit. A new spiritual door had opened, and I wanted to run through it as fast as I could into the arms of a forgiving, kind, loving God.

I decided to enrol in Bible college.

A deep hunger stirred inside me, an urgent desire to learn about the things of God. Who was Jesus? My Catholic upbringing had painted a grim picture of an angry God, full of wrath and punishment, surrounding me with guilt and shame. Fire and brimstones would fall on my head for all the mistakes I had made. This born-again experience was real. A tangible God wanting to communicate with me, to heal me and love me. After three years of study, I qualified with an Advanced Diploma in Theology and Leadership and a deepening love for my God. He had saved me… literally. I was able to begin to plant new seeds of forgiveness, faith, hope and love.

My parents were concerned by my newfound faith, noting the changes in my persona and my improved moods a little strange. The anger in my heart towards my mother softened to an understanding, perhaps of her own personal brokenness. I felt she had her own deep dark secrets. Had she been abused as a child? I would never know. The changes in me were soon embraced as my parents' gained reassurance that I had not joined a cult. I became more accepting of others and more forgiving, including learning to forgive myself. The drug induced volatility blurred into the horizon behind me, I turned my back on its wicked plan to kill, steal and destroy my life.

Could I forgive Brother Dave and all the others who had wronged me? Betrayal, lies, rape, abuse by evil perpetrators, did they deserve my forgiveness? No, probably not, but God had forgiven me. He had forgiven me for all my wrongdoings and the intense hatred I had in my heart. If you hate someone you are a murderer, it says in 1 John 3:15. I had been full of hate. "Be kind and helpful to one another, tender-hearted, compassionate, understanding, forgiving one another readily and freely, just as God in Christ also forgave you," Ephesians 4:32 AMP. Forgiveness is a process that occurs one step at a time. Forgive others so that I can forgive you, God instructs as a principle in life. Holding on to unforgiveness is like taking poison and expecting the other person to die. Unforgiveness only hurts you. It eats away at your soul. But my painful memories lingered in the darkness, waiting to return. The scab of an old wound could be ripped off causing it to fester once more. A familiar weeping ooze, the stench of bitterness, a reminder of my humanity. The pain of wrongdoing would return to my memories, and I would have to forgive repeatedly. How many times do I have to forgive?

"Seventy times seven," Jesus said.

So many victims of childhood sexual abuse do not survive with suicide being their final escape. The secret shame pushing a tormented soul over the edge.

NEW BEGINNING

"It was your fault" - "You are not good enough." - "Why didn't you stop it?" - "You deserve to die." These voices badger the victim in a relentless torrent, flooding a mind already riddled with guilt.

To silence a child after a crime by the perpetrator, embeds a shame so deep, that it alters the essence of that child's being. Children are pliable souls, moulded by the environment they live in and the experiences they live through. The adults in their world have the responsibility to protect and provide, to nurture and to love. The abused who survive often limp through life with depression, anxiety, PTSD, prostitution, addictions, and relational dysfunction. A life stolen, taken off course, forever changed. This made me angry. How dare these evil monsters fulfil their lustful desires on innocent children? It was a righteous anger, strong and powerful. I discovered that my forgiveness did not excuse the crime; I was simply freeing myself from guilt and shame. I began planting seeds of forgiveness and they needed time to take root and grow.

*****

"Would you like to go out for dinner?" David asked.

It had been five years since walking through those large glass doors of the church and I was curious about this man. We met through a singles group at the church that organised picnics, bus trips and other social gatherings. This night was a movie night and at the last minute no one else could attend. Only David and I were available, so he suggested a dinner, just the two of us.

David was tall with strong broad shoulders, soft light brown hair neatly cut but not too short, and a handsome face featuring an angular jaw and high cheek bones. He had a quiet demeaner, that allowed an occasional quirky comment to come forth and surprise us all with his cheeky wit. I was interested enough to say,

"Yes, let's go to dinner."

The Thai restaurant stood tall on the waterfront of Manly Beach in Sydney, decorated with red and green ornate Asian dragons. The air had a balminess, moist and soft. The moon was in the new moon cycle illuminating a darkness of royal blue on the Pacific Ocean. White lapping waves could be seen in the distance as they gently greeted the sand, then retreated to the vast body of water where they came from. I first met David over a year ago, but this was the first time we had been alone.

David's parents were both Dutch, leaving Holland after World War II to settle in New Zealand where David was born. Our evening conversation took some twists and turns with David sharing some of his troubled childhood, but not too much to spoil a pleasant evening. Stories of trauma intrigued me, as I would inwardly compare my own. We gazed at each other in a new light, the 40 years of life he had lived did not show on his younger face. After a few hours of talking and eating, the beach was calling us to a moonlit walk. David's large hand reached for mine, as I released the buckle of my sandals to allow my bare feet to feel the soft cool sand. He steadied me until both sandals were unbuckled, his hand wrapped in mine for the entire walk. We strolled along the long sandy shore, laughing at silly stories we took turns sharing. A sizable cluster of rocks offered an opportunity to pause - we sat taking a moment to rest in the stillness. David shuffled closer, pulling me gently into an embrace, my body melted, and we began to kiss. This new intimacy felt foreign; it had been over five years since I had kissed a man.

Six months later David and I were married. It was a dream wedding in the church, then a spectacular reception on the lawn at my parents' Hunters Hill waterfront home. My gown was white, a simple well-fitting style flattering my slender figure. The veil was short, flowing over my shoulders. I decided not to have a fine layer over my face, traditionally allowing the

NEW BEGINNING

groom to reveal his bride at the climactic moment of, "You can kiss the bride." I was sure David would be so nervous he would fluster and make a mess of it. Over seventy guests enjoyed the hot January evening before the newlyweds departed the shore in my brother Matthew's cruiser, sailing up my much-loved Lane Cove River.

Getting consistent employment proved to be a problem for David, causing tensions once we were settled in our new matrimonial home. David's frustrations were evident, his hidden source of numbing increasing. We both enjoyed sharing a bottle of wine with a meal, but I had no idea that drug use was his 'secret thing'. After an argument, David would leave the house and not return for weeks. Only a few months into our marriage and a new kind of rejection was tearing at my heart. Where had my husband gone? I had married a man with his own secrets, his own ugly demons. His childhood memories of a broken home, separation from his siblings and a violent father brewed frustrating anger.

Keeping secrets was easy for me. I had been well trained my whole life harvesting silence, so this new secret would be locked away with all the others I had in my secrets box. No one needed to know what was going on behind closed doors. In the first year of marriage, I became pregnant with a much-wanted baby. This was my new life. Marriage was "until death do, we part."

The police arrived at the front door of our West Ryde home. The house belonged to my late grandmother on my mother's side. Mum had inherited it and allowed David and me to make it our first home.

"There has been a report of suspected domestic violence," the police officer's voice boomed deep.

The two constables stood tall taking up all the space in the front doorway. They had received a call from a concerned neighbour. Red marks on my arms were apparent, with older bruises hidden behind my pyjamas. The meek look on my tortured face gave them the answer they were expecting, they didn't need to hear me speak. This look was familiar, a look they had seen many times before, a broken victim.

"Come with us," they barked a demand, gesturing David to follow them to the police car waiting in the driveway, red lights flashing.

Humiliation triggered me into dismay. The shame of my past rushing like a whirlwind to the surface, a shame that had not left me. I had been healed of many aspects of the abuse through my counselling sessions, but shame ran deep, its tentacles twisted around my soul.

"What about the neighbours? What will they think?" my mother's concerned voice was yelling inside my head.

I watched as the police car drove down the street, taking a right-hand turn then disappearing. Sitting on the bedroom floor I held my growing belly, the baby kicking slightly against my hand. I had to survive for her.

Hannah was born during the opening ceremony of the Sydney Olympic Games. The TV above my hospital bed was belting out the celebrations. Immediately after the opening ceremony the swimming races began with the 4x100 men's relay, an anticipated Australian win. I was in the middle of a contraction when the dutchman, Pieter van den Hoogenband took the lead in the final lap of the swim. The Australian, Michael Klim had done a sterling job on his leg, but now the win was in question. All eyes were on the TV, including David's and my obstetrician's.

"I'm having a baby," I yelled, getting no one's attention.

The Dutchman won by a hundredth of a second. I had a baby girl to 100,000 screaming people at the Sydney Olympic Stadium and two screaming men at my bedside. I wondered if David was more excited about seeing the country of his heritage win a swimming race than me giving birth to our first child.

NEW BEGINNING

Hannah brought incredible joy into my world, my heart exploding with an indescribable love. 'Unconditional love' was a term I had heard of but now it was my reality. I examined every detail of her body in total awe, a wonder that I never dreamed could exist. Her tiny hands, her curious looks, her total interest in the new world that she now belonged to. I could not believe that I was her mother.

Hannah's determination and inner strength were immediately evident. Our first family outing was to the Sydney Olympic Games Closing Ceremony. Hannah, just two weeks old, tucked tightly under my shirt, suckled contently on my breast. The world was celebrating great sporting achievements while I was celebrating a new life. I adored my precious gift from God.

The preparations for Hannah's first birthday were in place. A group of five other mothers and their babies were invited to meet in a nearby park for cake. These were mothers that the local baby health clinic had assigned as a group, all of us giving birth around the same time. This formulated group was intended to offer support, sharing advice and tips as first-time mums. The cake was ready to be iced and the Telly Tubbies offered a necessary distraction. Hannah's little eyes glued to the TV, while the meaningless babyish babbling captured every ounce of her attention.

The programme was interrupted. A horrific image commanded my observation. A news reporter's voice trembled with a fear I had never heard before. He was crying, shaking, and speaking all at the same time. The World Trade Centre in New York City, had collapsed, its Twin Towers were struck by two hijacked aeroplanes, the reporter informed. The deadly devastation was too large to grasp. The segway from the sweet sounds of the Telly Tubbies, to screams of horror sent shock waves through my body. It was too unbelievable to believe. Mass destruction with immense loss of life. Was Kyle, ok? He worked in finance in New York City. Was he in one of those buildings? A traumatic memory had been triggered, racing to the surface to sting once again. Those days on the game fishing boat where we had met, and my pilgrimage to America in search of his love were to no avail. A man who had used me and discarded me. Why was I concerned about his wellbeing? My heart ached for this hidden secret.

I turned off the TV.

In my third year of marriage, I was blessed with a second daughter, a sister for Hannah. Grace's sweetness lit up the room, her face wide with a beaming smile. She was an easy baby, eating and sleeping, rarely crying. The unconditional love I had for Hannah only grew deeper with a second child, my heart exploding with an uncontainable love. I thought of Joshua, the secret older brother I could never tell them about. How could they ever understand me taking the life of their brother.

I was grateful for the mothercraft skills I had learnt at the Tresillian hospital; I was able to put both my daughters into manageable routines. I coped day by day.

My mother had been an only child, and I often wondered if this exacerbated her narcissism. Motherhood forces you to reflect on your own upbringing. One of my first memories was my mother leaving me crying in my cot. Dad would sneak in and pick me up. Was this really a first memory, or a memory of a story Dad used to share with me over and over? He was my rescuer, saving me from the terror of being left alone.

I could not tell my father any of my secrets. I could not bear the look of sorrow and disappointment on his face. I wanted that kind smile to always be there, it was my safety net. He would never know my pain, knowing it would make it his pain, a pain he didn't deserve. I remained alone, counting my secrets.

I was to learn that violence has a cycle. There is a build-up period, an escalation before the explosion, the explosion happens and then followed by the honeymoon phase. The build-up period then starts all over again. The honeymoon phase is delightful. This is when David would show remorse and beg for forgiveness. He would promise to come back to church, stop the alcohol and drugs, and unstack the dishwasher. I would melt into forgiveness, believing every word.

The Women's Refuge was a haven. A safe house, a sanctuary for women experiencing domestic violence. On one of the police visits to our house, a female police officer had handed me a card. There was no address, just a help line phone number. The location was withheld, only to be given discreetly to protect the women and their children from their abusers. I began to attend a course, 'The Cycle of Violence'. Both shock and relief took hold as I discovered the truth of my existence. I was trapped in a cycle.

The violence continued. The lengths of the cycles were inconsistent to ensure you always walked on eggshells. An abuser likes to keep his victim to himself, we therefore stayed home most evenings. I would venture out in the day to take the children to the beach where they enjoyed building sandcastles and frolicking in the waves. David and I had moved into a townhouse on the Northern Beaches of Sydney. An idyllic, peaceful place to bring up a family, a direct contrast to my inside world of conflict. AVO's (Apprehended Violence Orders) were put in place by the police to try and curb David's temper. He was ordered to attend an Anger Management course, an eight-week course to try and educate abusers. Nothing changed.

It was a typical evening at home. Hannah was in the highchair making a wonderful mess forcing clumps of spaghetti bolognaise into her mouth. She managed to get the sticky red sauce in her hair, all over her face and on the kitchen floor. It was not long after her second birthday, yet she still preferred to eat with her hands rather than use a spoon. Grace was happily bouncing in her bouncer, a crocheted seat held by wire, designed to bounce when a baby jiggled. A great invention to pacify a baby.

David descended the stairs from the upstairs bedroom carrying a suitcase. It was red and black, a stranger to me. Our only suitcase was brown and was stored on the rafters in the garage. His descent was slow and measured, my eyes fixed on the suitcase in wonder.

"I'm leaving," he announced in a gruff voice, a tone encased in exhaustion.

David had left many times before but this time I knew it was permanent. There had been no discussion, he was simply leaving.

The door closed behind him leaving a silence. A wave of peace moved through the room, both children unaware of the magnitude of the moment. I wiped some sauce from the corner of Hannah's mouth, scooped up some spaghetti into a spoon and handed it to her.

Divorce was not in my life plan. I was to be married forever. My parents were married and had stayed married and so must I. What would the neighbours think? Would the doctor's wives snigger behind their hands while gossiping at a game of Bridge? I felt ashamed, a complete failure.

My parents became aware of one of my secrets, a secret life hidden in domestic violence. Shame turned into depression as rejection and brokenness pierced my heart. The reality that my children would be victims of a broken home hit hard. This was an infliction they did not choose. My townhouse became my woodpile. A place to hide from the world. For three weeks I sat and stared at the walls hoping they would change.

Chapter 30
A Single Mum

Over time, I began to pick up the pieces. In the same way I had learnt to block out the past with Brother Dave, and the other abusers, so I changed my environment. I packed up the townhouse and moved. New neighbours, new streets, new local shops, new friends, new thoughts, allowing me to be re-created. No one in my new world needed to know anything. I was just, 'a single mum'. Me, and my two girls, starting all over again.

The news of my failed marriage delivered a deep sadness, like an ominous cloud that rested on Dad's shoulders. He was angry but sadder at what had happened to his precious daughter. He had tried to warn me, aware of David's inner troubles, but I had not heard his warning or chosen not to hear it.

Parents often see into situations in which their children are blinded. An instinct, an intuition, unexplainable but so right.

Imagine if Dad knew about Brother Dave, Mr Blackman, Andre, Bobby Dazzler, Joe, Damien, Kyle, the list goes on. Why did I attract so much predatory abuse?

A person who, at an early age, experiences abuse can develop a connection between abuse and the abuser. A 'trauma bond' is formed. This is where a person forms a deep emotional attachment to their abuser. An abused person can develop sympathy or affection for the abuser. Stockholm syndrome is a specific type of trauma bond. This refers to someone who is captive, developing positive feelings for their captors. Brother Dave, through his grooming, developed a relationship with me. A trauma bond of love. As most victims of childhood sexual abuse know their abuser and often love their abuser, this connection creates confusion. A future attraction to abusers can be rooted into the subconscious. The person searching for love finds more abuse. This strange association to abuse becomes a familiar place to attach. More dysfunctional, co-dependent relationships become the norm, destined to fail. There is a 'familiar spirit', an evil presence disguised as an 'angel of light' luring the person through trickery into another abusive situation. My vulnerability was noticeable, and I was therefore targeted.

Dad's way of helping me was financial. It brought joy to his saddened heart to give me money, which I accepted with great need and appreciation. This enabled me to be a 'stay at home mum'. I delighted in motherhood, filling my days with trips to the beach, watching my girls play in the sand for hours. Sitting in the shade of the towering pine trees, I would spread the picnic rug and open a large wicker picnic basket with a red and black tartan lining, bursting with endless goodies I had thoughtfully packed for the days outing. Healthy snacks in individual Tupperware containers, celery and hummus, fruit salad of fresh seasonal fruits cut into bite size pieces, peanut butter and vegemite sandwiches cut into quarters and some Tiny Teddies, a favourite biscuit for a treat. Cooled bottled water would be wrapped snugly in a cooler bag, and the girls Sippy cups always topped up to keep them hydrated in the hot sun. Sometimes another Mum would join me, usually one from the Baby Health Clinic mothers' group who also didn't have to work.

The relationship with my mother continued to improve as I walked through motherhood. She had loosened the claw of control, now finally realising she was losing the battle. A child grows into an adult, eventually flying from the nest. My mother's grip held tight as long as she could, but in my motherhood, she began to let go. After giving birth to two children, my physical appearance changed, resulting in excess fat around my middle, those hard to lose extra kilos. I was tired, struggling to exercise and wore no makeup. Mum's obsession with my appearance had lessened but she would make a last-ditch effort to influence me.

"Are you wearing lipstick? You look better with lipstick," she would suggest handing me her bright red lipstick.

"Eat more salads, Sarah."

Five years passed quickly; it was time for Hannah to start school. Memories of my first day of school haunted me, as I remembered back to being the appointed interpreter for my brother, in a role I had not chosen. My primary school memories of marching around the school yard, chasing boys, threats of being caned, all came out of my locked-up mind. I couldn't find any lovely memories of early school life, but I knew Hannah would survive. Her strength of character was a force to be reckoned with. She had a tenacity I wished I had known at her young age.

Grace soon followed her sister into the school yard. I had a sense of relief that Hannah was there to fight off any enemies that Grace may encounter.

A letter came home from the school principal, warning parents of a suspicious white Toyota Hilux van that had been seen circling the streets around the school. It had been reported to have slowed down, a man calling out to children walking home from school. The police had been informed, and we were to remind our children to be on high alert. The mothers at the school gate whispered concerns, trying not to alarm the children too much and to instil fear. A tin box filled with souring warm milk was more of a fear to me. Fortunately, the government had put a stop to this compulsory sickening practice.

The feared man was in a van, only with a perceived possibility of harm. My abuser had been waiting at the school gate, invited into my home, planning his attack, with no warnings and no restrictions in place.

"He was spotted again yesterday afternoon," one of the mother's spoke quietly.

"I'm not worried," I added at a normal volume.

"If he grabbed Hannah and dragged her into the van, he would drive around the block and then come back and quickly return her," I said with a chuckle.

"Hannah's forceful, determined personality would scare the man out of his skin," I added.

My outburst was not taken kindly, and my humour not appreciated. I left them to dwell in their concerns.

I had developed a necessary resilience. An ability to brush off pain and move on. With two young girls to raise, this was my only choice. Their world was broken, I had to keep it together. There was no time for tears, no time for pity, no time to talk. Continuing to bury the truth was the only mechanism for survival I had. The pattern of abuse in my life continued to ebb and flow, attempts at relationships with men destined to fail, and they did. My radar always found selfish narcissistic, abusive personalities.

But God was my anchor. Like a boat being tossed around in the wind and waves, I was firmly held in place by His love. Church life was a constant resting place. A place where I could return without judgement, dust off my mistakes, and begin again. God's mercies are new every day, for this I was truly thankful and in great need of.

A SINGLE MUM

Hannah and Grace continued to grow into their teen years. Their struggles often mirroring mine, as they navigated the experiences in their worlds. I was operating out of my woundedness, a mother terrified that her children would find the suffering she had encountered. I was overprotective at times, filled with fear whenever they were out of my sight. The bad relationships I kept choosing had a negative impact on them, but I was too distorted and damaged in my views to see it. Despite all the turbulence, Hannah grew strong and resilient. A determined beautiful young woman taking on all that the world had to offer. Grace remained sweet, growing in beauty both inside and out. Emotional scars are inevitable from living in a broken family, yet both my girls remain strong and courageous.

Chapter 31

The Royal Commission

On 12th November 2012, the Prime Minister at that time was Julia Gillard and she announced a national investigation into institutional responses to child sexual abuse. She stated,

"The allegations that have come to light recently about child sexual abuse have been heartbreaking. These are insidious, evil acts to which no child should be subject. The individuals concerned deserve the most thorough of investigations into the wrongs that have been committed against them. They deserve to have their voices heard and their claims investigated. I believe a Royal Commission is the best way to do this." (2)

The Royal Commission into Institutional Responses to Child Sexual Abuse was a five-year enquiry from 2013 to 2017. The offices handled 42,041 calls, 25,846 letters and emails were received, 8,013 private sessions were held with the commissioners, and there were 2,575 referrals to authorities, including police.

The findings in the 'Final Report Summary', showed that children who were abused were predominately male at 64.3%, while females were 35.4%. The definition of 'Child Sexual Abuse' in the report reads:

THE ROYAL COMMISSION

"Any act, which exposes a child to, or involves a child in, sexual processes beyond his or her understanding or contrary to accepted community standards. Sexually abusive behaviours can include the fondling of genitals, masturbation, oral sex, vaginal or anal penetration by a penis, finger, or any other object, fondling of breasts, voyeurism, exhibitionism, and exposing the child to or involving the child in pornography. It includes child grooming, which refers to actions deliberately undertaken with the aim of befriending and establishing an emotional connection with a child, to lower the child's inhibitions in preparation for sexual activity with the child."

The findings revealed that the average age for male children who were sexually abused began at 10.8 years old where for girls it began at 9.7 years old. My grooming began at eight years old. I sat below the average. Men were the predominant abusers at 93.8%. Looking into all the religious institutions, the Catholic Church led the way in leaps and bounds at 61.4%. (3)

A statement taken from one of the victims in the report sums it up:

> *As a victim, I can tell you the memories, sense of guilt, shame, and anger, live with you every day. It destroys your faith in people, your will to achieve, to love, and one's ability to cope with normal everyday living.* (4)

The impact of child sexual abuse most evident in the private sessions and public hearings was around mental health - 94.9 % of individuals who had been victims of a sexual crime had displayed a range of psychological and behavioural reactions, including, depression, anxiety, and post-traumatic stress disorder (PTSD). Nightmares and sleeping difficulties, and emotional issues such as feelings of shame, guilt and low self-esteem were also common.

Victims reported having difficulties with trust and intimacy, lack of confidence with parenting, and relationship problems. Education and economic impacts were also frequently raised, as was addiction to alcohol and drugs to deal with the ongoing trauma.

Throughout the inquiry many survivors concluded that this ongoing trauma was a result of the institutions failing to respond appropriately to child sexual abuse. Some institutions responded by punishing and silencing victims, which caused further damage, it was reported.

Suicide attempts were reported at 16.4%, with one in five of the victims at the private sessions stating they had experienced suicidal thoughts. This number only represents the proportion of people who were selected and there were thousands more not at the hearings. Many victims were not able to tell their story as their suicide attempts were successful. They lie in their graves, their secrets buried deep.

The Australian Government put in place The National Redress Scheme running for 10 years from July 1st, 2018, until June 30th, 2027, where some victims will be offered compensation from $10,000 to $150,000 with the average payout $49,000. To have your life ruined then to be given less than one year's average annual wage, only adds to the trauma a victim has already endured. Taking this path precludes victims from ever pursuing their cases legally against the institution. Victims face the choice of either engaging in the legal process or signing their rights away for substantially lower NRS payments or not coming forward at all. This is how the law in Australia works. This is the system.

* * * * *

Two years after Ms Gillard's announcement of a national investigation into institutional responses to child sexual abuse, I sat snuggled under a faux fur green blanket watching the 6 o'clock news. It was a cold wet evening, a hot water bottle on my lap, I delighted in its radiating warmth.

THE ROYAL COMMISSION

The six o'clock news was turned on religiously in my house. I wondered why I subjected myself to such negativity. Someone died, global disasters, awful weather coming, fraud blah blah. A glass of wine and a bag of potato chips at hand, completing my evening ritual.

The news went to a break. A spokesperson made an announcement,

"There will be a Royal Commission into Institutional Child Sexual Abuse. For all information, please contact the number on your screen. Applications are now open."

Choking on a chip I gasped. Did I hear that correctly?

My phone instantly rang.

"Did you hear that? On the TV, a Royal Commission! There's going to be an investigation into those sick criminals," my friend Jean shouted down the phone in a voice at such speed I could hardly keep up with her words.

"Yes, I did," I replied.

"You MUST contact them," she insisted.

"This is your chance to tell your story. Ha, they tried to shut you up, now is your chance to expose them."

I had broken my silence and told Jean about the abuse shortly after my 20th birthday. It was an evening of copious amounts of red wine, and I didn't remember telling her when she brought it up the next day. Brother Dave had instructed me not to think about the abuse until I was 20, the resurfacing of the foul memory needed a lot of alcohol to push it back down.

I shuddered. Did I want to tell my story after all this time to a commissioner? A deep, familiar shame made me tilt my head to the floor, solemn and heavy. "Childhood sexual abuse," were words I could never say. They felt dirty on my lips. I could envisage the disgust in the eyes of people, looking at a filthy, damaged soul, only to pity and walk in the other direction.

"I don't think so, Jean," I replied.

As the days passed, the announcement seemed to follow me. I'd hear it on the radio, see it plastered on billboards, while the TV repeated a constant reminder to call the number on the screen. Did I want to relive the trauma by listening to words spilling from my mouth to strangers who may judge my character, not believe me, blame me for being too pretty, or shame me for not telling him to stop? The answer was "no," so I decided not to call the number.

A few weeks ticked past; the phone rang.

"The submissions to the Royal Commission are closing this week," Jean gently informed. "You really should call Sarah. This is an opportunity you should not let slip past. I love you. Just do it!"

Another frantic school morning, uniforms on, the one lost school shoe found, lunches in the bags, homework book packed, excursion note signed, kiss on the cheek, out the door! My cold cup of coffee sat on the bench waiting to be put in the microwave. Already exhausted and it was only 9am. Sitting in front of my computer I expelled a spontaneous sigh. I started a part time job working from home. For two days a week I would make cold calls. They are called cold calls for a reason; they make you feel cold. I reached for my green blanket, arranging it carefully on my lap, making sure there were no gaps around my legs. The list was long, name after name, alphabetically displayed on the excel spread sheet. Pausing to take a sip of my coffee, Jean's words entered my mind.

"This is an opportunity you should not let slip past. I love you. Just do it!"

I looked down at the Nike gym top I was wearing and began to giggle. The company's motto of 'Just do it' was an invisible elbow digging into my ribs. I always wore my gym clothes when I worked from home. Not that I was going to the gym, but active wear seemed to be the standard working from home uniform. No one could see me in my home office, so comfort was important, and I was 'actively' making calls.

THE ROYAL COMMISSION

Tapping the keys on my computer I clicked into the Google search,

"The Royal Commission into Institutional Responses to Child Sexual Abuse," the number to call was bold in large font.

This Royal Commission kept tugging on my heart. I could not allow the truth to be eternally hidden, not for my sake, but for the sake of my children and the generations to come.

I pressed the numbers hard into my mobile phone. My heart began to beat so fast I thought I was having a panic attack. Waves of heat flushed my face as I fought the urge to vomit up my coffee. I pressed 'END'.

Shaking profusely, I began to breathe. In 2,3,4 exhale 2,3,4, again and again. Controlled breathing was a tool I had learnt at the Women's Refuge. This was helpful when the panic attacks attacked you, waiting in ambush, always a surprise.

The following day, the same routine, except the one lost shoe wasn't found. Hannah went to school in her sports shoes, holding a permission note as she ran out the door. The microwave beeped its three long beeps, indicating my coffee was hot again.

Positioned in front of my computer I picked up my mobile phone and dialled.

"Hello, you are speaking to Steven. Thank you for calling the Royal Commission hotline. Are you a survivor or are you calling for someone else?" a kind gentle male voice asked.

A "survivor," he had said. This was the first time I had heard this term. Was I a survivor? I always had referred to myself as a 'Victim' with a capital V. Steven sounded quite young. I pictured a man in his early thirties, still struggling to grow facial hair.

"It's me," I responded quietly.

"I want to acknowledge your bravery and great courage for making this call today. May I take your name?" Steven quickly replied.

"My name is Sarah."

Steven continued to make me feel at ease and I warmed to him immediately. He was certainly the right person for this role, carefully selected and well trained. He asked me for a brief overview of what happened, when and by whom. Taking a deep breath while pinching my thigh as hard as I could, I briefly shared the facts in a matter-of-fact way.

"I want to thank you again Sarah for speaking with me today. You will be contacted should you be selected to speak before the commissioner. Goodbye."

Selected? I needed to be selected? What did he mean? Was my abuse bad enough to use up the Commissioner's valuable time? Was it to be put on a scale and weighed? Was I worthy? A sense of regret washed over me.

The following week the call came.

"Hello, Sarah. How are you? I hope you are well today. We would like to invite you to come before the Commissioner on the 9th September at 2:15pm."

Steven's voice had a gentle melodious tone, a syrupy sweetness of kindness. He must make these calls all day, yet he made me feel like I was the only one. I was important. I had been invited. I was to be one of the 8,013 who fronted the Commissioner for a private session.

Unexpected emotions bubbled up on the inside of me, a blend of excitement and dread.

It was a workday, so I had my usual active wear adorned. I closed my laptop, jumped in my car, and headed to the gym. My mind was swirling so fast, I knew that it would be impossible to make any work calls. Sweat was dripping off me as I entered the gym. I had not even started a workout yet. "9th September, 9th September, 9th September," was on loop in my head. A date I had to make sure I remembered.

I headed straight to the dumb bells. Six kilos in each hand I began to pump them high above my head until the pain in my muscles screamed at me. I kept going, counting the numbers out loud between groans. I only stopped when the lactic acid flooded my veins with a tingling stab, causing the muscles to fail. The pain was refreshing. A relief from the emotional pain that was agonising. Somehow by increasing physical pain, the emotional pain diminishes. I wondered if this was how victims who chose to self-harm would feel, the cutting into their flesh, a sharp blade piercing the skin, would this offer the same relief?

A few weeks before my allocated date, I received a call from Monique.

"Hello Sarah," she said gently in a high-pitched voice.

"We are so sorry for what happened to you. I will be your support person to help you prepare to meet with the Commissioner. Do you have any questions?"

I had 40 years of questions.

"No," I lied, I didn't know where to start.

Monique sounded compassionate and in control. I immediately connected with her.

"I am here for you Sarah," she said.

"I will walk you through the process on the day. You can prepare your story beforehand by writing it down and reading it if this will be easier for you."

Ok, there are options, I thought thankfully. This would be the first time I would share my story of abuse in front of significant people. Authority figures had let me down in the past, treating me like I didn't matter, that I was a liar. The approaching date was equally daunting and terrifying.

Monique's soothing voice added reassurance, telling me the process ahead was for me. It was my opportunity to tell my story, break the silence - I would finally have a voice.

That afternoon on the ferry as a brave 11-year-old girl, sharing my secret with Rebecca was still fresh in my memory. Then came the silencing. The Marist Fathers, Brother Dave, and the nuns, all knew the truth but remained silent. My voice had been stolen.

An extensive email arrived addressed from the Private Sessions Coordinator of The Royal Commission into Institutional Responses to Child Sexual Abuse – SENSITIVE.

The email outlined the detailed instructions for my private session: time of arrival, where to meet Monique, what to bring, who would be present and a map showing transport and parking details. There were two attached documents: Frequently Asked Questions and A Guide to Telling My Story.

Five white pages with blue inked handwriting sat on my desk. I had painstakingly written these words over and over, screwing up the pages and starting again. They carried a weight of importance, to present my distant memories in a factual and truthful way. Succinct recollections of disgusting violations towards an innocent unsuspecting child, matter of fact, no fabrications.

The day arrived surprising me as I awoke without emotion, numb and feelingless. The air was still and quiet. The kookaburras had forgotten to laugh; no birds were singing. I sat momentarily on the side of my bed, staring at the clock as the minute hand clicked forward. I was paralysed. Today I was to meet the Commissioner. I slapped my face hard enough to sting, awakening myself to the reality of the day ahead. Fear took a grip, and a tightening in my chest made me reach for my asthma inhaler.

There was no place for emotions. To let them out would be a disaster. Flood gates needed to be shut tight. To cry would make them win, or so I believed, even though none of the perpetrators would be present. I needed to remain in control, to keep dignified, and put on a shield of strength. No one could see my brokenness.

THE ROYAL COMMISSION

The drive into Sydney's CBD took longer than usual. The rows of shiny metal cars ahead were blocking my passage. The traffic was jammed tight. It was as though they wanted to stop me in my tracks, keep me quiet. The blue inked words sat next to me on the passenger's seat, my eyes rolled over and over them.

Monique greeted me as I arrived, showing no concern that I was 20 minutes later than our agreed meeting time. She was smiling ear to ear, her face soft and inviting. I guessed she would be in her early forties, her European skin adding a youthful glow.

This was the first time I was going to meet her in person and her sweet disposition was more radiant than on the phone. The foyer was tiled in white, with the blaring hanging lights making me reach for my sunglasses. A large marble counter stretched for four metres with five immaculately dressed staff standing positioned ready to answer questions.

Monique ushered me towards the lifts chatting happily as if she was about to take me to a delicious lunch at a rooftop revolving restaurant. I was swept up in her sparkling energy, forgetting the reason why I was there.

"Would you like a cup of tea?" she asked when we reached the 17th floor.

"Yes please," I replied.

A hot cup of English breakfast tea arrived with a small heart shaped shortbread cookie. I sipped and munched while she talked about her new cute puppy. It had not even entered my mind to eat breakfast earlier. Her happy banter was a perfect distraction, I listened intently.

Thirty minutes had passed when my name was called.

"It's time, Sarah. Don't worry, I will stay with you in case you need me," Monique promised.

I was flooded with relief as I followed her into the conference room. Three people were seated behind a large desk, formally waiting, their unspoken importance almost tangible. Two empty seats, in royal blue fabric were placed on the other side of the desk facing my attentive audience.

A grey-haired middle-aged man began the introductions.

"I'm Bob Atkinson, the Commissioner for this inquiry. Thank you so much for coming today. I would like to acknowledge your bravery for speaking up." His voice was deep and gruff yet also kind like a granddad's might be. I never knew either of my grandfathers, both dying before I was born. Yet if I had to choose a man to be my grandfather, this man would be the one.

A few more formalities about my name, address, date of birth and it was time to share. A cold chill sent goose bumps all over my body even though the room wasn't cold. I rubbed my hands furiously on my lap hidden from everyone's view.

"Would you like a glass of water?" a woman opposite me asked, her eyes shielded with thick dark rimmed glasses.

"Yes please," I replied gratefully.

She carefully poured water from a stainless-steel pitcher into a glass and slid it across the desk into my reach. My dry mouth was screaming for the much needed liquid. I took a sip while grappling for my papers.

A growing anticipation on the faces of the three in front of me indicated that I was to begin.

I hesitated, looking sideways at Monique.

"Go ahead Sarah," she gestured with a nod.

I began to read. The words flowed from the page, a little girl's story of abuse, the silencing, the shame, the guilt, the disgust, the addictions, the torment, the ongoing trauma. My audience sat captivated.

I stopped, a sudden stabbing pain piercing my chest. It was as if my heart was in a vice crushing life out of me. The tears I was not to display were uncontrollably welling up in my eyes. The little girl had jumped off the pages and entered the room. She was sad, displaying a gut-wrenching sadness from a broken heart.

"Do you need to take a break?" the Commissioner asked with concern.

I looked to Monique for the answer. Her hand reached under the table, taking mine offering a gentle squeeze of reassurance.

"I'm ok," I said as I reached for a tissue from the box on the table.

Gathering myself, I found my place on the paper and continued. I concluded the hearing with an Impact Statement, outlining how the effects of the abuse and the wrong doings of those in authority had negatively impacted my life.

The Commissioner showed compassion as he listened, nodding slowly in agreement. He then asked a few clarifying questions to make sure he had all the details needed for the report. The three thanked me for coming, commented on my courage and strength, then dismissed me. Monique escorted me into a quiet room handing me a white card, a brochure, and a pre-prepared stamped addressed envelope. The brochure read:

'The Royal Commission into Institutional Responses to Child Sexual Abuse is making a book called Message to Australia. (5) The information said that the book would be made up of messages from people who attended The Royal Commission's private sessions. This book would be kept at the National Library of Australia for the public to view and to be preserved for future generations.' It concluded with gratitude and thanks.

"This is an opportunity for you to write to the public, to share your thoughts, if you would like to. It's totally up to you, Sarah," Monique suggested.

I wrote from my heart, filling every bit of space allocated to me in the white box. This was a historical moment, and I was grateful to finally find my voice. The harvesting, a gathering of all my silenced traumas, had finally ripened and was presented to a field of believing ears. My hidden anger had been soothed with the relief of being heard. The Commissioner was presented with many injustices; the thousands of children who were violated, then silenced. The perpetrators were often sent away, relocated only to continue to abuse others. Historical documents were destroyed - truths were hidden, souls were destroyed, lives were never to be the same.

Exhausted, I drove home. Proud of my bravery.

Another brochure sat in the bottom of my handbag, 'After Sharing Your Story'. The following day I dug it out and read:

'Speaking out can bring up many mixed feelings, relief, elation, disappointment, grief. Sometimes it can bring up strong emotions about the abuse you suffered, such as anger, distress, fear, and grief. Many people coming forward to tell their story also describe feeling lighter, relieved, heard, believed, and respected. You may feel proud of yourself that you were able to do this. A few days later you may feel flat, depressed, with a mix of strong feelings. You can expect this after such a significant step'.

It followed with some strategies that could be helpful - talking to a friend, being kind to yourself, exercise, writing, crying and support numbers to call.

I had so many feelings, a pendulum of highs and lows. I never called a support number, preferring to hide my feelings and soldier on. To toughen up and get on with life. I had two daughters and two ageing parents to care for.

* * * * *

In early 2015, my beloved father passed away. His frail body hanging onto life into his 90th year. His frequent phone calls would announce,

"Just a friendly call from Dad," leaving a sweet melody on my answer machine. He always showed genuine joy when he heard my voice.

"How are you sweetheart? I don't know how you manage so well on your own. Is there anything you need from me?" he would ask.

His last week was spent at Royal North Shore Hospital. Tests had shown his kidneys were failing, his body was shutting down. The hospital where I had begun a nursing career now seemed foreign as I was on the other side of the desk. I was a desperate relative, watching her father die. My only sibling was away at Nelson's Bay on a holiday with his family, and I begged him to drive the three hours to come home and help me. Matthew refused, not believing that Dad was in fact on his death bed. Mum was so distraught that she could not take any phone calls or make any lucid decisions. She would visit the hospital for one hour only, her hair perfectly manicured into a higher than high tease, towering well above her petite 83-year-old frame. Eyelids flashed of blue powder, lips of vivid red darker than cherries, she sat with a blank stare not hearing a word any doctor tried to say. The medical staff soon realised that I needed to be her advocate, taking over the role of 'family member in charge', a position I did not want. When the hourly visit exhausted her, Mum required to be driven home.

"Is your father going to be alright?" she would ask. "He looks terrible." She was in complete denial of his failing body.

I knew that Mum losing Dad was going to be an immense shock. He had always taken care of her, provided for her, paid all the bills, managed all the necessary requirements to run a large family home. Mum's role was to shop, clean the house, cook average meals, and look glamorous.

I positioned her in front of the mirror at her dressing table, so she could begin to comb out her hair. It was then to be set in rollers in preparation to be brutally teased again the following morning. I would rush back to Dad's bedside to hold his hand and read scriptures from the Bible. He seemed to find comfort in my voice as I spoke of the angels in heaven and God's endless grace.

"We took your father for some scans, and he refused," the doctor informed me.

Dad could be stubborn if he wanted to be - these intrusive tests he did not want to endure.

Nights were long and torturous. I had never been with a dying person before and had no idea what was happening. The staff left me and Dad alone in a room way down the end of the corridor. A large lime green plastic reclining chair was positioned as close as possible to Dad's bed. I would lie awake all night listening to his moans and gasps for air.

I pressed the button, 'Call Nurse', desperate for help.

"He is choking, he can't breathe," I cried tears of panic.

"I'll get an injection to dry up the secretions," she said before leaving us alone again.

I hated being alone with Dad. I felt so helpless and useless. He would pull at my arm indicating for me to draw closer, words not forming in his crusty foul-smelling mouth. I silently heaved, before allowing myself to get so close that his warm breath brushed my cheek.

"I'm here Dad. I'm here," I said.

Dad was to be moved to Greenwich Hospital the following day; it was a palliative care hospital. The staff had tried to organise a transportation ambulance, but none were available. I was to spend my fifth sleepless night at Dad's side at Royal North Shore Hospital. I was beyond exhausted continuing with the pickups and drop offs for Mum's hourly visits that were now twice daily.

My brother arrived late that night at the hospital, carrying an angry frown at the sight of Dad's skeletal body, motionless on the bed. He had dropped his family home after completing his holiday and driven on to the hospital.

THE ROYAL COMMISSION

"The doctor told me you said to stop the blood transfusions!" he barked at me in a furious tone as if I was to blame for Dad's dying state.

"No, Matthew, the doctor said there was no point. I had to make all the decisions. You were not here. Mum is totally off with the fairies. I was stuck with making decisions I wanted you to help me make." I tried to justify myself knowing Matthew was taking no notice. I was to blame, and he was angry.

The transportation arrived early the following morning to my relief. I knew I could not survive another night with Dad's disturbing groans along with my inadequacies and exhaustion. I drove my car the 10 minutes to Greenwich Hospital, pinching my skin hard so as not to fall asleep at the wheel.

Dr Sarah was the admitting doctor; her angelic face took on a Mother Theresa glow as she greeted my half-conscious father with great respect.

"Hello, Dr Cook. I hear you are a wonderful doctor. My name is Sarah," the doctor said.

I saw Dad's eyes open momentarily as he looked up into her eyes. They were sparkling beams of light shining onto his pale-tired face.

Dr Sarah greeted Matthew and Mum as they arrived, both still panting from the rush to get to Dad's side. Mum's face was flushed crimson, and an asthma inhaler was held tight in her right hand ready for another puff. Matthew looked cool and calm yet concerned. He was not aware of the severity of Dad's condition - he was near death. I had tried to relay the gravity of Dad's condition days before, but he was too busy holidaying. Mum had a small transistor radio in her hand, Allan Jones was talking in a loud opinionated voice. This was her coping mechanism, blocking out the reality before her eyes. Matthew asked endless questions, all the questions I had already asked over the past week.

"Will he recover?" he asked, somehow not understanding that Dad was dying.

A sudden last gasp billowed stale air from Dad's lungs. I knew it was time.

"Go Dad," I shouted.

"Go and be with the angels. It's time to go, Dad. Don't worry about Mum, I will look after her," I promised.

I glanced towards Mum who seemed completely oblivious to what was happening, the radio pressed close to her ear.

His spirit was gone. An instant peace entered the room. No more moaning, no more gasping, just peace.

Dr Sarah moved forward, seeming surprised at Dad's sudden exit in the middle of her admission. I wondered if seeing her angelic smile and hearing her name, the name he loved so much, my name, Princess Sarah allowed him to let go and drift into heaven. I had seen the look in his eyes as he stared into hers, a look of acceptance, it was his time.

Dr Sarah confirmed the time of death on her paperwork, only moments after the time of admission.

Matthew and Mum left the room escorted by Dr Sarah; I chose to stay. Alone again with my much-adored father, a man I greatly admired, I looked intently into his face. His skin was soft, translucent, only a few lines showing any sign of age. He had kept a youthful appearance despite the hardships and strains of his ninety years of life. The still face before me had smiled a thousand smiles of unconditional love.

I placed my hand under his arm pit, savouring the last warmth of his cooling body. The chill of death rapidly lowering the generated heat of life. I stayed for some time not wanting to say a last goodbye. A tangible spiritual presence suddenly entered the room. I spontaneously leapt to my feet with euphoric energy and danced freely around the room laughing with unexplainable joy. I undeniably knew that Dad was now in heaven dancing with the angels.

THE ROYAL COMMISSION

A man entered the room,

"Have you had enough time? You can stay as long as you like," he said.

"No, I'm done," I replied, placing a gentle kiss on Dad's cool clammy cheek.

"Bye Dad, thank you for being the best Dad." I left the room.

I was glad my father never knew of Brother Dave's abuse, or any of my dark secrets. Knowing them would only cause him pain, unnecessary pain.

* * * * *

A formal thank you arrived in the mail. It was a card signed by two of the Commissioners from The Royal Commission, Bob Atkinson, and Peter McClellan.

"Thank you for sharing your story with the Royal Commission into Institutional Responses to Child Sexual Abuse. Your contribution by attending a private session is an important part of Australia bearing witness to the stories of survivors of institutional child sexual abuse. We acknowledge and value your courage in coming forward. Your story also assists the Royal Commission making recommendations to protect children, to improve laws, policies, and practices and to prevent and respond to child sexual abuse in institutions."

I held the textured cream card with royal blue indented font firmly on my heart. These words of acknowledgement meant so much to me. Men of position and power were valuing my courage and the importance of sharing my story. I had transitioned from a victim to a survivor. I found a new strength in this simple card, words of affirmation I would treasure forever. The harvest of silence had been broken by the courage I found to share my story.

Chapter 32

Seek and you shall find

In September 2020, I sat in deep reflection. The world had been locked down fearing a deadly virus. I had recently lost my job like so many others around me. Deep despair gripped the nation as people questioned their futures.

My large, grey corner desk displayed neat, labelled folders, with assorted pens standing like soldiers in a brown leather cup and a notebook at the ready. I always liked to have a pen and paper at hand to write my thoughts as they would often come and then suddenly disappear. Past trauma is known to impact memory, the mind becomes saturated and unable to retain information. My mind had been battered with trauma.

I would sit for hours at my desk, often staring blankly out the window at the deep green glossy leaves of the murraya hedge - it was well overdue for a prune. My gardener, also affected by lockdowns, was locked away behind closed doors. My mind would often drift visualising pictures and images carrying me to distant places. I pictured myself casting a stone into a smooth pond, bouncing across the surface of the water forming a moving pattern of beautiful ripples. My stone stopped and sank deep into the jet-black abyss. Sinking deeper and deeper. A black cloud entered the room. I needed to pray. Dark thoughts lurked around me wanting to steal my life, but God had a lifeline. I put on some soft worship music, a comforting peace quickly returning, shining light into the darkness.

Weeks passed. The continued lockdowns in Sydney cut me off from the world, allowing me way too much time alone to think. Grace, still living at home, was struggling with missing out on her Year 12 experiences. Locked in her room, attempting ZOOM call lessons that the teachers had thrown together in a poor attempt to educate. No school formal, no end of the year presentations, no celebration for completing the HSC and 13 years of school. Depression was rife among her friends during this dark time. Hannah worked in childcare as a private nanny and was therefore seen as an 'essential worker' and could continue in her job.

From out of nowhere, Brother Dave slipped into my mind like a slivering snake. Sharp fangs waiting to penetrate my isolated soul.

"Where was he? Was he still alive?" my mind questioned.

He had been sent away - never to face his crimes, even though the Commissioner knew his name. It was rumored that he was living in Japan where there are no extradition laws with Australia.

Why did he still have access to my subconscious mind? It was as if an enemy was waiting in the background to revisit, to remind me of the past. His visits were unexpected and unwanted.

I was like a deer standing at the edge of a dam ready to quench a deep longing thirst, unaware of the hidden enemy. As she stretched her long slender neck toward the cooling waters, a sudden sharp pain would engulf her body, sending violent shivers first from her neck to her heart, then throughout every cell. The enemy had attacked her from behind. She didn't see the ambush coming. Death was calling. In a matter of minutes, her limp body moistening from her own warm blood would soon become blackened, cold, dry and dead. The hidden enemy had come to kill, steal, and destroy.

I was shaking. I tried to steady my vibrating fingers as panic took a familiar hold. Panic attacks had claimed a part of my identity, sneaking up from behind, calling me by name. Fear followed me, lurking in the shadows, stealing my breath. A violated child lives with an ongoing, recurring trauma that is always present whether seen or not. A trauma that continues into adulthood. Triggers quickly transport you back to terror and pain. Flashbacks were also common. They would sometimes sneak up on me and side swipe me into that place where a memory becomes a reality once again. Dreams would turn into nightmares, sending me running back to the wood pile to hide, waking in a sweat.

"God, why am I still not free from this past trauma? Rescue me from my enemies," I cried.

Weekend getaways were medicine for me. One weekend I selected a stylish hotel with a riverside ambiance. The water continued to be a healing balm on my life, offering something soothing that I desired and needed to survive. I was now titled a 'survivor'. I was alive, I had therefore survived.

My hotel room was overlooking the pool where I planned to lie in the sun, turn off my mobile phone and read a magazine. Arriving at room 202, I needed both hands, with the help of my shoulder to push open the heavily weighted door. My small suitcase was on wheels, the one I liked to use as cabin luggage on overseas trips. It had faithfully been at my side for many years. I walked past the mini bar fridge, quickly opening it to see the selection of cold drinks and chocolates. A queen-sized bed, adorned with multiple cushions in deep apricots and luscious creams, dominated the middle of the room. The bedspread looked soft to touch, woven with golden velure stripes. I ran my hand over the velvety surface.

Suddenly, everything went dark. Not just a darkness as if the lights had been switched off, but a blackness deeper than charcoal. Fear gripped me, as I began shaking in a violent tremble. My hands immediately left the bed, reaching up over my head to cover my ears, protecting me from the dark silence. My chin tucked deep into my chest, forcing a folding of my body. My mind went blank as sheer terror was weighing down on my head.

The blackness halted time. I blacked out.

When I regained a semi-conscious state, I was trapped in what seemed to be a small box. With hard walls on each side, I lay in the fetal position not daring to move. I was in the hotel room wardrobe, with the door shut. Eventually, I pushed on the door, the light peeking through the crack a welcome relief from the inky terror. Slowly standing, dazed and giddy, I patted down my hair to tidy its mess in an automatic response.

A flashback had assaulted me, attacked out of nowhere, transporting me back to my childhood terror. I was suddenly back at the woodpile – hiding from 'him'.

Memories of Brother Dave sat with me at my office desk. Opening my laptop, I began to scroll my emails. The weekly update from my mother's nursing home was always marked 'Important'. My mother had deteriorated quickly after Dad's death. He was her rock, and she was lost without him. She had managed for five years in the big house on her own, my regular visits finding her sipping on brandy and milk, her way of self-soothing. Forgetting to eat, her body was shrinking by the day, it was a big concern for me. She was also becoming forgetful, perhaps from dementia or too much brandy. I made the difficult decision to find a nursing home, a five-star nursing home that would be to her liking. I had promised Dad I would take care of Mum; therefore, she would have to have the best.

Mum was furious when I first mentioned she needed help and wasn't managing at home. Stairs were a falls risk, and the stove had been left on by mistake on numerous occasions. Mum's cleaner took on an extra role as a carer, taking her shopping and to cafes to 'people-watch'. Claire loved Mum, and Mum loved Claire who quickly became her companion. But

Claire had concerns as well, noticing Mum's health deteriorating. A nursing home was the safe solution.

The group email from the nursing home informed all the relatives that the Covid 19 lockdown was to continue for another three weeks. I was devastated. My mother's joy was looking forward to my daily visits, usually to join her for an afternoon glass of wine. 'Happy hour' in the nursing home included entertainment, and cheese with biscuits and wine. The residents were given two glasses before the bottles were switched to non-alcoholic wine; they were none the wiser. I loved my visits delighting in getting to know the other residents and Mum's new friends.

The extended lockdown would mean that my mother's 90th birthday celebration could not go ahead. She was not permitted to leave the home, and no one was allowed to visit. A milestone would slip by her family and friends who were unable to give her a hug and congratulate her. I sat in despair.

The grey desk before me reflected the grey world I was now living in. People were isolated from loved ones, suffering loneliness, especially the elderly. This was for their protection from a virus we were told, but our elderly were dying from broken hearts.

Google had become my distraction. 'Marist Fathers Japan', I typed furiously into the search bar. My curiosity had been triggered. Would I be able to find him? I cast my net into a vast sea — the world wide web, hoping for a catch.

The Marist Mission Centre in Hunters Hill, where my mother dutifully volunteered, was linked to the Marist Fathers in Japan. Lionel Marsden, an Australian military chaplain and POW to the Japanese during WWII, decided to repay his captors with his faith in Jesus Christ. This began the Marist Japanese Mission. I remember Mum talking about the schools in Japan that the church was supporting through donations from the congregation. Her role included putting stamps on envelopes to send newsletters offering updates.

SEEK AND YOU SHALL FIND

An email address in Japan for the Marist Fathers glared at me. My hands were shaking slightly as I began.

Hello

I am trying to find my mother's long lost friend David Davenport who went to Japan in the mid-seventies. He was a Marist Brother at Hunters Hill Parish, and my mother is in a nursing home now and wanted to know if he is still alive.

Most of the family lost contact when he went to Japan, but Mum was in contact on the phone. Mum now has early dementia and can't try and contact him for herself, so I am trying to locate him on her behalf. She is now 89 years old, and David would be in his 70's I believe.

He may have come to your school to work. If you have any information on his life in Japan or how I can find out more, my Mum would be very grateful.

With thanks
Sal

I had adjusted the truth slightly using Mum as an excuse to hunt him down. I was now a self-appointed investigator, an Erin Brockovich. I had nobly been given the nickname Erin, after my hero Erin Brockovich. She took on a giant, strong and courageous and she won. A modern-day David, taking on the Goliaths of the day.

A single mother taking on a job as a legal researcher, Erin Brockovich uncovered that Pacific Gas and Electric, a huge company in the USA, had been poisoning the small town of Hinkley for over 30 years. People were dying and developing cancers, and it was only through Erin's tenacity that the company was exposed. In 1996, the utility giant was forced to pay out the largest direct-action lawsuit of its kind. The sum of $333 million was paid in damages to more than 600 Hinkley residents.

I loved Erin. I had taken on her persona when the nursing home tried to keep me out. Mum had fractured her hip and desperately needed me. I was on a mission. I found loopholes in the system, with medical letters and exemptions and I won many battles gaining entry.

I remembered many years ago, Mum mentioned that she had spoken to Brother Dave over the phone. I believe this is where the information came from regarding his 'being shipped' to Japan all those years ago.

I signed the email Sal as I did not want my identity known. A clever Erin move I thought. My real name may have triggered alarm bells, so I thought.

To my complete astonishment a reply came through within two hours. I sat and stared at the computer for the longest time. My head was up, my eyes were open, but I could no longer see. The screen began to blur. I was numb.

> *Dear Sal,*
>
> *Thank you for your mail.*
> *We would like to forward your email to the Brothers and Alumni association.*
> *Please confirm this is OK. It might be good to provide your full name and your mother's name.*
> *Good luck searching for David.*
>
> *Best regards,*
> *Yoko*

Focus slowly returned. I had been asked to reveal my mother's identity. I didn't think it would come to this. What had I done? I had opened a can of worms. What would Erin do?

Erin had a deep sense of justice. An innate knowing of right and wrong. I knew what had happened to me was wrong and I suddenly wanted justice. How can a crime be committed, on a child then be covered up? My email was the first bold step to find the man who had started the domino effect on my life. He had violated the sanctuary of my home to fulfill his lustful evil desires with no regard for my age or the effects his selfish acts would have on my future. I wanted to find him.

I replied gratefully, accepting the offer to forward my email. I included my mother's full name and corrected the 'typo', Sal to Sarah.

On October 13, 2020, an email arrived. This time from a librarian teacher from the International School in Kobe, Japan. It stated there was no record of David Davenport ever being at the Marist Father's Monastery in Kobe.

"What?" my brain screamed.

Maybe they were wrong but then I thought, did he ever really go?

My head was exploding with questions that threatened to drown my soul. All I could do was sit on the cold floorboards in my home office, knees to chest, head in hands sobbing, a gut-wrenching moan of disbelief. Over forty years had passed, yet that little girl inside me was still alive and suffering. The little girl who was never heard, never believed, never apologised to, never acknowledged, never counselled, never allowed to speak.

I continued my Google hunt, hoping for more clues. Website after website, I finally stumbled onto a story about a young boy who had been sexually abused by a Marist Priest, and he had won a compensation payout.

"*Wow,*" I thought with a satisfying smile.

Good on him. But no amount of money could ever compensate for a life that had been stolen. At the bottom of the article was a picture of a man with a kind face, Tony Tertullus, with the words written, *Abuse Law and Compensation Lawyers for Victims of Sexual Abuse.*

I immediately Googled the website, found a contact number, and gave him a call.

Tony's gentle soothing voice put me at ease. He listened intently and compassionately to my story and shared some traumas of his own childhood. We talked for some time as he explained the role of legal representation and commencing a civil lawsuit. This was all new to me as I had no idea that compensation was even possible.

"Will I get an apology?" I asked.

This was far more important to me than money. I wanted to be heard. I wanted an explanation as to why there was a cover up. I wanted an apology for the terrible consequences their decision had on my life.

"Did you go to the police?" Tony asked.

"No," I replied.

I was asked the same question at The Royal Commission and was told that a person could not be extradited from another country for this matter. I was also told an officer would contact me but that never happened, so I let it go.

"It's not too late Sarah," Tony offered.

"What… now? All this time later? Really do you think I should. How?" The questions were running off my tongue too fast.

A frantic hysteria came over me at the thought of speaking to the police. It was so long ago.

"All you need to do is go to your local police station and report it Sarah," Tony instructed.

We finished our conversation with Tony summarising the process and promising to email all the necessary information to commence a claim against the Marist Fathers Institution.

Mobile phone still in hand, I ran to my bedroom, threw on some jeans and a T-shirt, grabbed my handbag and drove to Manly police station. I wanted to act before I changed my mind. I had been given permission to report a historical crime. Maybe this time, I would find justice.

Manly police station is a two story, red brick building adjacent to the courthouse. As I walked through the towering sandstone arch, I pondered on all the criminals who had been brought to justice in this place since its establishment in 1863. But then I also wondered about all the ones who got away with it. What is justice? A validation presenting acceptable recognition of a victim while at the same time, the guilty is also recognised for the crime and punished. But proving guilt is not always possible. You are innocent until proven guilty the law states. There can be no reasonable doubt. How does an adult woman prove she was violated as a child more than 40 years ago? Was I wasting my time?

The waiting room at the police station was sparse. A row of red plastic chairs were all joined together, with large metal rods so that they could not be separated or easily stolen.

A woman sat behind a glass wall, reaching from floor to ceiling, beckoning me with a smile. "Can I help you?" she asked.

"Yes please. I am here to report a case of sexual abuse from a long time ago," I said.

I felt embarrassed as the words rolled off my tongue, and blood rushing, causing my face to blush. Was this embarrassment or shame? I questioned myself.

"Ok, are you reporting on behalf of someone else or yourself?" she asked.

"It's me," I said, feeling my heart racing even faster.

The woman smiled again.

"One moment please," she said as she disappeared through a side door.

I inhaled so deep that I thought I may be sucked into myself. I moved towards a noticeboard with a desperate hunger for distraction. A poster with a line of photos revealed faces of various ages and ethnicities. I looked closer to see if I recognised anyone. The word 'MISSING' was in large bold letters at the top. Where are all these people? How could they just go missing? Do people just drop off the face of the earth, or are they abducted for evil purposes?

My thoughts were interrupted as a beautiful blonde in her mid-thirties approached me. Her hair was tied up in a loose bun, soft yet professional.

"Hello, I am Detective Deborah Denis. I am a detective here that looks after Historical Crimes. You can call me Deb. Come with me please."

I was delighted my detective was a woman. She led me into a small interview room, a large window bringing a brightness to the space. Deb was very attentive, asking question after question while franticly writing my answers on a pad of paper.

"When did this happen? How old were you? Did you report it at the time? What is his name? How old was he at the time? I will be commencing a criminal case. It's not too late, Sarah," she reassured me.

I felt at ease with her as I sensed a genuine concern. Over an hour had passed and I was dismissed. An eight-page 'Statement of Witness' was signed and filed. Walking back to my car I spoke to myself with a sense of relief,

"Done."

A few weeks later, Deb called.

"Hello Sarah, I hope you are well. I need to inform you that I have been taken off your case as I am moving to another department," she informed me, a sadness evident in her voice. Disappointment flooded me.

SEEK AND YOU SHALL FIND

I was informed that my case was to be taken over by a male detective from Epping Station. This was closer to the crime and therefore was a more appropriate station to manage my investigation. I instantly disliked my newly appointed detective. He was dismissive and unrelatable.

Months passed and I heard nothing.

Eventually the Erin in me found the courage to call the station.

"I would like a replacement detective. I need a female please," I asked, hoping for understanding.

Michelle 'Mich' was allocated to me. She was calm and thorough, a perfect fit to hunt down a criminal.

Time continued to pass as Mich dug deep.

She obtained statements from Jean, Victoria, Emily, Rebecca, and my brother Matthew. My police statement detailed the events that took place during my childhood and the visits from the priests.

I had been allocated a 'solicitor' from Tertullus Lawyers. Kevin started the process of gathering information. He asked for the reports from the Royal Commission, including the transcript of my 'private session' with the Commissioner. I was able to obtain a recording. Listening to myself as I spoke to the Commissioner brought back the trauma of that day. The quivering in my voice resonated with both terror and courage. I listened intently as if it was someone else speaking, someone I knew from the past sharing their story. A familiar friend who had been through a difficult time, but not me.

He also asked for a copy of my driver's licence, my Medicare number, and any information from the police report.

"There are a few bad eggs out there," Kevin confirmed when I shared all the details of my past with him.

An email arrived with cost agreements from Tertullus Lawyers for me to sign. The seven pages, including General Terms of Business, were filled with legal jargon that I struggled to understand. I asked a friend who was a lawyer to read through the agreement. She told me it was standard for these kinds of claims. I signed hopeful that this would be a step towards my justice.

Kevin called,

"Now that there is a legal case established, your civil case will be put on hold."

He informed me that the two could not run together.

I was to learn that there are two types of cases. A civil case is a private case where someone sues someone else. This is also known as a suit or action. A criminal case is where the Crown, a government body, prosecutes an accused under a public-law statute. The criminal case takes precedence over the civil.

The continuing lockdowns due to Covid slowed Mich's investigations remarkably. I had to wait and wait.

"I wish to inform you that I will be leaving Tretullus Lawyers next week," Kevin's surprise email read.

Six months after engaging him as my lawyer, he was leaving. I felt abandoned. Just like with the police investigation, there was to be a change of guard. I was to be allocated a new person having to build rapport all over again, sharing the stories of my sordid past in a tedious repetition. A survivor of child abuse needs consistency - these kinds of changes only trigger an already fragile person. I stared at the email,

"I wish you well, Sarah." He signed off.

I was allocated a new lawyer, a 'partner' in the firm, Chris. According to the cost agreement I had signed, my lawyer's hourly rate was to double. A solicitor is paid $300 per hour plus GST while a partner is paid $600 per hour plus GST. I felt powerless accepting the change.

Chapter 33

The Reunion

A wet and gloomy week in Sydney preceded the day I was to meet with Rebecca. It had been over 40 years since our days at Loreto Convent and my confession on the ferry. The person I had blurted out my abuse to, while rocking back and forth on the waves of Sydney Harbour. Would she remember what I told her? Would she have the answers I was looking for? Would she be a witness in my case? I had searched for her on Facebook, surprised to find her familiar smiling face, older but the same.

The long lockdowns in Sydney had finally ceased, allowing us back out into civilisation. I grabbed the opportunity to set up a meeting with Rebecca and was delighted when she agreed. Rebecca was coming to Sydney to meet up with her brother, so the timing was perfect. She was living in Melbourne where she was working for the Australian Sports Commission. We had arranged to meet in a park on the Northern Beaches, not far from where I was living. The thought of meeting again after so long was exciting yet also bittersweet as the pending discussion was to bring to the surface a deeply hidden crime. I drove 10 mins to our meeting point in a trance. The details of my past trauma were etched in my mind clear and sharp, but would she even recall that day on the ferry?

Rebecca was instantly recognisable as I saw her waiting on a park bench. Her childhood features had carried through the years, a slim athletic figure, short dark silky hair, and thin metal rimmed glasses. Warm smiles were exchanged as we were transported back to our school days at Loreto. We asked each other questions, bringing us back to the here and now,

"Where do you live? What are you doing with your life?"

She told me she still played A grade soccer and lived with two loving dogs. We exchanged more pleasantries, both encouraging each other that we had hardly changed at all in the 45 years passed. Rebecca suggested we go for a walk. I was relieved, thinking it would be easier to broach the subject of my abuse and her memory of it, whilst walking. Fear remained a factor as I was mentally preparing for the conversation, I was desperate to have.

The walking pace was measured as was the conversation, but I knew I had to get to the nitty gritty. I was so hungry for the truth of what had happened after I told her of my abuse and my consequential silencing. Small talk continued as we walked along the tree-lined street towards the beach.

Rebecca seemed relaxed when I finally asked her the question that had been burning within me,

"Do you remember what I told you about Brother Dave?" I casually asked.

There was slight hesitation in her response as she calculated the many years that had passed.

Rebecca was a 14-year-old child herself when I confessed the details of my abuse on the ferry. This must have been very troubling for someone so young to hear.

"What do you remember? Do you remember what I told you?" I questioned gently but surely.

"Yes, I remember," she said.

THE REUNION

Rebecca seemed troubled by my question yet willing to search for memories. For me, it was easy to recall as breaking my silence was such a significant part of my life but for Rebecca it was a distance blur coated in a lifetime of other memories. She recalled telling Mummy Manns not knowing what else to do. I had told her not to tell anyone, but her telling put an end to the abuse. We hugged tightly as I thanked her for reporting to Mummy Manns. I told her how brave she must have been as a young girl with such difficult information, to speak up.

"Would it be ok if a detective calls you to ask a few questions? Her name is Michelle, she prefers Mich. She is investigating Brother Dave to hopefully bring him to justice," I asked.

"Sure, no problem," Rebecca said and smiled.

Full of thanks and relief I hugged her and said goodbye.

In the 1970's there was no mandatory reporting, yet Rebecca as a child knew she had to report a crime against a child. My request for secrecy was put aside as she had an inner sense that my secret needed to have the light shone on it. It had to come out of the dark place. But she wasn't to know that my secret was to be shoved back into darkness to be hidden away for decades.

I was so grateful for her courage to be the voice for me.

Chapter 34

The Arrest Warrant

Twelve months after I reported my childhood abuse to the police, an email arrived from Mich,

> Good evening, Sarah,
>
> I hope this email finds you well.
> An arrest warrant has been granted regarding the apprehension of David Davenport on his return to Australia.

My eyes fixed hard on the words, 'arrest warrant'. Bubbling joy exploded from within, tears flowed, breaking through laughing sobs. I buried my face in my hands in disbelief. Then the phone rang.

"Hello Sarah, did you get my email?" Mich asked, her excitement evident showing a vast difference from her usual unemotive voice.

"I contacted the Marist Fathers' Archives Department and spoke with Vicky. She was very helpful and found a document, containing a written report of a young girl who had been sexually assaulted in a family pool in Hunters Hill by David Davenport in 1976. This is very unusual Sarah.

THE ARREST WARRANT

Documents were not kept back then. If he steps back onto Australian soil, he will be arrested," Mich concluded.

"This is very unusual," repeated over and over in my head. Finding evidence of my report from so long ago was an absolute miracle. Historically, it was common practice to destroy all evidence that tainted institutional reputations. My report was documented and survived. I was overwhelmed with joy and relief. Somehow, I knew that God has His hand in this discovery.

"Thank you, thank you, thank you," I cried.

I forwarded Mich's email to my lawyer,

"We got him!"

Chris's reply came quickly.

"Fantastic news Sarah. Well done."

Mich had collected statements from my friends and my brother. Matthew recalled the family home visits and the dips in the pool. Jean recalled Brother Dave's charismatic nature, his visits to the school gate and his special interest in me. Rebecca spoke of my confidential disclosure and her passing on the information to the school. Victoria shared about my victimisation and decline at school. All their stories and recordings of events aligned perfectly with my truth. Mich's determination to gather evidence had resulted in an arrest warrant. This victory would be placed on the mantel piece of my heart, along with the cream "Thank You" card signed by the two Commissioners.

The legal case was now closed, or on hold until the possible event of Brother Dave returning to Australia, so my civil case could take off full speed ahead or so I thought. I was disappointed when I was informed that it would take at least another 12-18 months. It was now nearing the end of 2021, and the wait was not over.

There were to be three stages of the process for my case.

1. Evidence gathering- detailed statement, surrounding evidence, witness evidence, government records, medical records.
2. Joint psychiatric examination. Both parties agree to a suitable expert psychiatrist to conduct an examination and produce a report detailing the impact of the abuse upon you in clinical psychiatric terms (i.e. any mental health/psychiatric conditions the abuse has caused or contributed to, and the extent of that contribution).
3. Settlement conference/mediation. Both parties are to attend a negotiation to try and find a financial resolution to the case without the need to incur further costs via commencing litigation (court proceedings).

I was required to sign third party release forms for my lawyer to access all the private information from my entire life: education records, medical records, government records, transcripts from The Royal Commission, Medicare history, taxation records, education, and employment history. Statements from friends and my brother would be gathered and examined. I felt totally exposed, a dissected insect placed under a microscope, only to be picked apart and shamed once more.

Over the coming weeks, I received calls from doctors' offices and past counsellors' receptionists, asking if I knew all my records had been asked for. I felt a deep embarrassment with each call. Gathering evidence for my claim was going to take time but it was necessary to build a strong case. The other side, the Marist Fathers, would then conduct their own investigations before moving onto a psychiatric examination.

THE ARREST WARRANT

Really? *A psychiatrist* I pondered.

Was I mad? Mentally ill? This had never been a consideration for me. Yes, I had suffered anxiety, stress, panic attacks, trauma but a psychiatric examination?

The warrant for arrest showed that the abuse occurred, but the civil claim, was to pursue the institution that employed him.

I tried to get my head around this new concept. It would be the 'institution', the Marist Fathers, that would be held responsible. He was working for them when he regularly visited my primary school; he worked for them when he used his position to enter my family home. The institution covered up my confession, yet we had a legal battle to prove they were to blame.

My legal representation needed to show that the Marist Fathers knew, or ought to have known, of the threat the offender posed to children. This meant that they were on notice that he was an abuser of children, or was likely an abuser of children, prior to the time of my abuse. This was known as negligence. Or we needed to prove that the abuse was connected to the role they employed him to play, that they should be held liable for the abuse, simply because they employed him, regardless of whether they knew about the abuse or not. This is known as vicarious liability.

My lawyer informed me that vicarious liability was very difficult to argue and could be heavily disputed in negotiations.

"Heavily disputed?" I screamed.

What? Why would they dispute something that seemed so obvious to me? Was this the law? Was this justice? Were they going to continue to protect Brother Dave after all this time and take no responsibility for his behaviour? They had employed him, giving him a role to access children. My life had been irrevocably changed because of the trauma of abuse and subsequent cover up, and now they were going to try and argue against me? The legal system is not straight forward; a new beast for me to try and navigate.

I was told that it was critical to gather evidence by speaking with my criminal witnesses, which were now accessible as the criminal case was concluded.

There was not a case simply because the abuse occurred. To successfully pursue the Marist Fathers, we needed to put forward a convincing case for either negligence or vicarious liability. I was told I needed to complete a victim statement.

The Victim Statement document was attached to an email in my inbox. I had briefly opened it and instantly closed it again. Question after question, page after page, every sordid detail required.

My inner thoughts reflected:

> "Revisiting the details of the past and therefore the pain and frustration is confronting. Addressing questions that reflect on the impact of the abuse on my life is certainly challenging and incredibly sad. I have gone into survival mode which is now an automatic response learnt from childhood. When events and life experiences are too painful to face, I have learnt to mask that pain. Perhaps the fear of the deep-rooted pain that has been pushed so far down, may creep to the surface, and kill me. Therefore, keeping the beast buried is a safe place. Hence the hesitancy and fear of taking my mind back and pondering the life I may have had, if the adults in my world had protected me. If only the leaders of the Marist Fathers had comforted me as an example of Jesus's love. In the gospels, Jesus warned of harming little children in the book of Luke 17:2, "It would be better for them to be thrown into the sea

THE ARREST WARRANT

with a millstone around their neck than to cause one of these little ones to stumble." Yet I was left with silence. No one even acknowledged that it happened. As a child, I read this as guilt, blame and shame. To have brought my case to light now, only to once again be disregarded, only reinforces the shame. This is not a just world. The guilty get away with their crimes and the innocent are imprisoned, an internal prison, a life sentence."

What would have been the trajectory of Brother Dave's life if my reporting had been taken seriously? What if justice had been carried out? What if charges were laid for his crime? What if someone had taken me in their arms and offered counselling? My future could have been so different.

Tony Tertullus had informed me that when victims spoke out and identified their perpetrator, more victims usually came out of the woodwork. A wave of emotion stirred in my belly. Revisiting my trauma may have a purpose. It had never been about compensation for me. Yes, I wanted to be heard, to have an apology, but to help others come forward would be an incredible reward.

I had not anticipated my bravery might call out valour in other survivors. Making that first terrifying call to the Royal Commission, calling a lawyer and going to the police station to report a historical crime; I had not considered these steps could potentially help someone else. If I could do it, others could too. I wanted to be an inspiration, an Erin Brockovich, showing others that their Goliaths could be defeated as well. A new energy to keep going was seeded in my weary soul.

Chapter 35
Revisiting the Wooden Bench

My childhood friend Jean was coming to Sydney. We had lost contact when she moved to Brisbane to complete a master's in creative writing. My travels and parenthood had consumed me over the years, leaving little time for past friendships. Jean had been contacted by Detective Mich for a statement. Her memories were vivid of Brother Dave at the school gate and in the grounds of Villa Maria Church. She confirmed that I was his favourite. While she was at my house for a playdate, she reported that when Brother Dave arrived, my mother would instruct that she had to go home. She told of my increasing risky behaviours and drug use into my teens and early twenties. It had been 22 years since we had seen each other.

Phone conversations during the police investigations had us revisit our past, the stories of our adventures in my dinghy on the Lane Cove River and of the abuse. Jean continued to try to understand why I had only disclosed the abuse to her in my early twenties. She reminded me of a story I told her of a man coming into my bedroom when I was a little girl, leaving me trembling and crying. We were so close as children and yet I never spoke to her then of the abuse in my home. This proved how deep my silencing had been implanted.

REVISITING THE WOODEN BENCH

We planned to revisit Villa Maria Church. The autumn morning had the leaves beginning to turn to gold, still mixing with the greens of summer warmth. I wanted to walk the grounds, to go back in time, to revisit my memories, and to witness the wooden bench my silencer had walked me to. Was it still there? Would I remember the long walk into the forbidden ground? Would the old trees tell my story, whispering from 45 years ago?

I pulled on a large sun hat and dark glasses to disguise my identity.

"What if I'm recognised?" I exclaimed fearfully to Jean.

This was a ridiculous concern as with the passing of time I certainly did not look like an 11-year-old girl. But internally, I was that young girl again, encased in anxiety. Lingering guilt and shame were still trying to wrap me in chains.

Jean boldly entered the grand sandstone building of the church, while I gingerly followed. It was smaller than I remembered, or perhaps because I was smaller back then.

Jean marched ahead speaking loudly, relaying memories of our times in this building. The long-drawn-out Masses, the confessions, the penance, the boring hymns.

"Shhh, speak quietly Jean. Someone might be here," I said.

My indoctrination to be quiet in church, weighed on me in reverential fear. I looked up at the stations of the cross, a visual display of horrific last steps to death. Jesus looked traumatised, and I was transported back to the memory of my mother's long nails piecing my skin at her command to be quiet.

"Should we be in here?" I whispered.

The high vaulted ceiling was trimmed in dark cedar, its magnificence to behold. The stained-glass windows lit up, their primary colours illuminating to captivate all in their presence. Jean was still chatting away to herself as she approached the altar. I wanted to run. What if we got caught? I felt like a schoolgirl again, out of bounds with the threat of punishment. The large statues, including angels, the mother Mary, and the baby Jesus, were all watching me.

Leaving the building through a side door we then entered the gardens. I was relieved to be out of the religious oppression of my past. I was on a mission to find the wooden bench; the place where Brother Dave had taken me to say his last goodbye. The place where he silenced me, telling me I would understand when I was older. A lie! I would never understand the sick perversion of sexually touching a child. I had a deep need to take the walk through the church grounds to that place. The walk I had dutifully taken in terror at his invitation all those years ago. An obedient victim following her predator. Would it recreate the memory etched in my mind?

The grass was a fluorescent green, smooth, and soft rolling down the gentle hill. My heart quickened. There it was, exactly as I had remembered. It was a peaceful place, allocated for the priests from the presbytery to come and pray. The towering trees had only grown larger, offering a canopy of shelter.

"This is where he brought you, isn't it?" Jean finally broke the silence.

I nodded in satisfaction. This place was stored perfectly in my mind. Preserved over the years, a slight weathering, but the bench remained solid in form. I sat, the grained textured wood pressing through the fabric of my cotton pants. It was cool and damp. Closing my eyes tight, I felt gratefulness in my heart. I had trusted my memories, and they had served me well. I thanked the little girl for her bravery, for taking the walk to this place. I thanked the wooden bench for remaining here waiting for me to revisit. I thanked God that I had survived.

Chapter 36

The Assessment

The confirmation of my psychiatric assessment came via an email. Arrangements were made for my medicolegal assessment, which was to be conducted by an independent psychiatrist in seven months' time. This doctor, a male, had been jointly selected by both parties to provide an expert opinion on any psychiatric injuries that I may have endured and any treatment that I may require. This was to assist both parties in evaluating my claim for compensation. The doctor was bound by the Expert Witness Code and his opinions and report were to be impartial to all parties involved.

The psychiatrist was to take a comprehensive history regarding my entire life, not just the subject of abuse. He would also be provided with my statement and medical records prior to the meeting. I was informed that I could bring a support person along, but they would not be allowed in the actual assessment with me. I was also instructed not to consume any intoxicating substances or alter the dosages of any prescribed medication prior to the assessment. I was to take my time when answering questions, and if I did not understand something to ask for clarification. If I needed to take a break, I was to tell the psychiatrist so that he could accommodate me. This was not to be a therapy session, and that some questions may seem insensitive or abrupt but needed to be asked as part of the assessment.

These instructions for the assessment sent me into a panic. A comprehensive history of my entire life! A support person was not allowed to be with me while I was asked insensitive and abrupt questions. It was too late. There was no turning back. I had already signed the cost agreement, which contained a clause that if I changed my mind and pulled out, I would be charged all legal fees to date. I had already completed a grueling Victim Statement, with details that included my family background, my family medical history, the nature of the abuse, the reporting of the abuse, the consequences of the abuse, major life events, relationship history, general health, mental health, suicidal thoughts and attempts, surgeries, compensation history, employment and education, family employment and education history, financial situation, criminal history and what life looks like today. I was in too deep.

My last memory of being interrogated was by Sister Gigantor in year 7, where I was both terrified and humiliated. The thought of being put back onto a stand to be examined, every inch of my life, especially by a person of authority, a doctor, a man, a stranger, was unimaginable.

"NO NO NO." I took a deep breath and reached for the phone to call the lawyers' office.

"What does this mean? When? How many months? Why such a wait?" I was scrambling for answers.

A medical examination by Dr X, a neutral doctor, an expert in the field, was to assess my mental health. He was to produce a 'medicolegal' report, a legal report designed to stand up in a court of law. This was part of the process to be held via a ZOOM call.

THE ASSESSMENT

"How can a stranger who has never met me assess my mental wellbeing of over 50 years in an online meeting?"

I could hardly breathe. The thought of reliving the trauma over again, spiraled me into stress.

So much power would be placed in this doctor's hands. He had a few hours to make a judgement to determine my justice. Would he judge me? Would he believe me?

I felt like a victim all over again. I had fallen from the throne of survivor into traumatised victim. There would be months of waiting, feeling sick to the stomach, waiting for the insensitive and abrupt questions to be delivered.

I flashed back into the musty confessional booth in Villa Maria Church, waiting to confess my sins. In the dark space, the scary silhouette behind the window, waiting. A dark figure would be inside my computer, waiting. Figures of authority brought an impregnated fear, adults not to be trusted in a child's world. I would be made to regress into childhood memories in front of a stranger, ready with terrifying questions.

Memories of secrets, abusers, cruel nuns, school expulsion, losing my childhood friendships, bad relationships, abortion, drugs, and domestic violence, would be dragged to the surface. I had to draw near to God.

God was also ready. Waiting for me to call out. His grace was sufficient for me. I put on a worship song, soft and soothing and sat quietly. My hands resting on my lap, palms facing heavenwards, I took an extended breath inwards, he was with me calming my storm.

As Assessment Day approached, my senses were heightened, subconscious memories from the past abruptly visiting my conscious mind without warning. I began to reflect, as I had done many times before, on the damage that had been done to me, by a man's perverted attraction to children and his boldness to act on it. I also reflected on the Marist Fathers' protection of him, a paedophile, along with the nun's cruelty, coconspirators in hiding a crime. The silence was deafening. It had been a long seven months.

The subconscious is an intriguing part of the mind, influencing every action and feelings you experience without conscious awareness. I had developed hypervigilance, an increased alertness in unwarranted situations. When visiting restaurants, cafes, libraries, any enclosed space, I would scan the room before sitting in the corner, with my back towards the wall. This was a safe position, eyes scanning outwards to watch for danger. I was unaware of this pattern of behaviour until it was pointed out to me by a friend. Life choices are under constant guard of the subconscious mind. This inbuilt protection directs thoughts to save the inner child from harm. No area in my life had not been impacted by my past.

The word 'victim' glared at me from the page of the document titled 'Victim Statement'. A victim is defined as a person who has come to feel helpless and passive in the face of misfortune or ill-treatment. But I had been renamed, 'survivor' at the Royal Commission all those years ago and now I was expected to fall back into my old helpless state - victim. I wanted to shout to the world,

"No. I am Erin, the giant slayer. I'm a survivor."

I decided I needed to find a quiet place in nature to attend the assessment ZOOM meeting, so I booked an Airbnb. The drive through the lush green Gold Coast hinterland was captivating while the picturesque villages greeted me around each bend. The winding road led me up a steep climb to a ridge top where the quaint cottage stood. Once inside, the cathedral windows, glass stretching from the floor to the roof, framed a spectacular view, which stole my breath away. Rolling mountains stretched as far as

THE ASSESSMENT

the eyes could see, cascading down to the turquoise waters of the Pacific Ocean.

For a moment, my thoughts drifted, convincing me that I had come away on a beautiful holiday. In a sudden snap back to reality, I awoke to the fact that I was preparing to present myself as a victim.

I was permitted to have a support person, but that person was not to be in the assessment meeting. "What is the point of a support person if they had to remain absent?" I pondered in confusion. The pending ZOOM meeting with the male doctor, made my stomach churn with anxiety. The details of my childhood sexual abuse and subsequent abuses were to be presented on a platter, like at a smorgasbord for consumption.

My beautiful friend Amanda would join me. I met Amanda while driving through The Promised Land. That now familiar still small voice spoke to me telling me to go to Bellingen, a six-hour drive from Sydney. I took heed of the instructions, deciding to explore the area. The man at the front desk of the hostel advised me to drive the loop road through The Promised Land.

I entered the name into Google Maps, the location showing indeed it was a place. I giggled at God's sense of humour. The drive was extraordinary. Green pastures rolling through valleys meandering over acres of farmland that were dotted with cattle. Tall mountains lined the magnificent backdrop commanding the driver to take note of the distant vista. The next bend turned into dense forest, giant trees forming rich canopies over the road, creating a tunnel of shaded delight. I came to a narrow wooden bridge crossing a pristine creek, the Never Never River, crystal clear waters cascading across smooth river stones.

Suddenly, a large white creature bound out of the forest in front of my car. I pressed my foot hard on the brakes of my Lexus convertible. It slid to a stop. The creature now identified as a large dog stood staring at my low-lying bonnet. Pounding hard in my chest, my heart delivered a message of shock and relief at the same time. While I was still in wonder, a tanned muscular woman, looking like Tarzan's Jane came out of the forest in a skimpy bikini with an equally huge second white dog. She was smiling profusely.

"Thank you for not running over my dog," she exclaimed beaming happiness across her pretty face.

Who was this woman, appearing in the middle of nowhere and why is she wearing a bikini? The questions circled in my mind like in a whirlpool. I was equally glad not to have run over her dog.

"Why are you wearing swimmers?" I asked coyly.

"Oh, there is a stunning waterhole just in behind the trees, come and have a look. You MUST come for a plunge," she insisted.

I was in a rush to get to an appointment I had in Sydney, but I knew saying "no" was not an option.

I put on my one-piece swimsuit and followed her into the forest, the two Bull Arab Irish Wolf Hounds, Ishka and Lobo leading the way.

The water was cool and deep, the pool larger than four swimming pools combined. A paradise hidden in rays of light beams. We sat on a large smooth rock for three hours sharing intimate stories. I felt warm comfort in our conversation, a fellow survivor, and a new special friend.

Amanda arrived at the cottage, joining me on the large wooden deck. The lights of the Gold Coast sparkled in the distance, a twinkling fairyland far away.

Amanda sipped on her home made kombucha, while I tried to calm my nerves by drinking some wine. Alcohol was a comfort, offering the relaxation I desperately needed. Very few words were spoken that evening, Amanda's silent presence a gentle reassurance. Somehow our life traumas resonated, wounded souls now warriors.

THE ASSESSMENT

Amanda had achieved the title of three times Cross Fit World champion. Against all odds, conquering alcoholism, domestic violence, surgeries for abdominal tumours, running 1000 kms for suicide awareness, she went from strength to strength to become a true legend. My support person, the one God led me to in The Promised Land.

Retiring for the evening, Amanda gently hugged me good night.

The cold tiles of the bathroom floor pressed hard against my cheek. I lay curled into the fetal position, my nose pressing into a corner. The sobs engulfed every part of my being while I desperately tried to disappear. I had flashed back to the wood pile, hiding from my perpetrator. My name had become 'Victim' again.

Ishka and Lobo bounded into my bedroom, their tails wagging with glee, the morning sun heating the room. Amanda's beaming smile followed,

"Good morning," she sang.

Was it a good morning? The pounding in my head questioned.

Coffee! I needed coffee.

Minutes ticked by at high speed, my anxiety mounting at the same pace. I was to check my email for a ZOOM link, read through my Victim Statement one more time, then eat the scrambled eggs Amanda had prepared.

What would the doctor be like? Would he be abrupt like Sister Anne? Would he interrogate me? Do I put on lipstick? What should I wear?

"Wear something comfortable," Amanda suggested somehow reading my thoughts.

Sitting at the kitchen table, papers carefully arranged, the email finally arrived. Seven months of stress in anticipation of this assessment and now it was upon me. Amanda quietly moved out onto the deck so as not to be in the same room, her reassuring smile remaining visible through the slat glass windows. A calm nod indicated, "You've got this."

HARVESTING SILENCE

I clicked on the ZOOM link entering the meeting. A man in his late fifties appeared on the screen, his pointed head had limited hair receding at the sides, and thin rimmed glasses sat on the tip of his nose,

"Hello, I'm Dr X."

It had begun.

The next two hours I was to enter a clinical exploration of my life. Emotional health, physical health, childhood, family, friends, relationships, life traumas, abuse. A familiar fearful internal vibration rose in me as I answered each question, hoping to 'get it right'. I had formed a shield of protection, appearing fine on the outside. Going about everyday life, a masked smile indicating all was well. A falsehood when at times all was not well. Human nature tends to put on a brave face and get on with life. But this man needed to know the truth. The shield must come down to show him my deep anguish below the surface from a life torn in pieces by careless, cruel criminals.

"Has any counselling helped you?" he asked.

"No."

I had attended various counselling sessions over my lifetime, and not one of them seemed to grasp the magnitude of childhood sexual abuse, especially by a member of the clergy. One counsellor got angry at my perpetrator saying she wanted to "hit him with a bat." I didn't find that helpful.

"What are your hobbies? He asked. "Sewing?"

I was shocked by this question. Was I expected to have hobbies? I couldn't even thread a needle. Was there something wrong with me that I didn't have hobbies?

"When did your mother pass away?" he continued.

My mother passed away two and a half years ago. The lockdowns and separations during Covid had taken their toll. She had become depressed, losing the will to live. A fall causing a broken hip was the beginning of the end. After hip surgery she was left in excruciating pain, which became difficult to manage. There was a reluctance by the nursing home staff to increase her morphine dose, so she screamed out in pain daily. As her daughter and advocate, I did my best to fight for her. My childhood under her control had been forgiven, now I only saw a frail old woman, suffering and needing her only daughter. The fond memories of our trip to Europe flooded to the surface of my mind. I held her hand tightly, my face close to her ear as I retold the funny story of our trip together in France all those years ago at the St Maximum 'Mosquito' hotel. I reminded her of the countless mosquito bites dotted all over her face. She was alert and listening. Tears of laughter mixed with emotional pain filled my eyes as she took her last breath.

"I love you Mum," I whispered.

"And when did your father die?" the doctor's questioning continued without emotion.

"Dad died in my arms seven years ago, he was my hero," I said.

A sudden agonising awareness of my loneliness began to suffocate me - clawing its way to the surface, cutting a fresh wound. The piercing pain in my chest halted the rhythm of my breathing.

"Would you like to take a break?" he asked.

I looked towards Amanda's face at the glass window. Her gentle nod gave me permission to pause.

"Yes," I managed to reply.

In the bathroom I took a few deep breaths, regaining some form of composure.

On returning to my seat, I noticed Dr X had taken a break from the screen as well. I wondered if he needed time to process all the information I had shared so far. His job was to make a non-biased assessment of the abuse and its impact on my life. Did he see me as damaged? His return to the screen met me with a reassuring smile, a reminder that he was human after all.

"I need to bring something to your attention doctor," I said, my voice shaking slightly.

While sorting through some old boxes, I discovered a box of childhood memorabilia. A pile of school annual class photos showed my small face, positioned on the front row, notably becoming sadder with each passing year. My hair was pulled back into a tight ponytail, the rolled curl sitting softly on my shoulder where my mother had instructed me to position it.

The red dress with white spots was carefully folded and my first teddy bear, 'Pandy' stared up at me lovingly. A pile of school reports indicated my failing grades along with my deteriorating behaviour.

"Sarah is becoming increasingly withdrawn and disinterested in school," one report read. Another stated, "Sarah, seems to lack confidence and rarely participates in class."

The abuse and coverup clearly had an impact on my ability to function at school.

I also discovered the 1972 Harvest magazine, picturing me in the red dress wearing a forced cover girl smile.

I held the magazine up towards the camera in my laptop so Dr X could see it.

"See the young girl on the cover," I said.

"The cover girl, the pedo pin up girl, the pedo pet."

I then opened to the second page reading the information about the publication,

'Marist Fathers Christmas edition 1972'.

Dr X moved forward onto his seat to get a better look.

"That's me," I said firmly as I turned back to the cover page.

"Oh," Dr X sighed long and deep.

THE ASSESSMENT

My childhood innocence jumped off the page into the screen.

Dr X began typing notes furiously on his keyboard.

The girl in the red dress had been put on show for all to see - an innocent freckled faced child with long blonde locks. The cover girl for paedophiles in the church to ogle at. Had Brother Dave obtained a copy? Is this the reason I had become his 'special' girl at the school gate and why he would visit my family home? More unanswered questions plagued my mind.

The two-hour meeting came to an end.

"Thank you, Sarah," Dr X concluded.

Chapter 37
The Results

Time passes slowly when you are waiting for justice. Now in the third year since calling Tertullus Lawyers and reporting to the police, eight weeks since my medicolegal assessment, I continued to hear nothing.

"The report hasn't come back to us yet," was the reply when I called my lawyer's office again for an update. My life was on hold, and everything seemed to be pending on the report. The weight of my case, the decision regarding the effects of the abuse on my life was in Dr X's hands.

Trauma affects the frontal lobe. This part of the brain is involved in weighing values, understanding rules, making plans, and formulating predictions about the outcomes of our choices. It is also responsible for logical reasoning and emotional decision-making. These regulatory areas of my brain had been damaged, arresting my development. Arrested Development is a known condition caused by trauma, stress, or lack of care. It is where a person's development is stopped in its tracks at the age of the trauma. The stoppage can be physical, emotional, or mental development.

Everyday decisions were hard for me. Simple decisions like deciding what to order on a menu in a restaurant had a trauma response. A fear of making a poor choice, a wrong choice. Self-doubt had been rooted that day

THE RESULTS

I was told to forget. To wipe what happened from my mind for years only to breed confusion and create 'gas lighting'.

"Gaslighting is a form of psychological manipulation that causes the victim to question the validity of their own thoughts, perception of reality, or memories. It is a form of psychological abuse that can lead to confusion, loss of confidence and self-esteem, uncertainty of one's emotional or mental stability, and a dependency on the perpetrator" – Merrium Webster Dictionary.

Three years of police investigations, legal reports, and questioning, opening every part of my past had caused mental saturation. Trauma also causes mental overload, and I was overloaded.

A text came in from Jean. She had attached an article from ABC News, it read:

"Dismissed appeal finds Catholic Church liable for clergy's child abuse; *win for victim-survivors as Vic Court of appeal finds Catholic Church liable for sexual abuse by priests.*" This was music to my ears. A historical case, a five-year-old boy abused by a priest, and the Catholic Church was found responsible. My lawyer had stressed that we had to prove 'Vicarious Liability' that the respondent, i.e. the Marist Fathers were directly liable for the abuse or that it occurred because of their negligence. My legal team had to prove the abuse happened and that the Marist Fathers were responsible.

Chris had informed me that the next step was to go into mediation. This is where the two parties meet to agree on a settlement compensation before moving into litigation and the court system. The mediation was a pre-litigation negotiation to resolve matters. If my matter was not resolved, although terrifying, I was completely willing to go to court. I had been wronged, and I wanted justice.

The Marist Fathers, after hearing the report of my abuse in 1976, decided to say nothing. The churches' culture at the time, was to cover-up crimes amongst the brothers and priests. Their co-conspirators, the Loreto nuns, also decided to bury my story. My life trajectory was impacted by this choice. I wanted them to acknowledge their mistake and to apologise. No amount of money could bring back the life I lost.

"It is highly likely that, if the case proceeds to litigation, the respondent will ask the Court for a permanent stay," my lawyer informed me.

"A what?" I asked with no clue what this legal jargon meant.

A 'permanent stay' is where the courts have the discretionary capacity to halt proceedings indefinitely as to avoid undue or unfair circumstances. My case could simply be dismissed at the court's discretion.

"What do you mean? It's clear that they are guilty," I said in a panic.

"Yes, but a long time has passed. All the priests are elderly now or perhaps dead. There may be no witnesses, or they may be too old to testify. The courts would therefore see this as a waste of their time," Chris explained.

Why was he bringing this up now? Three long years into the investigation and there was a 'loophole' in the law?

"Litigation is an inherently risky exercise. Ultimately one-party wins, and the other party loses in court proceedings. Every lawyer has cases they expected to win, and lost, as well as cases they thought they would lose that ultimately succeeded. No experienced lawyer will give a guarantee of success in litigation," I was informed.

"What, I could lose?" I screamed.

I discovered that when an individual loses a court case, they are ordered by the court to pay the other side's legal costs. This could potentially be a six-figure sum. The shock of this information was overwhelming. The courts could charge me! The disbelief sent my heart into panicking beats causing my head to become light and spin uncontrollably. I rushed to the bathroom coughing up vomit, the acid burning my throat. I looked into the mirror, unable to recognise the face before me. An old and haggard face

THE RESULTS

looked back at me, the toll of the civil case etching its cost in the reflection. As I stared at the image before me, I hoped it would change back to the innocent little girl in the red dress so I could start my life over again.

The difficulties with historical abuse cases are that decisions are often open to appeal. Cases may take months or years to reach court. The case can go to the Supreme Court and in some cases to the High Court. A victim can win initially, then with an appeal can have the win overturned.

It is a matter of great difficulty to predict how judges will deal with the issue of vicarious liability in cases of historical abuse. When attempting to hold institutions liable for sexual abuse by their employees, it is very difficult to be confident about how cases will be decided.

My case could take years! I was already exhausted, completely drained. These risks now being brought to my attention, planted negative doubts in my mind. The regret for making that initial call to the lawyer was so heavy that I had to lie on the floor. In the foetal position I cried out to God.

"God, you are just. You love justice. Help me find my justice." A scripture immediately came to mind,

"For I the Lord love justice, I hate robbery and iniquity. In my faithfulness I will reward them and make an everlasting covenant with them." Isaiah 61:8

* * * * *

Four months had passed since the gruelling day of the medicolegal assessment when the email arrived in my inbox, stating that a copy of Dr X's report was attached.

The agonising wait was over. A shiver went through my spine, not a winter shiver of a southerly wind, but a deep cold in the marrow of my bones. A wood pile cold inching its way back into my memory.

Rubbing my hands briskly, I took three deep breaths before opening the 20-page document.

The report revealed that as a consequence of the alleged abuse, Ms Cook has developed post-traumatic stress disorder (309.81).

There before my eyes was Dr X's conclusion. Two hours of questioning and listening to my responses he had made a professional diagnosis. My diagnosis had a name and a number, PTSD 309.81. I wanted to ask Google what this meant, but not today. I shut down my computer and walked away. The next 19 pages had to wait. I knew deep within the essence of my being that the abuse and the cover up had damaged me. The consequences subsequently attracting more abuse in my life. I wanted to press 'delete' rather than return to the details in the report.

Three days passed before I revisited the email. I opened the attachment, glanced again at page one, then shut the computer, and walked away.

A week after receiving the report, I attempted once more to face its contents.

The report concluded that I had disclosed incidents, I had spoken to the Royal Commission, made a formal complaint to the police, an arrest warrant was granted, panic attacks, flashbacks. She felt humiliated, began to drink alcohol excessively, used drugs, became promiscuous, blackouts, difficulties going to sleep, impacted her education, affected her long-term employment, developed asthma, suffers anxiety. It had a negative effect on all relationships, suffered rejections and punished for disclosure, mistrust from authority figures, especially men, poor short-term memory from trauma, impairment of concentration, impairment to social and recreational activities, psychiatric and psychological conditions related to the abuse, extreme impact on mental health and overall wellbeing. It is unlikely she could return to the workforce. On a point scale of none, mild, moderate, severe, and extreme, the abuse by Brother Dave Davenport was

THE RESULTS

concluded to have had an 'extreme impact' on my mental health and overall wellbeing.

Shock can take many forms - silence, tears, laughter, anger, I was numb. Could this report really be mine? Staring into space I couldn't absorb the words. Every area of my life had been impacted negatively by Brother Dave's abuse and the Marist Fathers' cover up. Even though I knew this truth I desperately wanted to deny it. If only I could slide out of my skin into a new reality, an avatar, a distant world, but the hard cold cruel facts were in black and white in front of me. My life had been analysed, fifty years since the abuse and the truth had been revealed.

The little girl on the front of the Harvest Magazine in the red dress was curled up by the wood pile. Her arms over her ears to silence the pain, rocking slowly to ease the tormented soul. Crying tears never seen or heard. That little girl was still inside me.

Chapter 38
Mediation

The mediation meeting was booked. My legal team, along with the Marist Fathers' legal representative would attend. Brother Dave would not be present of course, yet the institution that had protected him would. I had requested a representative from the Marist Fathers to be present to hear me read my 'Impact Statement'. I wanted someone in a high position in the church. The justice I was seeking was for my perpetrators to hear the details of the impact their silencing had on my life. I was also requesting an apology, both spoken and written. The power of the voice cannot be denied, and I had an opportunity to be heard.

The day's proceedings were to be broken into two parts, the first being an apology, the second the compensation negotiations – the mediation. I was told I would be permitted to bring a support person to the apology but not recommended this person be in the settlement negotiation. My lawyer stated that the support person may influence my decision regarding accepting a payout.

"The person will have knowledge of the amount you are paid," I was told.

MEDIATION

I didn't care who knew. Every secret private part of my life was already known by my lawyers and the Marist Fathers' lawyers, who were all strangers to me. If my support person, my good friend knew, that would be totally fine. I wanted to shout the compensation amount from the roof top for all the world to hear. No more silence.

Two months before the mediation, my lawyer reiterated that going to court was not recommended, which only further depressed me. I believed three years earlier that I had an open and shut case. I was abused, the man has an arrest warrant, and the Marist Fathers, the order he worked for covered up my reporting – plain and simple.

I was to discover through Mich's police investigations, that Brother Dave had entered the Marist Order in the late sixties as a young man. In his early days, it was known by the Marist Fathers, that there were sexual indiscretions with women, including a nun and a single mother. He was known as 'shifty' and was asked to leave. One year's absence as a teacher at a primary school where he frequently spent time on home visitations, he was accepted back into the Order. It was understood that he had a lack of judgement and struggled with the sexual implications of his chosen profession. My report to the school of the abuse was discovered in a file – it read of an incident with a schoolgirl in a swimming pool, where sexual misconduct was alleged. My brave report had been preserved for all those years, locked away in a vault to be hidden from the world. A paedophile to be protected.

Seven months after my report to the school, Brother Dave was ordained as a priest. The Marist Fathers knew of Brother Dave's ongoing struggles with his sexuality, yet he was permitted to continue in the pursuit of the priesthood. A child had been abused, and he became a priest!

The Catholic Priesthood requires men to abstain from all sexual relationships to honour a life pure to God. Celibacy is a requirement. Yet

Brother Dave displayed behaviours that were a concern and totally against the requirements of the Catholic church. Paul, an apostle of Jesus Christ, spoke of celibacy as a calling from God, but instructed that if a man cannot control himself, it is better for him to be married. I cannot understand how a church can miss this message and create an organisation that requires all its men to abstain from sex. God created man and woman to be fruitful and multiply, this is a God ordained healthy relationship. I look at the history of overwhelming sexual perversion within the Catholic Church and conclude that compulsive celibacy needs to be addressed.

My legal team had to prove that there was 'vicarious liability', and Chris kept telling me there were risks. Even with this information, I could still lose, he informed me. I was fragmented and confused. The legal system has so many flaws only adding to the victim's suffering.

Chris's continuing reminders of the risks of taking my case to court put an invisible pressure on me regarding the pending mediation. I was expected to accept a settlement figure lower 'than I would like', he told me. The estimated costs of taking the matter to court would be deducted from my compensation payout. How was this fair?

"There has to be a compromise," Chris explained over and over.

"The risks are high," Chris kept telling me before mediation.

If I had known about this three years ago, I would not have chosen this path. A path obstructed with legal implications to strategically revictimise the victim. The civil case began simply with the gathering of information. There were no discussions about risks. The 'risks' conversations came later when I was already locked into an agreement with a signature. To pull out would only cause me to incur a substantial financial cost. I journeyed through immense re-traumatisation as a result, feeling trapped.

There were three scenarios presented to me:

1. Win in negligence, but not in Vicarious Liability.

2. Win, conservative damages awarded.

3. Win in negligence, but not Vicarious Liability and conservative damages.

Each scenario had calculated financial amounts in the following categories: general damages, interest, economic loss, past treatment, future treatment, legal costs. The payment amounts varied greatly depending on the outcome.

In the lead-up to the mediation, I was told the opening offer was to consider court costs. It therefore needed to be substantially lower than I had expected. This was to be a substantial drop that I was not prepared for. After everything I had been through, reliving the trauma and putting my life under a microscope; I was expected to reduce the amount of compensation before the discussions had even begun. This was to be a compromise.

No, I didn't want to compromise. I felt that my life was worth more.

"No that's too low," I cried.

I was trying to understand the rhythm of this legal dance. I was expected to make an opening offer, then the Marist Fathers were to put in a counteroffer.

"Can't they put in an opening offer?" I pleaded.

"No. This is the way it is done," Chris said.

I felt sick at the thought of laying my life bare on the table – my story, my pain, my very sense of self reduced to a number. A figure to be negotiated and debated.

"No, her abuse and trauma are not worth that much. Let's offer less." That imagined voice echoed through me, cutting deep.

The only other time I had witnessed this kind of system was at a property auction. Buyers placing bids, the vendor holding the power to accept or decline – numbers volleyed back and forth until an amount is accepted. Except this wasn't a house. It was my life.

I imagined the Marist Fathers as the vendors, hovering like vultures over my life- circling, watching, waiting. I felt as though they were playing with numbers, trying to break me down, hoping I would accept the lowest possible offer. My vulnerability, exposed and raw, would become a part of their strategy.

When I researched legal costs, I discovered there is a scaling payment plan that varies depending on the payout. For example, the lawyers would get $4000 for $10,000, $30,000 for $120,000, capping at $60,000 for a $320,000 payout or more. The amount is deducted from the client's compensation payout. There could be additional costs – for example if your lawyer seeks advice from a barrister plus other expenses that surface along the way. And then, there's the government's share. I was told I would also be expected to repay any Medicare benefits that had covered my healthcare from the compensation payout. Each new cost carving more away.

I was speaking with a friend who had recently presented a compensation claim. She informed me that there is a clause in the compensation agreement that states that should the client accept an amount on the mediation day, they are not permitted to disclose the amount. Here was another silencing! I was furious. How dare they tell me what I could or could not disclose. The same silencing that made me a victim was still trying to strangle me.

"I'm not signing the document with the 'gag' clause, Chris," I announced, the anger evident in my voice.

"You tell their legal team if it's there to remove it! There is absolutely no way I will agree to be silenced again," I continued.

"This is a standard clause," Chris replied.

"You are the first client I have known to ask to have it removed."

"I do not agree with the 'standard clause' and the fact that it has not been challenged before is not my concern. I have been silenced all my life,

MEDIATION

and a continuation of silencing is only ongoing abuse from this organisation," I responded.

My statement was clear and final.

I was deeply saddened as I thought of all the survivors who had gone ahead of me. Accepting the legal system, the last-minute surprises, the interrogations, the stripping away of dignity as their lives are put under a microscope and the payout compromised.

As time progressed and the mediation was drawing closer, I was continually being massaged to accept a lower amount.

"There are risks going to court," Chris's words echoed in my head.

I was exhausted, feeling like a whipped slave, begging for mercy.

Weakened into accepting a compromise, I selected a bottom-line figure in my head. I decided if it was not reached at mediation, I would go to court. This was my only chance for justice. I wrote the amount on a piece of paper to take to the mediation meeting. It wasn't about the money but the three-year battle plus my life's trauma was worth something.

The day arrived. The strange bed with stiff white sheets did not offer me comfort the night before. Intermittent sleep felt as if I had not slept at all. The rented apartment was stark, selected for its proximity to the Marist Fathers' legal team's offices.

Meg, my chosen support person, was slowly moving around the apartment. She had slept in the second bedroom to be ready to assist me with preparations. I had met Meg 16 years earlier, a fellow Christian I could pray with and this day I certainly would need some prayer. I dragged my crumpled body to the bathroom, trying not to catch my reflection in the mirrors that tried to engulf me on every wall. I succumbed to the mirror behind the bathroom door. I stared at my weighted shoulders, a visible indication of the day ahead of me. Clicking the door shut, I moved heavily towards the shower. The water ran cold over my shivering body as I waited silently for warmth.

"Would you like me to do your hair?" Meg called through the door.

My hair was long. I usually would leave it to fall freely, scrunching it into loose waves when wet. Today I wanted to look 'presentable'. Meg watched a u-tube video on how to twirl the hair into a bun-style ponytail. I loved the picture she showed me and agreed. After a few failed attempts my hair was swept back, tidy yet casual. I chose a black shirt spotted with yellow flowers, black pants, and ankle boots. The blazer was a soft grey offering a professional finish. Meg dressed equally well presented in a vibrant pink blazer, perhaps to try and keep me cheerful.

The walk to our destination would take 10 minutes. As I stepped outside onto the footpath, the bitter air grabbed me. I pulled on a pair of black leather gloves from my handbag wishing I was wearing a warm coat. Towering grey buildings robbed us of any chance to feel the morning rays of sunshine. A gloomy atmosphere was mirrored on the faces of the early morning commuters, frowning brows bracing the gusting wind. I quickened my step hoping Meg would too.

"We are 10 minutes early," Meg said as she glanced at her mobile phone.

I was glad to have someone who was aware of the details, the ones that I knew my mind could not contain. I was about to face 'them'.

Chris had informed me that the Marist Fathers were sending their head man along with a woman. I was pleased that at least my case was considered significant enough to send their leader. Or was it because they were concerned that my case held some weight. A weight that could bring embarrassment to their church.

Meg and I arrived at the towering city building. While waiting in the foyer a man approached me from behind.

"You must be Sarah," he said.

I turned quickly, assuming this must be Chris. I had never seen my lawyer, so I had no idea what he looked like. He was younger than I expected, less than forty with short combed brown hair. His plain brown suit was absent from a tie delivering an unkempt appearance for a lawyer. A woman in her twenties was with him.

"This is Louise," he said as an introduction.

Louise was wearing an almost white T-shirt shapelessly sagging at her neck. Her pencil-thin skirt was far too tight for her voluptuous figure and her black blazers buttons were struggling to meet. She kept pulling at the lapels trying to cover her middle. She looked disheveled.

"Hello," I said, unable to get any eye contact from her.

"Are these the people representing me?" a disturbed thought suddenly struck me.

In three years, I had never been invited to meet my lawyer. No visit to their office, no meet up for coffee, no ZOOM meeting, nothing. These people knew my documents but didn't know me. I felt uncomfortable around these strange faces now wishing that I was offered an opportunity to meet them prior to this crucially important meeting.

We took the elevator up to the legal offices where my mediation was to take place. It was the opposition's legal offices; we were in their territory. We were led to a small room. Bottles of spring water lined the table that we were to sit behind. Meg and I on one side, Chris, and Louise on the other. Irrelevant chatter began between Meg and Chris while I waited, each minute that passed increasing an unbearable anxiety.

A man appeared at the door immaculately dressed in a tailored black suit. The shirt was crisp white and the tie neat. He beckoned Chris outside into the corridor. Chris returned after a few minutes,

"Father Brown is going to be late. He is on a ferry that has broken down," Chris informed.

Father Brown was delayed. My waiting agony was to be extended.

"Would you like a cup of tea?" Louise suggested.

I sipped the hot black tea only as a token to pass the time. Louise spoke with Meg sharing stories of overseas travel while I remained silent. All my concentration was on the Impact Statement I was about to read.

I had painstakingly sat for days and days, writing then rewriting about the impacts that Brother Dave's actions, the Loreto nuns, and the Marist Fathers shameful coverup had on my life. Physical, emotional, relational, and spiritual impacts over every area of my life.

"He's here," the well-dressed man announced.

Stuart was the Marist Fathers' legal representation. His high standards were evident as he held his head tall on his shoulders, leading us down a corridor into a large conference room. Father Brown was seated, looking flushed from rushing. Next to him was a gaunt elderly woman, sadness evident in each deep wrinkle on her tired face. I suspected this wasn't the first mediation she had attended.

Stuart also had a legal assistant on his team, an elegant young woman who looked like she had stepped out of a Vogue magazine. I couldn't help thinking that their team looked better than mine.

Introductions were completed and it was time for me to speak. I laid the papers of my Impact Statement in front of me on the large oval table, inner vibrations flooding the core of my existence. This was it. My opportunity to tell this Catholic institution what they had done to me. To no longer be silent.

I began to read the words; words I had read over countless times. They rolled off my lips as if they had a life of their own. The dam had broken, it was their time to flow. As I spoke out the disgusting details of Brother Dave's actions, I saw Father Brown squirm in his seat. The chronological account began in my childhood, journeying through adolescence into adulthood. My unhappy school life tormented by the nuns, alcohol and drug dependency, risky behaviours, anxiety, shame, low self-image leapt

MEDIATION

off the pages for 25 minutes. An empowerment gripped me amongst the anxiety as Erin Brockovich came to the surface. I was a warrior, and this was my moment. I had the command of the room, every eye fixed on me. As I addressed the Marist Fathers' coverup I looked directly at Father Brown, his eyes exhausted from repeatedly listening to these kinds of atrocities.

I finished reading. The room was still. Father Brown broke the silence.

"I am very sorry this happened to you," his words were soft and humble. "He was indeed a wolf in sheep's clothing".

An apology, finally! He went on to comment on some of the impacts on my life, seeming saddened by my stories. The woman with him was equally drained as she forced a smile of understanding.

Chris ushered me out of the room back to the small original room for the mediation to commence.

"Would you like a break? Some lunch?" Chris asked.

I was sapped. The adrenaline in my blood diluted as the anticipation of the apology wavered. It was over. I wanted to go home.

"No, thank you," I replied.

I knew that I could not eat. My stomach was coiled into a knot preventing anything from entering.

Father Brown and his team had decided to take a lunch break.

I grabbed the crumpled piece of paper from my handbag and placed it on the table. Clutching Meg's hand tightly, I begged her not to leave. The earlier suggestion that the person leave after the apology, and not remain for the negotiations, was no longer something I could accept. I could not to be alone.

"Please don't leave me Meg," I pleaded silently, the words caught between my heart and my throat.

Meg saw the fear I couldn't voice. She read my eyes and stayed.

The mediation was about to begin.

"I will go and begin discussions," Chris began eager to get started.

A number had been proposed significantly lower than what I had believed was achievable. This was to start the proceedings.

"Ok," I replied quietly, trying to stay composed.

Chris had prepared me to believe that I had power over the decision. But the sudden drop in expectations left me disheartened.

Then a piece of paper was placed in front of me – full of unfamiliar figures, much lower than I had previously been told. I blinked in disbelief.

"What is this? Why wasn't I shown this earlier?"

"You were Sarah," Chris replied.

I later checked all my emails and attachments and concluded that I had not seen these figures before. I looked at Meg, eyes wide and stunned.

The aim, as I understood it, was to achieve the best result possible on the day. I was then to decide whether to accept or reject it and whether to commence litigation. I believed I would be supported in making the final decision.

Chris stepped out to continue the discussions. He returned soon after, delivering a response from the other room. Humiliation pounded my face.

"What?" I gasped.

"This is standard, Sarah," Chris said, as if I should've expected it.

"Why so low?" my voice trembled with panic.

"We will go back with another offer, don't worry," he said.

"But I don't want to go any lower." Tears were welling up in my eyes begging me to leave the room. I reached for my crumpled paper. My bottom-line amount staring up at me seemed hopeless.

"They won't accept that, we need to compromise," he replied.

MEDIATION

Chris's certainty unsettled me. How could he know what they would accept or would not accept?

"I have already compromised so much," I pleaded.

Time passed. Chris and Louise laid out reasons why my case may fail in court. I reluctantly agreed. I felt an intense pressure to comply with the process.

Another proposed amount was shared. Again, the numbers felt like a knife piercing my heart. I turned to Meg, searching for a lifeline.

"Let's step outside for a minute," she said gently.

In the reception area, I hugged Meg whilst holding back sobs, my body inwardly convulsing.

"What do I do?" I asked, eyes wide with desperation. I felt as if I had been put back on the victim's seat. I felt powerless.

Meg seemed puzzled watching the game that was being played out before us. The toing and froing back and forth between the rooms seemed to be a familiar rhythm for Chris and Stuart. They had played on this court together many times and I felt like I was the 'ball' being smashed. We returned to the game.

I glanced down at the figure scribbled on my crumpled piece of paper; we were well below this amount. A wave of failure washed over me as the numbers blurred through my tears. Why was I under such tormenting pressure to accept something that felt so far beneath my worth?

I didn't feel prepared for this – not this kind of process. After pouring my heart out in my Impact Statement, I was emotionally raw. The negotiation, the uncertainty, the quiet strategising happening around me – it was all too much. Panic surged through me, thick and inescapable. I sat frozen, every muscle locked, while inside I was screaming, "I can't take this anymore". I desperately wanted to put a stop to this. I wanted to go home.

"We're below the amount I said I wouldn't go under, Chris," I finally said, sliding the paper toward him again.

He shook his head. "It's still too high," he responded.

Reluctantly, I suggested something lower – less than I had ever intended to offer, but still not as low as what had been presented earlier.

"They won't go for that," Chris said immediately, dismissing it before even trying.

My heart pounded. "How do you know?" I questioned, startled by how quickly he had overridden me. Wasn't he supposed to represent me? Wasn't I supposed to have a say in this?

"I'm not going to them with that offer. They won't accept it," Chris said firmly.

His tone had shifted—his frustration now plain in his face. Meg and I looked at each other, dazed, unsure what was happening.

"How do you know they won't accept it?" Meg asked, her voice cautious.

"I just know. They've reached their limit," Chris replied.

But I had not. What about my limit?

I was the one who had lived through the abuse, the one sitting here trying to find some measure of recognition for what I'd endured. Yet somehow, I no longer felt like the one steering this.

When did Chris get this information? Had something been said outside the room? Had decisions already been made—before today, before I even walked in?

MEDIATION

I felt like a puppet, my strings pulled by others while they watched to see how long it would take me to break.

It was beginning to feel like the number had been decided long ago.

"I want to go to court," I said quietly.

Chris looked furious. "I've already explained all the reasons you'll lose if you take that route," he snapped. His eyes burned with the kind of fire usually reserved for unruly children.

We were at deuce. And it felt like they were playing for game, set, and match.

Wearily, I glanced at my phone. It was 4:45pm—nearly five hours into negotiations. I was already drained from reading my Impact Statement earlier that day. After almost eight hours in these legal offices, I was emotionally spent.

Now, caught in the thick of this brutal process, one thing had become painfully clear; the apology and the mediation should never happen on the same day.

How could anyone be expected to endure two such deeply confronting events; one about truth, the other about bargaining within a narrow window of time?

My lawyer told me months earlier that once we had concrete offers on the table, we would discuss the options in detail so that I could make an informed decision. If a satisfactory resolution could not be reached, they would support me in taking the matter further to potential litigation. This promise was supposed to be an option.

I truly believed my legal team would stand with me if I chose to go to court. But now, in this exhausting moment, it became clear that that option had quietly slipped away. The only option left was to accept the Marist Fathers' final offer.

I sighed, the sound heavy with defeat and despair.

A form was placed in front of me, pages of legal jargon with a space for my signature. Weary and deflated, I attempted to read it.

There it was, the clause, screaming at me, "gag order".

"I told you Chris, I would not sign the compensation agreement with the confidentiality clause, silencing me, preventing the disclosure of the amount I would receive," I said, the last of my strength flaring into a righteous stance.

I had made it clear, in emails and conversations, I would not be silenced. I would not allow the terms of this process to become another layer of secrecy. I would not sign a deed that states I cannot disclose the amount they choose to compensate me.

But there it was. Still in the agreement, sneering at me.

"We had to leave it in. I spoke to Stuart, and he said there was a potential risk of being sued," Chris said.

Sued? I didn't understand. Broken and defeated - I signed.

The pages of legal jargon meant nothing to me, I did not fully understand what I was signing. Couldn't I go away and think about it? Take time to read through it slowly with someone explaining what it all meant? I was like a fragmented vase smashed on the floor. They had won. Their manipulation tactics had worn me down to submission. I wanted to get out and run for my life. The auction was over.

Later, reading the document with another lawyer – one outside the mediation, I discovered that the clause extended beyond the financial amount. It included documents and therefore I could not include the Marist Father's letter of apology in this book. The documents were silenced.

The bar next door to the legal offices was beckoning us. Meg and I remained speechless as we scanned the menu. I ordered the most expensive bottle of wine available, thinking its value would give me some value. I felt valueless.

A shudder woke me from a nightmare. The proceedings from the day before tormented my mind, a black evil presence was in my room. The nightmare was real. I lay on my bed in disbelief. It was over. The day I had waited for, more than three torturous years of preparation was done, and I had failed. The crumpled piece of paper with the fading figure stared at me, mocking my weakness. The invisible power that forced my signature on the gag clause laughed at my foolishness.

"You are weak," it taunted. "You said you wouldn't, but you did -ha - you are so stupid."

A gripping weight held me motionless to the bed. I wanted to die. With all the trauma in my life I had never felt suicidal until now. There was no point in living. I had ruined my only opportunity. I had said I would go to court, but that option was taken off the table at the last minute of the mediation meeting. Over and over in my head, every minute of the gruelling eight-hour day was on loop. You should have said this, you should have done that - it was too late. The depression and sleeping tablets kept me in bed for days, my mind blank in hopelessness. There was no escape from the inevitable desire to die.

My mobile phone rang again, its piercing tone to be ignored. But this time, I mindlessly reached for it.

"Hello," my dry voice whispered.

"Helloooo," Meg sang in her always cheerful voice.

"Are you ok?" she asked.

Silence!

"Sarah, are you there? How are you? Are you ok?" she persisted.

"No," I answered slowly. I wasn't ok and I wasn't there. I had gone to another place, dark and alone.

"Let's pray!" Meg suggested.

She began a beautiful prayer to our Heavenly Father, asking him to comfort me. She reminded Him that He is a just God and asked for His peace, that surpasses understanding to guard my heart and my mind.

A warmth came into my body, a gentle touch of His love. I thanked her, got out of bed, and walked to the shower. There was hope. I had gone through one of the most traumatic days of my life, facing the Marist Fathers and the manipulated legal mediation, and survived. Somehow, I sensed there had to be a reason. Maybe I was meant to share this—to help others know what to expect, so they could be better prepared.

Chapter 39
The Harvest

Awakening from the depths of suicidal thoughts, I knew I needed professional support. The stress of the past few years, taking on both a legal and civil case put a huge strain on my life. Seeking justice takes bravery and tenacity. I had to find an inner strength to last the distance and to survive.

The Royal Commission in 2014 had given me the opportunity to break my silence, telling my story to the Commissioners, but I needed more. My soul cried out to be believed and to be acknowledged by the Marist Fathers. The abuse happened and they knew about it. I reported my abuse as a brave 11-year-old child, only to be shamed and silenced. It was crucial for me to receive an apology. Finally, after 50 long years, I had a glimpse at justice as I looked into Father Brown's exhausted, sorrowful eyes. The sorrow of a leader in a broken system. These eyes reflected an era of immense abuse of innocent young children, and a church that covered it up. A church that protected paedophiles and silenced a generation.

Even though I had achieved an arrest warrant for my perpetrator should he return to Australia, he remains a free man. I still wait in silent anticipation for the day that I could get a call, "He is back in the country and under arrest. You need to face a court hearing, Sarah."

The despairing disappointment of the mediation process just a few days earlier had left me exhausted and broken. I had wanted to go to court but the door was firmly shut. The gag clause was pushed in front of me, and I felt coerced to sign, worn down by the lawyer's tactics. That gruelling eight-hour day still doesn't make sense to me. My hope is that by sharing this experience, others might be better prepared if they chose to pursue a civil case. The Australian legal-mediation system I encountered, wasn't built to support the victim – it was built to serve the system itself.

A Google search led me to a retreat which resonated with my spirit. 'Saprea' is a nonprofit organisation offering survivors of child sexual abuse a full emersion 4-day retreat into self-discovery and healing. In October 2023, I boarded a plane to the USA stepping into an unknown vulnerability. On arrival, a blanket of compassion and understanding greeted me. Clinical specialists guided me with gentle reassurance through education and healing techniques. Their love was immeasurable. I looked to God, spending time walking in the woods, meditating on His word in the book of Psalms, "Those who look to him are radiant; their faces are never covered with shame" Psalms 34:5. The seeds of silence that had been planted into my young life had brought forth a harvest of silence in every area of my life. But now the little girl in the red dress had come out from hiding, out from behind the wood pile to let go of shame. The harvest of silence was continually being replaced with new seeds of hope and healing. I had become 'new voiced', a fruitful harvest with a victorious voice.

Reflecting on my past, I was born into a generation of children who were to be seen and not heard. I was abused and silenced. My only sibling was cruel, and I married into domestic violence. I identified a syndrome which I call the 'Silencing Syndrome' where symptoms are embedded into the core of a person's mental, emotional and physical health. There were so many skeletons in the closet, allowing shame to know me by name. My soul had been conditioned to silence, hidden deep in my subconscious. The abuse had caused my brain to develop new neural pathways creating hyper-vigilance as a means for survival. Arrested Development had gripped many areas of my life, my damaged frontal lobe transporting me into flashbacks coupled with crippling anxiety. Trauma bonds had attracted me to more abusers, narcissistic relationships including gaslighting. Mental overload and overwhelm had become a daily condition to manage. I had journeyed into hatred and blame, turning my back on a God who I believed had not protected me from a wolf in sheep's clothing. My life's course was altered when that little girl in the red dress was violated, and the crime covered up.

But finally, it was time for shame to go where it belonged - with the people who had wronged me. It was no longer mine to own. Even though my healing journey had begun the day I accepted Jesus Christ as my Lord and savior, the harvest of healing takes time to be cultivated. The old dead wood of the past needed to be uprooted to allow the light to shine in, bringing fresh growth. New seeds were then able to be planted and carefully watered and fertilised to bring forth a new harvest. A harvest of joy, peace, forgiveness, self-worth and love. These delightful fruits began to be evident in my life. Seasons will change, but with God you can weather the storms until it is time for the final feast.

I now realise that God has nothing to do with the evil in this world. He is a good God full of love. He has always been with me. I hear people say, "Why doesn't God stop evil?" God hates evil and there is a time coming soon when He will destroy all the plans of the enemy. His battle is already won. Jesus Christ is coming back for those who call out to him, "Everyone who calls on the name of the Lord will be saved" Romans 10:13. His still small voice is calling you, knocking on the door of your heart, all you need to do is let Him in.

A short time ago I visited a local market, and met a woman in her late seventies, who had written a book about growing up in rural Australia. She was eagerly offering autographed copies for sale. I told her that I was also writing a book.

Towards the end of 2019, I started to hear a still small voice speaking to me,

"Write your book," it whispered.

The same voice that called me to "find a church" all those years earlier was still directing my steps. This voice, that I was now familiar with, I knew as my Heavenly Father.

"Write your book," it persisted.

"No," I replied.

The voice continued to follow me over the months, gently reminding me. It wasn't demanding, just persistent.

Eventually I gave in and started to write.

"What is your book about, dear?" the woman at the market asked with a smile.

"I was sexually abused in my childhood by a man training to be a priest," I stated with a newfound bravery.

Her face went pale as she pressed her fingers into a tight ball.

"Me too," she whispered, her eyes dropping to the ground. "I was sexually abused as a child too, and you are the first person I have ever told."

Tears welled up in both our eyes as our souls connected deeply in that instance.

"I am so sorry that happened to you," I offered with sincerity.

"Thank you for being brave enough to tell me. It wasn't your fault. Let go of the shame."

She had been five years old when her abuse had begun. I saw a new freedom on this woman's face, a peaceful acceptance that she was not alone. All those years of silence were finally broken.

On my healing journey, I have discovered that your past and what others have done to you do not define you. I was born an adventurous, free-spirited, vibrant girl with purpose and this is who I still am today. I am the essence of the human I was created by God to be, "wonderfully and perfectly made" Psalm 139:14. I have been able to forgive those who have wronged me, share my hidden secrets, find my voice and write this book.

I initially believed that writing this book was for my healing alone. But over time, I realised it was meant to be shared. I was being called to step into total vulnerability, not just for myself but to help others. If any part of my story resonates with you or someone in your life - if it brings a glimmer of hope, then my purpose is fulfilled.

To those who have been silenced and shamed, I want to say:

It is never too late to find your voice.

It is never too late to tell your story.

It is never too late to seek justice.

Now is the time for the 'New Voiced'.

I have launched www.newvoiced.com as a space to share my healing journey and the tools that have helped transform me – from victim to survivor.

YOU too can make that transformation.

From stuck in silence ... to standing in strength.

From carrying shame … to shouting truth.

From hushed … to being heard.

There is power in numbers. When we gather in solidarity – linking arms, lifting one another – we become a force that cannot be ignored.

Together we cry out:

"I have a voice. I am valued. My story matters".

"I will not keep silent …. I will not remain quiet" Isaiah 62:1

Epilogue

Sarah Cook's Impact Statement

I am writing this statement directed to David Davenport and the Marist Fathers.

I want you, David, to hear of the destruction you have caused in my life and others through your criminal actions. I want to personalise this message and would welcome the opportunity to look you in the eye. I want to watch your face as I tell you of the pain you inflicted on me and how you stole my childhood, you changed the course of my life.

You violated an innocent child by first grooming her mother under the banner of 'Marist Father'. You targeted me and used your vile perverted plan to seduce, manipulate and gain trust. You wormed your way into my family home, my place of comfort and my refuge, the place I would look for nurturing and protection from the world. The home my parents purchased to raise their family, the home I was born in. My father, Dr Peter Cook, a war hero and a highly respected doctor, along with my mother Wilhelmina Cook, a professional opera singer, would hold fundraisers at our family home for the Marist Fathers' Missions work.

As a so called "man of God", you put on spiritual falsehood to gain trust and to identify your victim. You separated me from the pack, like a wolf in sheep's clothing, you prowled my territory and stole my innocence. As a small pre-pubescent girl, I had no idea what sex was or anything about sexual touching. I had been taught by the Catholic Church that the Brothers in training, the Priests and the Nuns were Godly holy people reflecting the goodness of Jesus. They were his hands and feet on earth to carry out good works and to protect the young and innocent. There was no doubt in my young mind that I would be 'safe' in their care. This was a given, to state otherwise and to be abused was unfathomable.

But, how far from the truth was this, as so many victims who have been broken by the incessant sexual abuse of children, which was rife in the Catholic Church, especially the Marist Fathers in the 60's, 70's and 80's. Have they ever read the Bible where Jesus instructs, "Do not call any man on earth 'Father'"? Matthew 23:9. Our Father God is in Heaven. Judges were put in a place of authority to bring order and justice to mankind, laws were created to be upheld to bring those who break the laws to justice. But you David, escaped the law.

I have many unanswered questions. Did you ever think of the effect your behaviour would have on me?

I remember that day you led me to the back grounds of Villa Maria Church after you had been 'found out'. I obediently followed you as you commanded, in terror of more abuse but somehow still hypnotised under your evil spell and religious power. You told me not to think about what had happened and that when I got older, I would understand. Well, yes you were right. I do understand. I understand that your despicable calculated strategy, a plan to corner a little lamb, white as snow, pure and innocent, naïve and trusting destroying her life was achieved. On 25th March 2021, I visited Villa Maria Church in Hunters Hill, to see if I remembered the

EPILOGUE: SARAH COOK'S IMPACT STATEMENT

wooden bench you led me to, to silence me, was it still there? It was there, exactly as I remembered.

Studies have shown that sexual abuse of a child has a lifelong impact that haunts, causing pain and brokenness to every aspect of the victim's life. Many do not make it with drug and alcohol abuse, risky behaviour and suicide taking them out. As a primary school child, shame and confusion dominated my mind. Fear beyond fear, the adrenalin rush and terror of seeing your car in our family driveway, knowing you were inside waiting to devour me, your prey. Waiting for me. Salivating, eyes flickering, demonic anticipation of my entrance imminent. I was walking to a slaughterhouse with no escape. A child, not even safe in the sanctuary of her own home. A mother tricked into a delusion also under your spell. The melodies of your piano playing sounding a false sense of joy.

Where was my father? You must have known his work hours and planned your visits carefully. You knew when the school bell would ring, what time I was expected home and how you could isolate me to have your way. Did you see me as the cover girl for the 1972 Christmas edition of the Marist Fathers Harvest magazine?

So, let me take you on my life journey. Have you ever wondered how I was? You never contacted me to ask. After I confided in a girl at Loreto two years above me in year 9 in 1976, the chaos began. I was summoned from my year 7 classroom by Sister Anne to be interviewed in her stark cold office. She rocked on her chair, suspended on two legs, listening in disbelief as I spoke the truth of my molestation. Mortification was drowning me as I tried to articulate evil male sexual behaviour, that I did not understand. It was not thinkable to a child of my age. I never spoke of it to any friends as they would be shocked, and I was so fearful of being labelled as 'that girl'. The corners of Sister Anne's mouth curled into a snarl – I was confused how my honesty had got me into trouble. I was marched back to my classroom and that was it. I was never asked about it again by anyone. Never! I was left to wonder what was going to happen with my secret, which was now known to the nuns.

I later heard that the girl I had confided in, overwhelmed by my story and feeling helpless, shared it with Mrs Manns, a lay teacher at the school fondly known by the girls as 'Mummy Manns'. She shared my secret story to the nuns and the Marist Fathers. It was out in the light. Finally, I would be set free as "the truth will set you free" it says in Luke 8:32. I had been taught this but no, the uncovering of a hideous crime against a child, was carefully put back into a secret place. The police were not informed and once again the supremacy of the clergy was protected above all, including the law.

I had been silenced again, deepening my fear and shame. I began quietly going to my father's bar at home, selecting random bottles of spirits (usually white as it seemed to have less of a foul taste), blocking my nose between my pointer and thumb and quickly sculling large gulps. The fiery fluid would burn my throat sliding down my esophagus to my stomach. Wiping the corners of my mouth with the back of my wrist, I would hurry back to my bedroom not to be noticed. The alcohol would begin to numb my body with a gentle warmth, lightening the load of tormenting thoughts from which I could never escape. These were my first experiences with alcohol. Not a sip of champagne at a family celebration at the age of 16 with Mum and Dad gingerly allowing a supervised first sip, mine was a private indulgence, way too early in life trying to drown my tormented reality.

I saw you the day you walked through the gate of Loreto into the Year 7 playground. I was playing elastics with my best friends, my heart skipped a beat when I caught your figure approaching. The secret was out and so you must have been informed I thought, you were 'busted'. My initial shock to

EPILOGUE: SARAH COOK'S IMPACT STATEMENT

see you, so out of context, froze me momentarily followed by that familiar fear I had known so well.

Anxiety has followed me all my life. An internal vibrating of intense discomfort that cannot be escaped. As I bring my hand before my eyes, fingers outstretched trying to hold them steady, only to witness a shaking across all fingers, the pinky finger shaking twice as fast. The more I try and still its dance, the more I realise it has taken on a life of its own. Anxiety is a crippling illness that brings dysfunction and debilitation. I remember when it first entered me as I crouched beside the wood pile at home. I had seen your car yet again, in my driveway after school, and ran up the side of the house to instinctively hide. My heart was beating out of my chest, sweat forming on my brow, and I had a strong urge to pee. The wood pile was about chest high, I went down on my haunches, curling into a ball hoping to disappear. My breaths were deep and laboured, yet I tried to silence their rhythmic sound so as not to be discovered. But my mother would be getting so worried and angry that I was late home from school, so my panic made me leave my hiding place and face you. I had never known this level of fear, yet it was now a part of my life forever.

My teenage years were extremely unhappy. The nuns and teachers at Loreto seemed to think my story of 'Brother Dave' and what you did to me was somehow my fault. That's if they even believed me at all. I was victimised and punished unjustly. The nuns, after nearly four years of bullying me, used me as a scape goat and expelled me two weeks before the Year 10 School Certificate. The results of your behaviour stole my education as I could not succeed in my mental state, and in this victimised environment.

I then attended Roseville College where I was deeply unhappy and alone after losing all my Loreto friends. I only lasted two terms in this school before moving to Hunters Hill High School to do my HSC. I remained troubled and silent. My final results were poor as I dropped rapidly from an A grade student to a C grade student from when your abuse began. I did not achieve a score for university entry.

My obedience from your command at the back of Villa Maria Church, to simply forget your abuse until I turned 20, only caused more confusion as the flooding memories ripped my soul apart on my 20th birthday. This led to an increasing need to be numbed through excessive drug and alcohol abuse and promiscuous sexual behaviour, looking for love and comfort. I took foolish risks and attracted destructive relationships. I was all alone yet appearing to the world as an outgoing young adult. I would run away, moving to new environments to try and escape my inner turmoil.

I eventually came back to Sydney at 30 years old, financially broke and wounded from many unhappy, abusive, casual relationships. I married a man when I was 35 years old called David. He was also an abuser, who put me through psychological and physical abuse. There were AVOs and bashings, isolation from friends and family, and two children conceived while on a four-year journey of confusion and heart ache. It is interesting how I attracted another David to abuse me. Studies have shown that this type of life pattern, repeating choices due to trauma, is common for victims of childhood abuse.

My life continued with a nervous breakdown, flashbacks, panic attacks, more abusive relationships, mental health issues including anxiety, depression and substance abuse, unemployment, and continued memories of what you did to me in my home, my innocence perverted and stolen.

When I sent an email in September 2020 to Japan, curiously seeking to find out if you were alive, I received a response saying, "yes" you were alive and well. I became angry. The pain had been triggered again. Has all this destruction of my life had any effect on you? You went on to become a priest, to travel to Japan with no justice for your crime. It is a crime to sexually abuse a child, and you need to be brought to justice. Are you

EPILOGUE: SARAH COOK'S IMPACT STATEMENT

aware there is a warrant out for your arrest? The moment you step foot on Australian soil, you will be arrested. You will face your crime. But will you continue to hide in Japan? What a shame there is no extradition with Japan for this crime. I believe there should be! I have heard you have left the priesthood and have married. Is this true? Did you have children?

I would now like to speak to the Marist Fathers

I had the courage as a young child to break my silence and report my abuse. As a year 7 girl, only 11 years old, I found my voice. Filled with fear I spoke. A deep sense of relief to no longer hold this terrible secret. When I discovered my confiding was passed onto Mrs Manns, I was devastated that my secret was out in public, but also relieved that finally I would be helped and cared for. But the opposite happened. I was victimised again and silenced. Why didn't the Marist Fathers call the police? Why didn't the Loreto nuns call the police? Why wasn't I protected? Why wasn't I counselled and spoken to in love? Why didn't anyone care? Why was Brother Dave protected? Why was he allowed to stay in the parish and be ordained as a priest? Why was he able to continue working with children? Why? I have so many unanswered questions. So many whys!

You are equal criminals in this case. Both you as an organisation and Brother Dave committed a crime against me. Although mandatory reporting was not law at the time, you had a moral obligation to protect the young as ministers of God. You had a duty of care. You further vicimised the victim and protected the perpetrator. Why? To protect the name of the Catholic Church? You would sacrifice me to protect your reputation? You destroyed my life for your gain. I hold you equally responsible for my abuse, you caused an ongoing life of struggles and PTSD by your actions. A life of shame, no longer able to trust authority, particularly male authority.

A lifetime of mental illness, and your disregard of my abuse by a man who was under your guidance. In my view, you are criminals! If anyone should take the stand it's you! You state in your response to the Royal Commission into Institutional Responses to Child Sexual Abuse, that you "make a firm commitment to continue supporting justice and healing for victims of abuse", yet you are an abuser in my case. How dare you silence me. How dare you protect a grown man, a perverted pedophile over an innocent child. How dare you impact my life in every way, destroying my education and my ability to have stable loving relationships in my life. My mental health issues and past addictions show me that it is only a miracle that I am still alive today. I have been to doctors, psychologists, and counsellors seeking help yet not finding it. The trauma you have inflicted on me by protecting my abuser has devalued me as a person. Not allowing my voice to be heard or have any meaning is disgusting. Yes, I want justice and healing. Yet no amount of counselling or money can ever make up for the damage you have caused me and my family. As you consider the action, or lack of action by the guidelines of your institution at the time, I continue to wait for an apology, answers to my questions, an explanation and compensation.

To be in a religious position of authority, makes a man powerful to the vulnerable.

He should have been removed from this position. If he had, he would not have been at my school gate in his priestly robes. He would not have gained access to my family home. He would not have groomed me and sexually violated me, an eight-year-old girl, over the period of four years.

Would this have happened if you had not made me the pin up girl on the cover of your Harvest magazine? Even though you knew of my abuse, as a young schoolgirl, David Davenport was ordained a priest, seven months after I reported his sexual abuse.

EPILOGUE: SARAH COOK'S IMPACT STATEMENT

The past three years, as I have sort justice with a criminal and civil case, every area of my life has been dissected and put under the microscope as if I am the criminal. This has caused me extreme stress and distress. It is only by the grace of my God, Jesus Christ that I am alive and have found the strength through my faith to stay the course and stand before you today. I believe in justice. God is a just God and HE WILL BRING JUSTICE.

"For I God Love Justice," Isaiah 61:8.

Sarah Cook

Supports

Lifeline on 13 11 14.

The National Sexual Assault, Family and Domestic Violence Counselling Line – 1800 RESPECT (1800 737 732) – is available 24 hours a day, seven days a week for any Australian who has experienced, or is at risk of, family and domestic violence and/or sexual assault.

C.A.N clergyabusednetwork.org.au
If you were abused in a religious context as a child or as an adult and need support to speak out.
PH 0411 108 465

SAPREA saprea.org
Saprea is the nonprofit known for using proven, practical methods for confronting and overcoming child sexual abuse. With clinically proven tools and resources, we empower survivors, parents, and community members with the knowledge they need to protect, heal, and put a stop to child sexual abuse.

SNAP - Survivors Network of those Abused by Priests
SNAP Leader Australia

SNAP Aotearoa New Zealand Trustee
Phone 0061 411565691
International Website: https://www.snapnetwork.org
National Website: https://www.snapnetwork.org/australia
Facebook: https://www.facebook.com/groups/snapaustralia

Footnotes

(1) Gisele Pelicot and her ex-husband Dominique Pelicot give final statements at French mass rape trial in Avignon - ABC News
(2) Quote Julia Gillard from the Royal Commission into Institutional Responses to Child Sexual Abuse - www.childabuseroyalcommission.gov.au
(3) Statistics from the Royal Commission into Institutional Responses to Child Sexual Abuse - www.childabuseroyalcommission.gov.au
(4) Victim Statement from Royal Commission into Institutional Responses to Child Sexual Abuse - www.childabuseroyalcommission.gov.au
(5) Message to Australia from the Royal Commission into Institutional Responses to Child Sexual Abuse - www.childabuseroyalcommission.gov.au

All scriptures quoted are taken from the Holy Bible New International Version, NIV, or otherwise indicated at the scripture.

Appendix

SNAP - Survivors Network of those Abused by Priests

News

21st April 2025 – Pope Francis dies aged 88 years

"Abused survivors do not want to see another conclave that elects a Pope who has shielded and covered up for clergy offenders," Sarah Pearson, a SNAP spokesperson.

- The next pope must institute a **zero tolerance law** for sexual abuse that immediately removes abusive clergy and leaders who have covered up abuse from ministry and mandates independent oversight of bishops. He must use his authority to enact fundamental, institutional changes to end the systematic practice of sexual abuse and its concealment.
- The next pope must not have any history of having covered up sexual abuse.
- None of Francis' reforms or initiatives have produced actual "zero tolerance" for abuse or ended the culture of extreme secrecy and control that enables it.

8th May 2025 – Robert Francis Prevost elected pope and will be known at Pope Leo XIV, the fist pontiff born in the United States of Amaerica.

Rome, Italy — As white smoke rises, the Survivors Network of those Abused by Priests (SNAP) extends its acknowledgment to Pope Leo XIV on the gravity of the role he now assumes.

Pope Leo's record on abuse management

As provincial of the Augustinians, Pope Leo XIV allowed Father James Ray, a priest then accused of abusing minors whose ministry had been restricted since 1991, to reside at the Augustinians' St. John Stone Friary in Chicago in 2000, despite its proximity to a Catholic elementary school. When Prevost was Bishop of Chiclayo, three victims reported to civil authorities in 2022 after there was no movement on their canonical case filed through the diocese. Victims have since claimed Prevost failed to open an investigation, sent inadequate information to Rome, and that the diocese allowed the priest to continue saying mass, attaching photos of the priest saying mass after their complaint to their letter.

SNAP filed a complaint against Prevost under Pope Francis' 2023 decree Vos estis lux mundi on March 25, 2025.

SNAP is calling for decisive action within the first 100 days:

- An independent Global Truth Commission with full Vatican cooperation;
- A Universal Zero Tolerance Law adopted into canon law;
- International legal agreements mandating transparency and accountability;
- A survivor-funded Reparations Fund supported by church assets;

- And a Global Survivors Council with the authority to oversee and enforce compliance.

"You can end the abuse crisis — the only question is, will you?" SNAP asks Pope Leo XIV.

www.snapnetwork.org

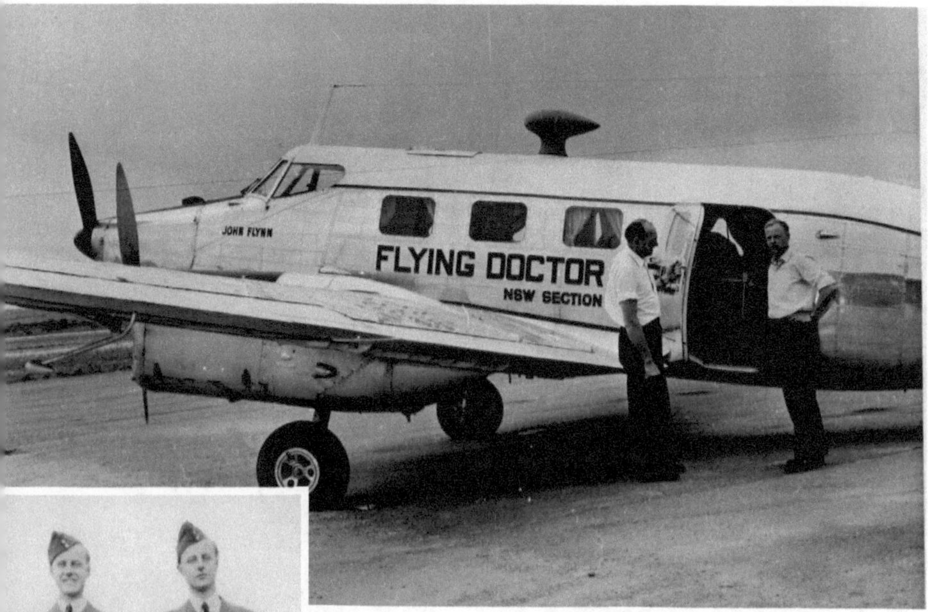

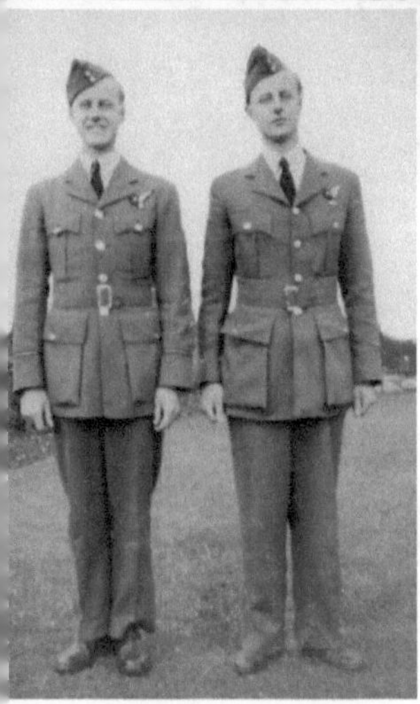

Clockwise from top: Peter Cook as a Flying Doctor serving the outback in Australia; Sympathy letter from King George VI; Peter and Wilhelmina at their bar in Hunters Hill; The twins Peter and John Cook, going to WWII in the UK.

BUCKINGHAM PALACE

The Queen and I offer you our heartfelt sympathy in your great sorrow.

We pray that your country's gratitude for a life so nobly given in its service may bring you some measure of consolation.

George R.I.

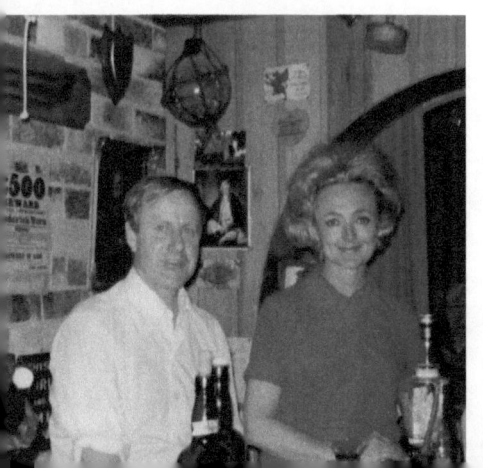

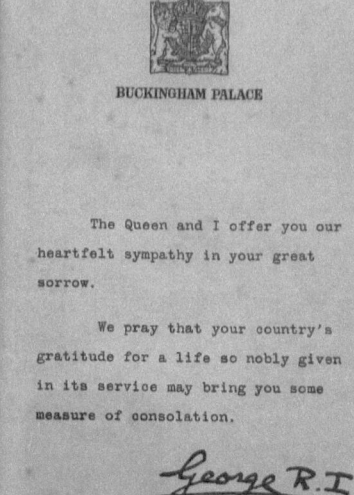

Clockwise from top: Wilhelmina staring in the pantomime, *Jack and the Bean Stalk* at Wimbledon Theatre, London 1959; Wilhelmina singing the Italian opera, Aida; 'Princess Sarah' ready for a school fancy dress; 1972 *Harvest Magazine*.

Clockwise from top: View of the Lane Cove River and the pool from Sarah's family home in Hunters Hill; Sarah as an unhappy teenager in her pink wallpapered bedroom; Tresillian Graduation 1986; Overseas trip to Nepal - Sarah with the local children.

Clockwise from top left: Sarah at the helm; Kayaking in Cape Tribulation, Queensland; Sarah Watering skiing Hamilton Island, Queensland Sarah working on one of the Superyachts.

www.ingramcontent.com/pod-product-compliance
Lightning Source LLC
Chambersburg PA
CBHW030102170426
43198CB00009B/456